Assessing Sex Bias in Testing

A Review of the
Issues and Evaluations
of 74 Psychological
and Educational Tests

PAULA SELKOW

Contributions in Psychology, Number 3

Greenwood Press
Westport, Connecticut • London, England

Library of Congress Cataloging in Publication Data

Selkow, Paula.
   Assessing sex bias in testing.

   (Contributions in psychology, ISSN 0736-2714   ; no. 3)
   Bibliography: p.
   Includes index.
   1.   Sexism in psychological tests.   2.   Sexism in
educational tests.   I.   Title.   II.   Series.
BF176.S44   1984   153.9'3   84-564
ISBN 0-313-24447-2   (lib. bdg.)

Library of Congress Catalog Card Number: 84-564
ISBN: 0-313-24447-2
ISSN: 0736-2714

First published in 1984

Greenwood Press
A division of Congressional Information Service, Inc.
88 Post Road West, Westport, Connecticut 06881

Printed in the United States of America

10 9 8 7 6 5 4 3 2 1

Copyright Acknowledgments

   The author and publisher are grateful for permission to reprint from the following
sources.
   "Criteria for Evaluation," from *Guidelines for Evaluation of Instructional
Materials with Respect to Social Content* (Sacramento: California State Department
of Education, 1978).
   Personal communication from representatives of American Guidance Service,
Inc., American Testronics, Consulting Psychologists Press, Inc., CTB/McGraw-
Hill, Educator's Publishing Service, Jamestown Publishers, Scholastic Testing Ser-
vice, Inc., Science Research Associates, Slosson Educational Publications, and
Western Psychological Services.

TO MAURICE

Contents

Preface

The selection of sex-fair tests concerns psychologists, counselors, and educators, as well as the millions of individuals tested each year. Those in the position of having to choose appropriate tests must often weigh many diverse factors. The goal of the Project for the Elimination of Sexism in Testing (Project T.E.S.T.) was to make this task somewhat easier. This is the report of the activities of that project.

The author would like to thank those people who assisted in accomplishing these goals. I am grateful to Roberta Kalmar, whose inspiration and expertise helped me to begin this undertaking. At William Paterson College, I am indebted to Edith Silverstein, who performed with grace and apparent ease the myriad tasks that fall to the unsuspecting person who accepts the title of research assistant. I also appreciate the efforts of the eight psychology students who served as test raters.

This research was funded through a grant from the Women's Educational Equity Act Program (WEEAP) at the then U.S. Department of Health, Education and Welfare. Several people on the WEEAP staff were very helpful, among them Doris Shakin, my project officer, and especially Leslie Wolfe, the director of WEEAP. At the Educational Development Center in Newton, Massachusetts, Vivian Guilfoy, Renée Wilson, Lynn Shreihofer, and Tyra Sidberry were consistently supportive and hardworking in preparing the manuscript.

I received invaluable assistance from many people at Trenton State College in the Office of Funding of Grants who helped me to obtain grant funds and later kept the project fiscally sound. My sincerest appreciation goes to Ray Wheeler, director, for his expertise, good humor, and helpfulness all along the way. I am also indebted to many others in the Office of Funding and Grants, particularly Beatrice Rosetty, Irene Dominguez, and Robert Kamping.

Rebecca Lubetkin of the Consortium for Educational Equity at Rutgers University was helpful at many stages of the study. She also provided several highly competent evaluators who are too numerous to mention individually. I would also like to thank Nancy Breland in the psychology department at Trenton State College and Carol Norman of the WEAL Fund for their useful comments and suggestions.

Our editor Kerry Kern and our typists Mary Ellen Wawrzossek and Susan Calish deserve special thanks.

I
The Study

Introduction

During the past several decades women and, to a lesser extent, men have been moving into programs, jobs, and recreational pursuits previously restricted to members of the opposite sex. Yet despite news accounts of women being selected for training as astronauts, having businesses as carpenters or welders, and sailing solo around the world, or of men teaching nursery school and being househusbands, the media still tend to portray males and females stereotypically. Until recently, educational materials also presented these stereotypical images. However, due to the pressure brought to bear by educators and parents (see, for example, Women on Words and Images, *Dick and Jane as Victims*, 1975), several publishers have issued guidelines designed to ensure fair representation of the sexes. For the most part, these guidelines have resulted in positive changes.

Unfortunately, the same cannot be said for tests, some 200 million or more of which are administered annually (Holman and Docter, 1972). Perhaps one of the reasons that tests have not been modified to the extent that other materials have been is that in general the public is not privy to them. This has been especially true for certain standardized tests such as the Scholastic Aptitude Test (SAT), and is still the case for psychological tests, although various "truth in testing" bills have been enacted and others are pending. Another likely explanation is that since substantial changes in a test instrument might result in altered validity or reliability, these aspects of testing would have to be studied—a costly task.

Despite the difficulties, the question of whether a test is fair to both sexes cannot go unanswered. We rely heavily on tests in making decisions for ourselves and others and will continue to do so to an even greater extent

(Fiske, 1980). Many of these are important decisions, such as education and job choices, and potentially determine critical life events. In addition, test results are often a deciding factor when one makes diagnoses, or decides on placements and treatment plans for adults and children with psychological or organically based problems (Wade and Baker, 1977). With increased compliance with Public Law 94-142, which mandates the education of youngsters with special needs, it is likely that there will be more evaluation and testing to identify the estimated 7 million handicapped children in the United States.

Finally, tests are used in research in order to expand our knowledge about human capabilities and behavior. Much of our information about sex differences has come from studies reporting test results. It is obvious that if a test instrument is biased against one or the other sex, its use cannot result in any valid conclusions about differences between males and females.

DEFINING SEX BIAS

Several psychometric methods for determining whether or not a test is sex-fair have been advanced. These will be discussed in the chapter entitled "Validity, Reliability, and Sex-Fair Selection."

Diamond (1976) points to two major sources of test bias: test content and the use of test results. The former includes two considerations: a test may contain a majority of items on which one or the other sex excels and/or it may reinforce sex stereotypes, either through the use of sex-restrictive language or sex roles. Coffman (1961), Donlon (1973), and others have looked at sex bias in terms of item difficulty, that is, whether some items are more difficult for one sex than for the other. For Holland (1975), tests are sex-fair if "they have effects or outcomes for both sexes that are about equal in number and magnitude, although such effects may differ in kind" (p. 19).

The American Psychological Association (1974) has urged that both validity and content be assessed:

A test user should investigate the possibility of bias in tests or in test items. Wherever possible, there should be an investigation of possible differences in criterion-related validity for ethnic, sex, or other subsamples that can be identified when the test is given. The manual or research report should give the results for each subsample separately or report that no differences were found. (p. 43)

Test content should be examined for possible bias. . . . One may investigate such bias in terms of carefully developed expert judgments; studies of the attitudes or interpretations of items in different subgroups might also present useful information. (pp. 45-46)

The National Institute of Education has proposed guidelines (Diamond, 1975) that specifically address the assessment of sex bias in interest inventories, and Diamond (1980) has offered recommendations concerning achievement tests. Each will be discussed more fully in the chapter entitled "Interest Inventories and Achievement Tests."

LEGAL CONSIDERATIONS

Whereas none of the above-mentioned guidelines has the force of law, the Vocational Education Act, the Civil Rights Act of 1964, the Fourteenth Amendment to the United States Constitution, and Title IX of the Education Amendments Act of 1972 do have. Fitzgerald and Fisher (1975) and Schiffer (1978) discuss the interpretation of these laws as they apply to sex bias in testing. According to Schiffer, the Civil Rights Act of 1964 "prohibits discrimination in employment on the basis of race, sex, color, religion and national origin." Therefore, she asserts, "counselors will want to assure themselves that they are [not] using career interest inventory instruments, which are in many cases themselves currently biased, for purposes of job selection, and that they are expressly encouraging students and employers also not to do so" (p. 138).

An amendment to the federal Vocational Education Act (Title II of the Education Amendments Act of 1976) gives grants to states so that they may eliminate sex bias in their vocational education programs. In addition, many states are required to monitor their vocational counseling programs, including testing, for sex discrimination (Schiffer, 1978).

According to the Equal Protection Clause of the Fourteenth Amendment,

In public schools career guidance, including test selection and use, must assure equal opportunity for all careers to male and female students. Public schools using tests that are not bias free themselves must, to comply with the U.S. Constitution, provide ancillary counseling and backup services sufficient to assure that students are being accorded equal opportunities regardless of sex. (Schiffer, 1978, p. 136)

The Title IX Education Amendments Act of 1972 has decreed that no person in the United States shall, on the basis of sex, "be excluded from participation in, be denied the benefits of, or be subjected to discrimination" under any educational program or activity receiving federal aid. More specific guidelines provide that

a recipient may not discriminate on the basis of sex in counseling or guiding students. . . . A recipient may not use tests or other appraisal and counseling materials which use different materials for each sex or which permit or require different treatment for students of each sex. Exceptions can be made if different materials used for each sex cover the same occupations and they are essential to eliminate sex bias. Schools must set up their own procedures to make certain that counseling and appraisal materials are not sex-biased. (Project on Equal Education Rights, 1975, p. 2)

Schiffer (1978) summarizes some additional interpretations of Title IX that were set forth in correspondence from the Department of Health, Education and Welfare. In order to meet Title IX requirements, a test should

provide technical information that gives a rationale for separate scales and/or separate norms by sex which demonstrates that such separation is essential to the elimination of sex bias.

Indicate the same vocational areas and/or occupations for each sex, with the sex composition of the norming groups for each scale clearly indicated.

[Support] the reporting of scores for one sex on scales normed or constructed on the basis of data from the other sex by a pattern of evidence of validity established for males and females scored on pairs of similar or same-named scales measuring the same constructs.

[Explain] how to interpret scores on own-sex and other-sex norms . . . in the interpretative materials for counselor and counselee, and in such way as will help them see there is virtually no activity or occupation that is exclusively male or female. In addition, where separate norms are given for each sex, steps are taken to insure that the counselee receives his or her test scores on both sets of norms. (p. 137)

Additional guidelines that will be useful for counselors in interpreting Title IX were published by the U.S. Office of Education and can be found in Tittle and Zytowski (1978).

Methods of Selection
and Evaluation

Despite the interpretations and clarifications that have been made available, schools and institutions are still primarily responsible for educating themselves and monitoring their own compliance with the law. Private practitioners and certain nonpublic agencies have even greater latitude. However, even those practitioners and/or agencies that wish to adopt nonsexist instruments may find it difficult and costly to devise assessment guidelines and to evaluate the plethora of available tests. Therefore, it was the task of this project to evaluate the most regularly used tests on a number of criteria and to present the results, along with a review of the literature, to those who select and use tests. In addition, an attempt was made to elicit comments from publishers and authors of the instruments that were evaluated. In some cases they offered modifications to reduce sex bias that could be made in administering their tests. It should be noted, however, that it was not the intention of this report to recommend one test over another or to set any "acceptable" level of sex bias.

Whereas the use of these results may assist in the decision making of those who select, administer, and use the results of tests, it should be noted that, due to various limitations, not all forms of potential sex bias were assessed in this study. For example, pass/fail rates by sex for each item of a test were not analyzed. In some cases these statistics may be available from the publisher. Further, since the results presented here are based on total tests, it may be the case that a balanced overall picture masks biased subtests. For example, if most arithmetic problems focus on males and most clerical items focus on females, there might appear to be a balanced representation of the sexes in the test as a whole. Of course, any test under consideration must be carefully evaluated for other types of bias, such as race or age bias, in addition to sex bias.

TEST SELECTION

We evaluated 74 psychological and educational tests for sex bias and stereotyping. These instruments fell into three main test categories: intelligence, personality, and diagnostic. This study purposely excluded vocational interest tests and most achievement tests, which have been extensively studied and reported on elsewhere (Diamond, 1975, 1980; Tittle, McCarthy, and Steckler, 1974; Tittle and Zytowski, 1978). However, some achievement test batteries that have not been reviewed or that have been updated were included because these are often relied on in making decisions in lieu of diagnostic and/or intelligence tests. This is especially true since the latter are no longer administered en masse in most states. In addition, achievement tests are sometimes used as a part of individual diagnostic studies, particularly when the presenting problem is a learning disability. Certainly, their results are a consideration in school placement decisions.

We selected tests from Buros's *Tests in Print* (1974) and the *Seventh* and the *Eighth Mental Measurements Yearbook* (1972, 1978), choosing instruments that are widely used for evaluation and/or research. We culled an initial group of tests from tables prepared by Buros (1972, 1978) that identified those instruments most commonly referenced during the past fifteen years. In addition, we selected several newer tests. Some of these instruments are revisions of tests with long histories of popular use. We selected the remainder of the tests because of the relatively great number of times they had been referenced, considering their recent publication dates, and/or because of the favorable reviews they had received in the *Eighth Mental Measurements Yearbook*.

In all cases, we reviewed the most recent edition available from the publisher or distributor. Tests that were out of print were eliminated. Some of the instruments reviewed are available in more than one form. Since specimen sets were purchased, the form (or forms) of the test that was provided by the publisher was the one evaluated. This would probably be the same form available to any psychologist or educator making a decision about the sex fairness of a test. Although supposedly equivalent forms of a particular instrument may vary somewhat in the way the sexes are represented, Tittle, McCarthy, and Steckler (1974) found these differences to be insignificant.

Many of the instruments studied had separate tests for particular age, grade, or achievement levels. Each test provided by the publisher was evaluated. In a few cases, a level was omitted from the test package and could not be obtained within the time limitations of the project. Consequently, these tests were not reviewed.

RATERS

Eight advanced psychology students (seven females and one male) elected, as part of their course work, to rate the tests. Due to the great number of tests, each student was assigned to rate half the total number of instruments. Students were paired randomly, and each pair of students rated the entire group of tests. The particular batteries assigned to each member of a pair were determined by random selection. Each test was evaluated by three to four raters. (Some rater attrition occurred near the end of the project.)

Ratings were made using the Sexism Rating Scale (see Appendix A). Students were familiarized with the scale and were also given criteria for evaluating the tests (see Appendix B) based on a set of standards for educational materials developed by the California State Department of Education (1978). Each rater was required to demonstrate her or his understanding of the procedure by evaluating a practice test, which was not included in the study. Interrater reliability for the entire study was .88.

THE RATING SCALE

The Sexism Rating Scale and accompanying guidelines were adapted, with the permission of the California State Department of Education,[1] from its *Guidelines for Evaluation of Instructional Materials with Respect to Social Content* (1978). The scale is the product of two major revisions. The original instrument, which was less quantitative and more open-ended, revealed during pilot testing that it was not likely to be able to provide comparable data. The second revision involved the elimination of some questions that, although probably applicable to educational materials, did not yield useful data when applied to tests.

There are two kinds of criticism one may receive when presenting data related to a controversial area such as sex bias. One is that offering counts of males and females engaged in this or that activity or occupation is meaningless. The other is that subjective reports suggesting that a test or procedure is biased are not reliable. Therefore, in constructing the Sexism Rating Scale, we attempted to include both quantitative and qualitative measures. And, indeed, we have now received both kinds of criticism.

We examined both illustrations and content in order to compare the actual numbers of males and females represented. Separate totals were derived for adults, children, and animals. In addition, roles, activities, and occupations engaged in by males and females were noted. Raters were required to make some judgments. For example, they were asked whether a particular activity, vocation, or emotion was sex-stereotyped and whether the language used in a passage or an item excluded one or the other sex unnecessarily.

The following kinds of information were used by the raters in evaluating each test.

Illustrations

The numbers of male and female adults, children, and animals appearing in illustrations were compared. Raters were instructed to count *each* illustration. Same-sex groups of three or more people were counted as one person of that sex. When sex was indeterminate or when the number of people of each sex represented was approximately equal (as in large groups), the illustration was not counted. Inanimate objects (such as toys) that resembled people or animals were included.

Content

Male and female adults, children, and animals featured in questions or stories were counted. Each person or animal was counted only once, despite the number of times his or her name appeared in the story or questions. References to same-sex groups of people or animals were counted as one character of that sex. For example, in the statement "The boys in her class helped Mindy with her arithmetic," *boys* counted as one male character.

Occupational and Nonoccupational Roles

Male and female participation in occupational and nonoccupational roles was tallied separately. Both illustrations and content were used to derive these results. Raters were also asked to judge whether particular activities were sex-stereotyped. The total number of *different* occupations depicted for each sex was also compared.

Famous Men and Women

Males and females appearing in stories or questions who have played a role in history or current events, or who have made contributions in art, science, literature, and so forth, were each counted once.

Questions

The following questions received *yes* or *no* responses.

Are women or girls only shown wearing dresses or skirts?

Are there any questions or statements which demean or stereotype females or males, e.g., "She's only a girl" or "All boys are mean"?

Are the emotions expressed either verbally or non-verbally by males or females sex-stereotyped? (Emotions—for example, fear, anger, aggression, excitement, or tenderness—should occur randomly among characters regardless of gender.)

Does the language of the test tend to exclude females? (Note instances when sexually neutral language, for example, *people, men and women*, or *they*, could be substituted without changing the intended meaning.)

Are there separate forms of this test for males and females?

Are there separate norms on this test for males and females?

Results

Results of the test evaluations are presented in tabular form in Appendix H. For every test, ratings were averaged for each of the 24 questions. These means are presented along with their standard deviations. Where a dot (•) appears in the standard deviation column, it indicates that only one rater responded to that particular question and, therefore, there was no standard deviation. The final six questions are presented with *yes* or *no* responses. An average score was derived by assigning numerical values (yes = 1, no = 2) to each rating. Means that were below 1.5 are presented as *yes* responses and those at 1.5 or above are presented as *no* responses. Some questions were not applicable to particular tests. These are designated as *NA* or by a dot (•) in both columns.

A summary of the overall results is presented in Table 1. Totals of all raters' responses are shown along with male-to-female ratios for each category of response. Ratios that exceed 1.00 indicate a preponderance of male referents.

As can be seen in Table 1, males outnumber females in all categories,

Table 1

Ratios of Male and Female Referents, All Tests Combined

Category	Total Number Reported by All Raters, M/F	Ratio M/F
Illustrations		
Adults	3422/1739	1.97
Children	3390/2695	1.26
Animals	28/42	0.67
Content		
Adults	2572/1427	1.80
Children	2591/1917	1.35
Animals	235/119	1.97
Illustrations and content		
Nonoccupational roles		
Stereotyped	610/321	1.90
Total	818/488	1.68
Occupational roles		
Stereotyped	1057/307	3.44
Total	1210/473	2.56
Number of different occupations	1164/430	2.71
Famous men and women	304/39	7.79

except for illustrations of animals, which is the smallest classification. Males appear more often than females in occupational and nonoccupational roles, which are generally gender-stereotyped. They are also shown in many more different types of vocational and avocational pursuits than are females. Most striking is the comparison of the numbers of famous men and women, which approaches a ratio of 8:1. In summary, the results indicate that, on the average, males are referred to more than twice as frequently as are females.

Comparisons of the numbers of tests in which references to males outnumber those to females are presented in Table 2. It should be noted that each rater was randomly assigned half of the test batteries and, therefore, no two raters evaluated exactly the same set of tests. Despite this, Table 2 illustrates that in 86 of the 96 comparisons, raters found more tests in which references were made to males than to females in both illustrations and content of the test materials. Overall, there were more than twice as many tests that featured males to a greater extent than females in the categories studied.

Table 2

Comparisons of the Number of Tests in Which References to Males Outnumber Those to Females

Category	Raters								Totals
	1 M/F	*2* M/F	*3* M/F	*4* M/F	*5* M/F	*6* M/F	*7* M/F	*8* M/F	*Totals* M/F
Illustrations									
Adults	22/14	15/5	19/8	27/11	25/10	25/7	16/7	25/8	174/70
Children	31/8	14/6	19/10	21/17	28/12	19/13	9/14	26/12	167/92
Animals	1/0	0/0	3/2	1/1	0/2	3/4	0/5	2/2	10/16
Content									
Adults	53/18	20/8	24/14	32/13	35/18	29/10	8/4	23/10	224/95
Children	34/30	18/4	23/8	22/28	35/20	16/12	6/4	18/11	172/117
Animals	18/8	4/1	6/0	8/4	10/3	8/2	0/5	7/1	61/24
Illustrations and content Nonoccupational roles									
Stereotyped	23/19	12/8	13/8	34/9	18/13	5/7	10/2	16/6	131/72
Total	31/21	14/8	13/12	31/11	22/9	6/7	10/2	17/7	144/77

Occupational roles								
Stereotyped	43/7	16/6	17/8	32/7	18/1	10/4	14/3	20/9	170/45
Total	47/3	15/5	17/9	35/8	21/2	12/2	13/3	20/8	180/40
Number of different occupations	48/5 170/43	11/5	12/10	29/7	10/5	28/5	14/2	18/4	170/43
Famous men and women	18/2	11/0	10/2	13/1	11/1	11/2	3/0	7/0	84/8
Totals	369/135	150/56	176/91	285/117	233/96	172/75	103/51	199/78	1687/699

Note: Test batteries were assigned randomly to each pair of raters and therefore no two raters evaluated the same set of tests.
M = Numbers of tests in which there were more references to males than to females.
F = Numbers of tests in which there were either an equal or greater number of references to females than to males.

Dialogue with Publishers

It has been pointed out by Boehm (1980), among others, that "few investigators and reviewers send test authors the outcomes of their studies or reviews, a gesture that is greatly appreciated" (p. 473). Boehm suggests that sending test authors this information should become standard policy among members of the American Psychological Association. Others (for example, Tittle, 1974, 1979) have indicated that researchers need to alert publishers to the sex inequities they encounter on test instruments and urge them to make whatever changes are necessary to eliminate bias.

Since one purpose of the present study was to encourage the reduction of sex stereotyping and other forms of sex bias in psychological and educational testing, involving test publishers was considered essential. Each publisher (or publisher's representative) was contacted by mail and informed of the study (see Appendix C). Summary tables (as produced in Appendix H) were provided for each test, and publishers were requested to complete individual response forms (see Appendix D). These forms requested information about planned revisions of the tests and asked publishers if any modifications of their instruments could be made in the interim to reduce sex bias. After the deadline for the return of forms had passed—about a month after the initial mailing—follow-up phone calls were made to each publisher that had not responded. When requested, duplicate materials were forwarded.

RESPONSES FROM PUBLISHERS

Responses were received from the publishers of 62 (or 84 percent) of the 74 tests studied. A total of 17 of the 26 publishers responded, 16 by mail and one by phone. Some of the respondents chose not to use the form provided, but made general comments in a letter.

Whereas most publishers endorsed sex-fair tests, many felt that any changes made by test administrators in order to reduce sex bias (for example, changing proper nouns or pronouns to create a balance of males and females) would invalidate their instruments:

We discourage any changes because these tend to render test results invalid due to departure from procedures used in the standardization program. . . . We uniformly take a rather negative view of any changes in the test content or administration procedures that deviate from the standard procedure or standard content used in the norming program.[2]

Changes in test items, after standardization, should not be made lightly. Uneven percentages of males and females, for example, found in illustrations and stories of an already published test, do not constitute grounds for making changes in the test booklets, in the absence of evidence that uneven percentages of males and females in materials create adverse social attitudes on the part of children.[3]

Any changes made would be extremely disruptive and would probably invalidate the testing.[4]

Changing item content without effecting [sic] test validity may well work for achievement and criterion-referenced tests, but I have seen no evidence that such a procedure would result in equivalent external validity for behavioral/personality measures, where separate norms by sex have always been necessary, and are the standard. Such evidence must come from the professional community before such changes can be instituted.[5]

However, several publishers suggested that until formal revisions were completed that would reduce or eliminate sex bias, certain changes could be made by those administering their tests. These changes are enumerated below.

CTB/McGraw-Hill

Comprehensive Tests of Basic Skills: The examiner may change nouns and pronouns as well as use sex-neutral language in the instructions only. Actual items, however, cannot be changed without risking the validity of the norms. (Changes apply to forms S and T, copyrights 1973 and 1975.)

Lee-Clark Reading Readiness Test: Language in the instructions may be changed so that it is sex-neutral. Changes to items could affect norms. (Changes apply to test copyrighted 1962.)

California Test of Personality: May change the language in the instructions only (see above). (Changes apply to test copyrighted 1953.)

Prescriptive Reading Inventory: Proper nouns and pronouns may be changed so that males and females are equally represented, except for items that test pronoun usage and items in which the proper noun or pronoun is either the correct response or a distractor. Sex-stereotyped language may only be changed if it is not contained in item stems or answer choices. (Changes apply to tests copyrighted 1972, 1973, 1974, 1975, 1976, and 1977.)

Consulting Psychologists Press

Inpatient Multidimensional Psychiatric Scale: Proper nouns and pronouns may be changed to equalize the representation of males and females. Language that excludes females may be changed to sex-neutral language, and demeaning or stereotypical statements about males or females may be revised.

Educators Publishing Service

Pre-reading Screening Procedure and Slingerland Screening Test: For both of these tests, proper nouns and pronouns may be changed by the examiner in order to equalize the representation of males and females.

Jamestown Publishers

Oral Reading Criterion Test: The following changes will be made at the time of the next printing and may be made now by examiners in their old editions in order to equalize the representation of males and females:

Question 2A
"He said to the *boy* sitting there."
Change *boy* to *girl.*
Question 2B
"Then they gave the pig *his* breakfast."
Change *his* to *her.*
"It was fun to watch *him* eat."
Change *him* to *her.*
"*He* seemed to like it."
Change *He* to *She.*
Question 3A
"When the man had gone the *boys* were surprised."
Change *boys* to *girls.*

Question 4
"Then came the long, thin *cowboy*."
Change *cowboy* to *cowgirl*.
"*He* was the last one to enter the contest."
Change *He* to *She*.
Question 6
"*Businessmen* from suburban areas."
Change *Businessmen* to *Workers*.
Question 7
"*His* audience comprised two thousand foreign-born men [addition] who had just been admitted to citizenship."
Change *His* to *The* and add *and women* after "foreign-born men."

Science Research Associates

Primary Mental Abilities Tests: Proper nouns and pronouns in the test may be changed by the examiner to equalize the representation of males and females and language that excludes females may be changed to language that is sex-neutral (for example, *policeman* could be changed to *police officer*, *him* could be replaced with *her*, *he* with *she*). These changes should not be made for vocabulary items. In addition, the sentence structure and context should not be altered.

Slosson

Slosson Intelligence Test: Proper nouns and pronouns in the test may be changed by the examiner to equalize the representation of males and females and language that excludes females may be changed to language that is sex-neutral. Items that depict either sex in stereotypical roles may be revised to reflect nonstereotypical roles.

Most publishers indicated that one or more of the tests that had been evaluated was under revision or was being considered for revision. Some tests were specifically identified as not being slated for any changes. The Lee-Clark Reading Readiness Test was said to be out of print, with no revisions planned. The California Test of Personality, also not slated for revision, was described as "out of date," having been normed in 1953. The Bernreuter Personality Inventory was reported by the publisher to be very old and likely to go out of print in the next few years.

CONCLUSIONS

The results of the present study suggest that many widely used tests present males and females differently. Females tend to be underrepresented in both the illustrations and content of tests. They are less often depicted in occupational and nonoccupational activities than are males and are only infrequently accorded historical importance. Although most test publishers who responded endorsed sex-fair instruments, it appears that changes in that direction will be slow. It is likely that when a particular instrument is next due for restandardization, representation of the sexes will be reconsidered. However, it seems less likely that the acknowledgment of sex bias in a test will make revisions of that test any more urgent.

It is interesting to note the differing responses of test publishers regarding their willingness to suggest modifications that might alleviate sex bias. It is apparent that some publishers believe that changes to their instruments, even those that would merely alter pronouns (such as *she* and *he*) or proper nouns (such as *Jim* or *Sue*), might have a significant effect on test results. Recent research has not borne out this conclusion (see, for example, Boyd, 1978; Gottfredson, 1976). However, since the previous research has been of a limited nature and one cannot be assured that such changes would not affect validity, perhaps it is prudent to be cautious on this point. On the other hand, if publishers are concerned that changes in the representation of males and females will so drastically alter the results produced by their instruments, it would seem that they should themselves be initiating studies to find out exactly what changes might occur and for whom. Unfortunately, there is little evidence that this is being done.

NOTES

1. T. R. Smith, personal communication, March 13, 1980.
2. G. J. Robertson, personal communication, June 5, 1980.
3. L. A. Munday, personal communication, May 29, 1980.
4. T. Sorenson, personal communication, May 2, 1980.
5. D. Lachar, personal communication, June 6, 1980.

II
Review of the
Research Literature

Test Content and Bias

Dwyer (1976) has identified some variables for consideration when one assesses sex bias in the content of test instruments. Basically, there are two types of questions that need to be answered. First, are the sexes role-stereotyped (for example, in terms of occupations, activities, or emotions); are the questions sexist (do they denigrate either sex or suggest limitations based on sex); and do they reflect unequal representation of the sexes? Second, are the types of items presented, the contexts of the items, or other technical aspects of the test biased? Assessment of the first group of concerns, according to Dwyer, must be guided by social values; the second, by psychometric methods.

Although there is likely to be some disagreement about which social values should be reflected in a particular test, establishing some guidelines in this area is essential. Tests are so frequently used in the United States as a part of educational and counseling programs that their cumulative effect is substantial. In addition, the results of tests are taken quite seriously by teachers, parents, and students (Tittle, 1973).

Lockheed-Katz (1974) suggests the use of three criteria to judge whether there is equitable treatment of the sexes:

1. Tests should be constructed of items which contain either no sex references or which are balanced for male and female references.
2. The status of the males and females within the test should be equal.
3. The content of items should not reinforce traditional or stereotyped images of men and women. (p. 12)

Lockheed-Katz concludes that "if a test is biased according to these criteria, it is not intrinsically fair as it does not represent males and females equally, whether or not the test discriminates between male and female test takers" (p. 5).

REPRESENTATION OF THE SEXES

Schneider and Hacker (1973) offer evidence that the word *man*, even when used generically (to refer to both men and women), is not always perceived that way. They found that students confronted with generically masculine words were more likely to choose masculine symbols to represent them than were students given sex-neutral words.

Even without considering such generic words as *man*, research has shown a definite imbalance in the use of masculine- and feminine-oriented items in tests. Tittle, McCarthy, and Steckler (1974) assessed 29 achievement test batteries that were included in the California Achievement Tests, Comparative Guidance and Placement Program, Iowa Tests of Basic Skills, Iowa Tests of Educational Development, Metropolitan Achievement Tests, Sequential Tests of Educational Progress, SRA Achievement Series, Stanford Early School Achievement Test, and the Stanford Achievement Test. They found that although the content of test items was generally biased in favor of males, the bias they found was not due to language usage. That is, even after removing generic nouns and pronouns (such as Western *man*), 21 of the 29 tests still had male to female ratios that were greater than 2:1.

Tittle et al. found that the tests they studied were similar to other educational materials in their sex-stereotyped portrayal of males and females. Females were presented mainly as homemakers and as less active than males, and it was insinuated that most professions are closed to them.

Tittle et al. also reviewed college admission test materials and concluded that explanatory information designed to acquaint students with these tests was also sex-biased. In a related study, the authors analyzed educational measurement textbooks and found a lack of discussion about the effects of sex stereotyping and sex bias on item construction.

Rowell (1977), who studied reading tests, found that males and females are not given equal representation and are presented in stereotypical roles on the Diagnostic Reading Scales, the Durrell Analysis of Reading Difficulty, and the Classroom Reading Inventory. Similar trends were noted by Tanney (1974) for interest inventories. She found instances of sex stereotyping and sex bias in the Kuder Occupational Interest Survey Form DD, the Self-Directed Search, and the Strong Campbell Interest Inventory.

ITEM CONTENT

According to Donlon et al. (1977), "Test outcomes are the result of an interaction between test taker and test content. The content of tests, however, frequently reflects the very stereotypical expectations about sex and identity that prevail in the society" (p. 3).

Dwyer (1976) notes that there is a good deal of "nonconscious sexism" that is perpetuated in standardized instruments. For example, on verbal tests, in which females traditionally excel, specifications often limit the proportions of various types of items and mandate that more male-oriented items be included. On the other hand, this has not generally been the case for exams in mathematics, which tend to favor males. Dwyer points out that changes in the content emphasis of a particular test, both from one edition to the next and from one grade level to another within the same edition, may be overlooked when conclusions are drawn about sex differences. For instance, girls and boys perform similarly on math computation, whereas boys seem to excel, beginning in adolescence, in problem solving. The proportions of each type of item included in a particular test would likely determine the degree of disparity between males' and females' scores. In addition, speeded math tests favor males. Dwyer concludes that "since sex differences are often small, one or two biased items may make a significant contribution to a reported sex difference" (p. 6).

The effect of test item content on sex differences in test performance has received remarkably little attention from publishers and researchers. In fact, disparities between test performance for males and females are often attributed to native differences between the sexes (Tittle, 1974). (Of course, evidence for these "differences" comes from the results of other tests.) Publishers seem to see no need to provide proof that sex-biased item construction does not have an effect on test scores. The majority of those studies conducted, however, confirm that for some items gender orientation of content or context does have a differential effect on male and female performance.

Early research by Milton (1959) controlled the content of math problems so that equivalent skills were tested using either "masculine"- or "feminine"-type items. Having found that women did better on feminine-oriented questions, he concluded:

It is not entirely that men have a better developed "general reasoning" capacity or solely that they have learned more skill, but apparently that they are responding in part merely to the stimulus properties of the immediate situation, which in the case of problem-solving research has been predominantly appropriate to the male role. That is, the role-appropriate stimuli motivate S to attend better, to work harder and longer, and perhaps, to experience less task anxiety. (p. 707)

The conjecture that motivational factors may be critical to test item success is also suggested by the work of Breland (1974), who found that black subjects did better on reading test questions related to a passage about a television program oriented toward blacks than they did on other equally challenging items.

Milton's study (1959) is one of the few that attempted to control content variables. Other research has compared test results to determine if males and females performed differently on items. If significant results were found, hypotheses were generated after the fact to explain why particular types of items were more often passed by members of one sex.

Graf and Riddell (1972) found that women took more time to solve a masculine-oriented question than did men, an outcome that was not found for a feminine-oriented item. Females also perceived the masculine-oriented question to be harder than did males, although both sexes found the feminine-oriented one equally difficult.

Coffman (1961) analyzed males' and females' responses to the 1954 version of the Scholastic Aptitude Test-Verbal (SAT-V). He found that women did significantly better on three items, each of which contained words that were related to personal feelings or personality characteristics. Of the six items on which males excelled, three focused on business or mechanics. Coffman also found that a test specialist he was working with was able to predict the direction of the sex differences with a high degree of accuracy.

Donlon (1973) notes that since 1930, males have remained superior to females on the Scholastic Aptitude Test-Mathematical (SAT-M), but females have lost their edge over males on the SAT-V. In his study Donlon looked at the content of both the verbal and mathematical portions of the 1964 SAT. His results are similar to Coffman's regarding the SAT-V. Eight items favored males and eleven favored females. Those items that were easier for males could be classified as "World of Practical Affairs" or "Science," while those on which females excelled could be categorized as "Human Relations," "Humanities," or "Aesthetic-Philosophical."

On the mathematical portion of the SAT, differences were even more substantial, with 29 items favoring males and only two favoring females slightly. One of the two, although no less mathematically oriented than the others, is a question relating to laundry.

Donlon notes that the 17 items on the SAT-M that referred to real-world things or "subject matter items" were all male-oriented. Although males were sometimes referred to, there were no corresponding references to females. It is interesting to note that compared to the other three categories of questions—"geometric figures," "algebra," and "other"—this group of questions showed the largest mean differences favoring males.

Donlon points out that if all of the SAT questions were of the "subject matter" variety, the male advantage on the SAT-M could have been as much as 60 points, rather than the 40-point difference he observed, However, if "algebra" questions were used exclusively, the difference could have dropped to as low as 20 points. Donlon does not conclude that it was the content of the SAT-M items that made them more difficult for females, since other factors that could have accounted for the difference may also have been present. He does suggest the need for further research.

In a subsequent study, Strassberg-Rosenberg and Donlon (1975) examined the SATs administered in 1974. The authors performed several analyses that included statistically locating items whose rank order of difficulty was dissimilar for males and females, and studying their content. Language bias, sex stereotyping, and sex bias were also studied.

Although males and females had similar mean SAT-V scores, males did significantly better on nine items, whereas females were superior on three. In classifying the content of these items, the authors found that males excelled on questions that fell into the categories of "World of Practical Affairs," "Science," and "Reading Comprehension." The two questions in the last category on which males performed better could be classified as "Historical-Political." Females did better on items which could be classified as "Aesthetic-Philosophical" and on items that, although the raters agreed they could be called "World of Practical Affairs," the authors considered to be person-oriented.

For the nine items on which males surpassed females, six were biased toward masculine interests or skills, such as time and space relations, transportation, communication, science, political science, mechanics, electronics, and war. The three items favoring women involved personality traits and cooking.

Although the authors found that the SAT-V included more references to males than to females, this imbalance did not appear to affect performance. Portrayals of both sexes were stereotyped, men being depicted as more powerful than women. Although questions were asked pertaining to famous men, no prominent women were included. The researchers concluded that, like the 1964 edition of the SAT-V, the 1974 version was male-oriented.

On the SAT-M, Strassberg-Rosenberg and Donlon found that males attained higher overall scores than females. Breaking the test down into "data sufficiency" and "regular math" items, the authors ascertained that although males did better on both types of questions, the former were relatively easier for females. However, there were far fewer questions of this type and it was noted that this category of items was scheduled to be eliminated from future versions of the SAT-M. Although no relationship was established between item content and performance by sex, it was found that there were more than twice as many references made to males than to females on the SAT-M.

Other achievement tests have also been analyzed for sex-biased content. Donlon et al. (1977) reviewed the Sequential Tests of Educational Progress, the California Achievement Test, the Iowa Tests of Basic Skills, and the Metropolitan Achievement Tests in Reading. The authors determined that content factors and sex differences in performance were related. Items tended to contain more references to males, and this imbalance corresponded (on the fifth, ninth, and tenth, but not the second grade tests) to sex differences in performance. That is, more females than males passed items when female references predominated than they did when items depicted greater numbers of males or equal numbers of males and females. This was true even after the effects of item achievement, content, format, and test length were removed.

Brown and Moss (1979) recently reported two studies that explored the effects of sex referents in test items on performance. In the first study, they examined teacher-constructed tests in an educational psychology course and found that students' relative performance increased on items that contained same-sex nouns or pronouns. The authors pointed out, however, that the actual item content, which was not taken into account, may have contributed to these results.

A second study attempted to control for content. Masculine or feminine forms of a passage and corresponding test items were presented randomly to psychology students. No significant interactions were found. However, there was a tendency for subjects to perform better when presented with materials corresponding to their own sex. The authors suggest that "while the effects of sex bias on any single test will be small, when cumulated over a course, or several years of education, the effects could indeed become significant. Thus, test constructors should attempt to balance sex references on their tests'' (p. 10).

Several studies have concluded, after finding negative or mixed results, that sex-biased items do not relate to sex differences or otherwise affect performance. One such study, by Plake, Hoover, and Loyd (1978), analyzed math items on the Iowa Tests of Basic Skills. Although it was found that there were several items in the Mathematics Problem Solving subtests that were stereotypically male-oriented and that contained a preponderance of male pronouns, these items did not clearly favor either sex. The authors did find significant sex interactions for every math and verbal subtest they studied. However, their analysis of the data yielded no systematic advantage for either sex.

A similar conclusion was reached by Shaffer (1976), who used three different procedures to determine if there was a relationship between sex bias and performance on two scales of the Ohio Vocational Interest Survey. Although Shaffer found that items on the two scales, Machine Work and Clerical Work, were favored significantly more often by males and by females, respectively, he did not find significant item-sex group interactions. He concluded, therefore, assuming that the actual items were not consistently biased, that no sex bias in performance exists for the two scales. Finally, using an item-total score correlational analysis, he found that some items on the Clerical Work scale may function differently for males and females and thus may possibly be sex-biased. Shaffer concluded that since the latter two analyses did not support the conclusions based on using the item favorability data, this method was probably inappropriate for use in detecting sex bias.

Gottfredson (1976) tested the assumption that sexist wording may affect performance on interest measures. Using an experimental edition of the Vocational Preference Inventory and the Self-Directed Search (SDS), he found that high school girls did not choose nonsexist items any more frequently than they chose sexist ones. Although Gottfredson pointed out that his study had its limitations (one was that only four occupations were compared), he concluded that his results were not consistent with the idea that interest inventories are sex-biased.

A similar study by Boyd (1978) utilized a revised form of the SDS that contained non-gender-specific occupational titles and sex-neutral instructions. Boyd found no differences in the final summary codes between college women who took the revised test and those who took the standard version. However, subjects' evaluations of the two tests were significantly different; those who completed the sex-neutral form perceived it as more sex-fair. Boyd concluded that revising the SDS had no significant effects and suggested that researchers spend their energies studying other areas instead.

An alternative conclusion might be that the psychometric integrity of a test can be maintained, even when it is changed so that the language it contains is sex-neutral. Such results "suggest that no author or publisher can be excused for using masculine-toned language or items" (Tittle and Zytowski, 1978, p. 15).

CONCLUSIONS

The results of studies that attempt to relate item content to sex differences in test performance are far from conclusive. However, some researchers have found statistically significant (if not always highly meaningful) effects. Obviously, more work in this area is indicated.

Little research has been attempted to ascertain the psychological effects of taking a test (or test after test) that is in some way sex-biased. One study referred to in this section does indicate, however, that people seem to be sensitive to such biases.

One frequent rejoinder made by publishers and others to the suggestion that females and males be represented in less restrictive roles is that tests should reflect only what a person has learned in society. They conclude, therefore, that it is not up to the test publisher, but rather to those preparing educational materials, to accelerate change. In light of the tendency to separate "educational" materials from those designed to assess educational outcomes, it should be considered that test taking is a part of an individual's education and that tests, like all educational materials, convey information. Institutions, especially publicly supported educational and medical facilities, must recognize that they hold powerful positions in the lives of their clients. The use of sex-biased tests by such institutions must be considered an endorsement of inequitable treatment of males and females.

Since there is now evidence that tests can be "sex-neutralized" without adverse psychometric effects (see the chapter entitled "Interest Inventories and Achievement Tests"), there does not seem to be any valid reason to accept or utilize instruments that do not treat the sexes fairly.

Validity, Reliability, and Sex-Fair Selection

VALIDITY

In determining the value of any test instrument, the question that must be confronted is, is it valid? That is, does it measure what it purports to measure? As Kerlinger (1964) states, "There is no one validity" (p. 445). Different users may have different purposes for a test and an instrument may be valid for some and not for others. Naturally, a separate test of validity is needed on each criterion. Three types of validity can be related to test bias: face validity, criterion validity, and construct validity.

Face Validity

According to Anastasi (1976), face validity "concerns rapport and public relations" (p. 139). Face validity refers simply to whether or not a test appears valid. It is based on the subjective judgments of testees and others not necessarily trained in test and measurement theory. Anastasi makes the point that "if test content appears irrelevant, inappropriate, silly or childish, the result will be poor cooperation, regardless of the actual validity of the test" (pp. 139-40). Obviously, an uncooperative test subject is not likely to perform to the best of his or her ability.

Insofar as sex bias is concerned, it is apparent that test items that demean or stereotype women and that are predominantly oriented toward males and highly masculine activities might not motivate females in the same way as they would males. This, of course, would also be true for men taking a test that was degrading in its references or irrelevant to males.

When face validity is poor, a simple solution is to rewrite the items so that they will appear more appropriate to the group being tested. Anastasi warned, however, that simply improving face validity will not necessarily improve a test's objective validity, nor can it be assumed that such changes will not affect objective validity.

Criterion Validity

Criterion validity includes both predictive and concurrent validity. Predictive validity refers to an instrument's ability to foretell a particular outcome. Concurrent validity is a similar measure based on current, rather than future, performance. A test that is unbiased, therefore, should be able to make predictions for different subgroups with equivalent accuracy.

Determining Test Criteria

One problem, often overlooked, is that the criterion itself is not easy to define and may be a source of controversy. For example, in the case of interest inventories, the relevant question at hand is whether the criterion should be accuracy of prediction or the encouragement of more diverse vocational options on the part of men and women.

Diamond (1972) proposes that the criteria, in order to be useful, should be current so that they reflect social change adequately. Few are likely to disagree that it is desirable to obtain up-to-date information on which to base test criteria. However, the proposal that interest inventories be validated on their ability to encourage testees to explore a wide range of career possibilities (Tittle, 1978a) has met with some resistance. Holland (1975) states that interest tests should be able to provide highly predictive information: "Interest inventories are assessment, not social-action devices. Attempts to make them otherwise are an anti-intellectual, anti-scientific, destructive activity" (p. 43). Gottfredson and Holland (1978) also express concern that if sex differences were removed from interest inventories, the scores would decrease in construct validity because personality constructs depend on experience, and experience is different for the two sexes.

Holland and Gottfredson (1976) tested a revision of the Realistic and Competency Scales of the Self-Directed Search (SDS). Although they found an increase in scores for females taking the revised form of the SDS, they also found that the new scales were lower in concurrent validity. The authors note that their small and nonrepresentative sample was a flaw in their study, yet conclude that "the revising of scales on intuitive grounds to reduce sex differences is not a promising way to improve the vocational welfare of women'' (p. 227).

As has been pointed out by van der Flier and Drenth (1977), when the goal is to make substantial changes in an existing system, the criterion-oriented approach is inappropriate, since it only reinforces those discrepancies that already exist. According to Cole and Hanson (1975), there are two hypotheses that apply to career selection. The hypothesis of socialization dominance suggests that ''until the areas of socially accepted interest options become broadened during a person's development, the careers in which such people will be satisfied will not broaden'' (p. 10). The hypothesis of opportunity dominance states, ''When career opportunities widen, people will find satisfaction in a wider range of careers in spite of limiting aspects of their earlier socialization'' (p. 10).

Prediger and Cole (1975) recommend that the opportunity model be used to validate interest inventories. Occupations could be suggested to men and women whose interests were similar to the interests of members of those occupational groups, regardless of current employment patterns. Like Prediger and Cole, Hanson, Prediger, and Schussel (1977) point out that it is a rather minimal accomplishment to be able to predict future vocations accurately, especially for women. One has only to look at the census, for example, to determine that the majority of women choose social service occupations. The authors state that, having only this information, one could attain a high ''hit rate'' (rate of accuracy of prediction). Prediger and Cole contend that ''an interest inventory that does not suggest social service, or nursing, or clerical occupations to large numbers of women and business, or technical, or trades occupations to large numbers of men would produce a relatively low hit rate because of the very nature of current occupational distributions'' (p. 245). In other words, the predictive validity of such an instrument would be low.

Another consideration is that even if we do agree on test criteria, we cannot assume that these criteria themselves are valid. For example, as Wild and Dwyer suggest (1977), grade point averages (GPAs), frequently used criteria, are made up of nonequivalent units that reflect different experiences for each student. The authors point out that course selection varies from one individual to another and the general fields from which courses are selected also tend to differ for each sex. In addition, grading practices may be affected by sex bias. Even if GPAs were equivalent for individuals, they might also be insufficient as criteria since they are not capable of measuring many educational objectives. Wild and Dwyer warn, however, that some criterion measures that have been suggested for use instead of test results or GPAs may be even more biased. For example, basing judgments on a candidate's early history or relying on letters of recommendation may only serve to reinforce traditional stereotypes.

Selection Models

Various models have been devised to equate the selection of subgroups. They have been discussed in depth by Jensen (1980) and comparisons among them have been made by several authors (Cole, 1972; Linn, 1973; van der Flier and Drenth, 1977). Therefore, they will be described here only briefly.

The classical or regression definition of test bias (also referred to as the Cleary definition) states:

A test is biased for members of a subgroup of the population if, in the prediction of a criterion for which the test was designed, consistent nonzero errors of prediction are made for members of the subgroup. In other words, the test is biased if the criterion score predicted from the common regression line is consistently too high or low for members of the subgroup. With this definition of bias, there may be a connotation of "unfair," particularly if the use of the test produces a prediction that is too low. (Cleary, 1968, p. 115)

Linn (1973 notes that Cleary's definition has been the one most widely accepted among psychometricians who use prediction to assess bias.

The Equal Risk Model (also known as the Employer's Model) is proposed by Einhorn and Bass (1971). The maximum level of selection error risk that an institution is willing to take is specified, and applicants who are below this level are selected, regardless of group membership. According to this model, a test or selection procedure would be unfair if people who were equally likely to succeed on a given task were not equally likely to be chosen.

The Proportional Representation Model is an attempt to equalize opportunties for groups that may otherwise be underselected or overselected based on test scores. The top-ranking proportion of the group, equivalent to its proportional representation in society, is selected. In other words, bias would exist when a particular group was not proportionally represented.

Thorndike (1971) proposes a Constant Ratio Model whereby members would be selected from each subgroup in proportion to the numbers who would be successful if everyone were selected. That is, equivalent proportions of successful candidates would be selected from each group. According to Thorndike, even if there were equal regressive equations, the lower-scoring group would be underselected as compared to the higher-scoring group. In other words, fewer members of the lower-scoring group who would have achieved success on the criterion would be chosen.

Cole's (1972) Conditional Probability Model (or Equal Opportunity Model) suggests that a test is fair if members of both groups who achieve satisfactory performance on the criterion are equally likely to be selected. This model utilizes cutting scores for each group so that the proportion of those successful on the criterion is the same for both groups. In other words, "given one member of the majority group and one member of the minority group, both of whom succeed if selected, the procedure is unfair unless they have the same probability of being selected" (p. 4).

Petersen and Novick (1976) have offered models based on premises that are the opposite of those proposed by preceding models. Their Converse Constant Ratio Model and Converse Conditional Probability Model are based upon rejecting rather than accepting equal proportions of subgroup members.

Frazer, Miller, and Epstein (1975) compared Cleary's and Thorndike's models with the traditional single equation regression model. They found that by using the single equation regression, selection was biased in favor of the subgroup with the lower mean criterion score. Using the Cleary model favored the subgroup with the higher mean criterion score. Only the Thorndike model, since it chooses proportionally from each subgroup, did not result in any selection bias in either direction.

Frazer et al. also compared these three models for the accuracy with which they selected successful individuals. They defined bias in selection accuracy as the identification of a greater number of successful individuals from one subgroup than from the other. Using the Cleary model, they found selection to be consistently biased in favor of the group with the higher mean, but only slightly. The traditional regression equation resulted in a slight selection bias in favor of the group with the lower mean.

Darlington (1971) suggests a Culture-Modified Criterion Model. He points out that the two optimally desirable goals of test construction—maximizing validity and minimizing a test's correlation with cultural variables—are incompatible. The problem lies in how one should balance these two objectives. Darlington concludes that since no "mechanical" solution to the problem is feasible, the weight given to each of these goals must be derived subjectively. An outline of the procedures he recommends for doing so can be found in Darlington's articles (1971, 1976).

Construct Validity

Construct validity may also be a consideration in assessing test equity. The question here is, does the instrument measure the trait(s) it purports to measure? This can be gauged either internally or externally.

External validation includes intercorrelating the test in question with others that supposedly measure the same thing, or administering the instrument to people who are known to have the particular characteristic being assessed (known groups method). For examples of these procedures, see Kerlinger (1964).

Internal validation methods include analyzing item intercorrelations, computing group X item interactions, conducting factor analyses, and comparing characteristic curves.

Fishbein (1975) considered items biased against a group if they showed a group X item interaction. That is, if a group's average scores on particular items are inconsistent with those that would be expected based on total test scores, bias is present. He points out that merely using analysis of variance to assess this interaction is insufficient because this procedure will not identify which items are contributing to the interaction. Fishbein also notes that finding no interaction does not necessarily indicate that a test is fair. Rather, it may be that all of the items are biased against the group in question. If this is the case, the possibility exists that no one item would show an interaction because all are similarly biased. On the other hand, he states, this could also mean that an item found to be biased might be fair, having been identified only because of its difference from the majority of biased items.

Strassberg-Rosenberg and Donlon (1975) explain item-sex bias as an "aberration in the pattern of difficulty for males and females on a specific item when that item is compared to the performance on other items within the test or section" (p. 1). In their work, plots of item difficulty were used to determine item-group interactions with those items that were far from the major cluster of points in the plots being designated as adding to the interaction. That is, those items that were not in the same rank order of difficulty for males and females were considered biased. Once these items were identified statistically, the authors tried to assess subjectively whether the content of these items might account for the varying levels of difficulty for the groups.

Another method of assessing bias was used by Shaffer (1976), who examined item-total score correlations for males and females on interest inventory subtests. Correlations were derived for each individual's total score and her or his score on each item.

Scheuneman (n.d.) proposes that an item is unbiased if people who are equal in ability are equally likely to pass it, regardless of the subgroup to which they belong. She considers that subtests, since they are comprised of similar items, are more appropriate to compare than are the scores attained on an entire test that might measure various abilities. A subtest item is considered unbiased if equal numbers of individuals from each subgroup who have scored similarly on the entire subtest are able to pass it.

Potthoff (cited in Burrill, 1975) offers another definition of fairness. He suggests that a fair test would result in equivalent total mean scores for each subgroup. In other words, although items might be responded to differently, these differences would be balanced out.

Still another way of assessing bias, suggested by Veale and Foreman (cited in Burrill, 1975), is to analyze incorrect, rather than correct, responses. This method supposes that the distractors (incorrect choices) may be biased.

Diamond (1976) suggests a model for studying sex bias in aptitude and achievement instruments that involves calculating for each item or subtest the percentage of males and females in the upper- and lower-scoring groups who respond correctly. Comparisons could then be made of the results for males and females and the combined sex data could be obtained. Diamond proposes that the differences between males' and females' performance in each group should not average more than 5 percent in either direction and that their average test differences should be smaller. She recommends that the above procedure be used during the pretesting phase of test construction.

RELIABILITY

Although no test can be valid if it is unreliable, we often do not consider that a particular instrument may not be equally reliable for males and females, thus making it less valid for one sex than for the other. When one uses a regression model to predict performance, the lower-scoring group will be overpredicted when the reliability is less than one. The less reliable the predictor, the more important it is to make adjustments in the regression equations (Wild and Dwyer, 1977).

CONCLUSIONS

Since it appears that it is not difficult to predict future vocational membership for females and males, with or without traditional interest inventories, it seems appropriate to demand more of these instruments. If we are to spend time and money on their distribution, administration, and interpretation, it would seem reasonable that these inventories should offer counselors and counselees more than they could already guess using common sense. Using the opportunity dominance model or a similar one to assess validity would seem less constricting to both women and men than the traditional validation procedures generally used for interest inventories.

As with other types of tests using validation criteria that may be biased, it appears that we need to be cautious in interpreting their results. It may be that although we can gain very dependable data from these instruments, these data do not really reflect what we may think. The fact that one is successful or unsuccessful in a situation in which a particular bias is operating may reflect luck (that one is in the favored group), skill (at getting around the bias), socialization, intelligence, or a combination of these. Although there are no perfect instruments, systematic criterion bias can and should certainly be tempered by assessing or selecting individuals in a variety of ways.

There does not seem to be a lack of models for defining test bias. Although it is probably impossible to choose the one best means of determining whether or not a test is sex-fair, it should be noted that the choice of a particular model is likely to influence that conclusion. As has been mentioned in countless statistics books, one can "prove" almost anything by presenting the "right" set of data. Therefore, it should be made quite clear in the information provided for test administrators why a particular set of statistics was chosen to demonstrate test fairness.

If possible, it is suggested that more than one means of demonstrating sex fairness should be reported and that subjective as well as objective reports be considered. Those who use tests will often find in the test manual no information available to answer questions about sex bias. However, the more feedback that test publishers receive indicating a desire for such information, the more likely they are to begin studying and reporting it. Further, since many models have already been derived, it is not unreasonable to suggest that individuals can begin to apply these models to the tests they use and offer their results to publishers and test authors.

Interest Inventories and Achievement Tests

INTEREST INVENTORIES

Interest measures were among the first tests to be identified as sex-biased. Although they are discussed separately here in order to highlight the changes they have undergone, many of the criticisms and recommendations mentioned are equally applicable to all tests.

In 1972 the American Personnel and Guidance Association appointed the Commission on Sex Bias in Measurement of the Association for Measurement and Evaluation in Guidance (AMEG Commission). Its task was to study alleged sex bias in the Strong Vocational Interest Blank (SVIB). The commission defined sex bias in career guidance as "that condition or provision which influences a person to limit his or her consideration of career opportunities solely on the basis of that person's sex" (AMEG Commission on Sex Bias in Measurement, 1973, p. 172). The commission noted the following inequities in the treatment of males and females on the SVIB:

1. Different occupational scores were provided for each sex and there were some occupations (e.g., certified public accountant and public administrator) on which women could not be scored and some (e.g., medical technologist and physical education teacher) on which men could not be scored.

2. Males and females who took the SVIB opposite-sex form received scores that were different from those they would receive on the same-sex form.

3. The SVIB manual questioned women's occupational interests and suggested deference to "practical considerations," including training or job experience in

fields "providing backgrounds that might be helpful to a wife and mother, occupations that can be pursued part time, are easily resumed after periods of non-
employment, and are readily available in different locales." (p. 171)

The commission made several recommendations for revising the SVIB. It
suggested that a single test form be used for both sexes and that occupational choices on that form be sex-neutral (for example not *saleslady*, but
salesperson). Also recommended was that same-sex norms be provided for
homogeneous interest scales (scales composed of clusters of items related to
occupational interests) because responses to these types of tests typically
differ along sex lines.

The commission noted that occupational interest scales (scales developed
by empirical correlation of interests and occupations so that characteristic
interests associated with members of an occupation can be identified) are
usually derived using separate-sex criterion and reference groups. In
general, the responses of males and females in both groups differ. However,
some researchers have questioned the importance of these differences. The
commission implied that perhaps items could be devised that would be able
to differentiate among vocational groups without separating the sexes. The
commission pointed out the problems inherent in reporting opposite-sex
scores and concluded that if a report was of questionable validity, no scores
should be reported.

Campbell (author of the Strong-Campbell Interest Inventory, the SVIB's
revised version published in 1974) indicates (in Campbell et al., 1974) that it
was pressure for change, largely the result of the women's movement, that
prompted the decision to merge the separate-sex forms into a common
inventory. Campbell et al. explain that other modifications were also made
during the revision. For example, scores are now reported on the same form
for both sexes. However, sex is still a consideration in scoring because,
according to Campbell et al., "Men and women still differ markedly in their
responses to this inventory—even when samples of both sexes are drawn
from the same occupation" (p. 94). In addition, the report allows males and
females to compare their scores to those of members of their own and of the
opposite sex. Other modifications include the elimination of the
Masculinity-Femininity Scale, changes in occupational titles so that they
could apply to either sex, and the addition of scales normed on women in
nontraditional occupations. However, Tittle (1978a) indicates that many
items on the Strong-Campbell Interest Inventory are still highly sex-
stereotyped.

In 1974 the National Institute of Education (NIE) published its "Guidelines for Assessment of Sex Bias and Sex Fairness" (in Diamond, 1975) to serve as a supplement to guidelines included in the American Psychological Association's *Standards for Educational and Psychological Tests* (1974), to the selection guidelines of the Equal Employment Opportunity Commission (1970), and to Title IX of the Education Amendments Act of 1972. The NIE guidelines focused on three areas of possible sex bias: the inventory itself, technical information, and inter-pretive guidelines. In summary, NIE suggested standards that, in large measure, are applicable to most tests.

As concerns the test itself, the guidelines indicated that the same form should be used for males and females unless separate forms have been proved to be significantly more efficient in reducing sex bias. Scores in all areas should be reported for both sexes and the derivation of those scores should be clearly designated (such as male, female, or combined-sex norms). It is preferable that items be equally familiar to both sexes. If this is not possible, then a balance of items familiar to each sex should be achieved within each scale. Sex-specific occupational titles, as well as the generic use of *he* and *she*, should be eliminated and replaced with sex-neutral terms on both male and female forms.

The NIE guidelines also made a number of recommendations concerning technical materials accompanying tests. The group suggested that these materials should indicate what a publisher has done to comply with the guidelines. The technical materials should report the breakdown by sex of criterion and norm groups and should explain the use of same- or combined-sex norms and their impact on test validity. If scores for one sex are to be reported on scales derived using the opposite sex, the validity of this procedure should be indicated. In addition, NIE proposed that publishers include the distribution by sex of career options suggested by a particular inventory. It also recommended that the validity of an inventory for minorities should be studied and reported on and that all aspects of a test be assessed at least every five years and updated if necessary.

The NIE guidelines also addressed interpretive information that might be given to counselors or to the testees themselves. Some of these recommendations are similar to those made concerning the inventory and its accompanying technical information. For example, recommended are the use of sex-neutral language, the presentation of case studies that include both sexes and that are not stereotypical, and explanations of the types of norms employed. The guidelines also detailed suggestions for increasing the user's awareness of possible sex biases in tests and in society and for helping counselors and testees to broaden their occupational outlook regardless of sex.

Guidelines such as those devised by NIE represent the ideal, however. Studies of interest tests have found many severely lacking, even as concerns the most basic aspects of sex fairness. Birk (1974) points out that, whereas the U.S. Department of Labor has indicated a need for women to train for nontraditional as well as traditional occupations, interest inventories and manuals are replete with overt and covert messages to the contrary. She found that manuals and interpretive guidelines could, if adhered to by counselors, result in restrictive recommendations for women. She recommends, as did NIE, that manuals should not be written as if all counselors and clients were males, that case examples should represent both sexes equally, and that both males and females be represented in nontraditional pursuits. She suggests that interest inventories might include a statement indicating that the entire range of occupations is open to either sex, but, unlike AMEG, she supports the use of opposite-sex norms.

Prediger (1978) points out that sex-restrictive interest inventories seem to be based on the premise that these instruments "simply report the facts of life" (p. 1). Prediger defines an interest inventory as sex-restrictive "to the degree that the distribution of career options suggested to males and females is disproportionate. Conversely, an interest inventory is not sex restrictive if each career option covered by the inventory is suggested to similar proportions of males and females" (p. 2).

Prediger distinguishes between sex restrictiveness and sex bias. A test may have to be sex-restrictive in order to be valid. However, if a test is sex-restrictive and sex restrictiveness is not necessary for its validity, then the test is sex-biased. Prediger points out that the burden of proof for justifying the necessity for sex-restrictive tests must be borne by the publisher. One alternative to sex-restrictive tests that Prediger suggests is to use same-sex norms, since these have been shown to yield similar profiles for males and females. Another is to try to match interests and occupations without consideration for the accuracy of prediction. In other words, the identification of career possibilities, rather than probabilities, would be the criterion used to validate interest inventories.

Of particular importance is Prediger's finding that construct and criterion validity are not compromised when sex-balanced reporting is utilized. In his review of ten studies, Prediger found that using sex-balanced (same-sex) norms produced scores that were at least as valid, and in some cases more valid, as those based on sex-restrictive criteria.

Another way of reducing sex restrictiveness suggested by Prediger would be to use items that are sex-balanced. He points out that about half of the items already in use would meet this criterion. If all items were sex-balanced, then combined-sex norms could be utilized. Sex balancing has already been achieved to some extent in the Unisex Interest Inventory (Rayman, 1978) and in the Unisex ACT Interest Inventory (Hanson, Prediger, and Schussel, 1977). Prediger's review of the research suggests that similar levels of validity are reached when one uses these sex-balanced scales as when sex-balanced reports are employed.

A more individualized career-interest approach has been developed by Dewey (1974). Her Non-Sexist Vocational Card Sort for men and women is based on the Tyler Vocational Card Sort. Occupations from the male and female Strong Vocational Interest Blanks and the Kuder Occupational Interest Survey (KOIS) are placed on 3 " x 5 " cards and coded according to Holland's six personality types. All occupational titles are non-sex-specific and there are no norms. Clients sort the cards according to their interests and are counseled on vocational possibilities.

In 1974 the Association for Measurement and Evaluation in Guidance (AMEG) Commission was asked to evaluate 11 widely used interest inventories. In 1975 and again in 1977, publishers of these tests were contacted to find out what measures they were taking to counteract sex bias in their instruments. The AMEG Commission (1977) found that the publishers surveyed were working toward reducing identified bias. However, others have found that revisions were sometimes less than complete.

Harway et al. (1976) reported that the KOIS Form DD placed males and females in separate criterion groups. The authors felt that this procedure reinforced the idea that sex differences are a prominent concern in occupational decision making.

These authors also reviewed Holland's Self-Directed Search and found that, since one's career predictions are made, in part, by considering one's past experiences, the test may reflect a woman's insufficient opportunities rather than her interests or abilities.

Holland (1975) has defended his test and has taken strong objection to NIE's definition of sex bias. He contends that "assessment devices must score or note the effects of a lifetime—to fail to do so would lead to invalid assessment" (p. 24). Holland states that the AMEG and the U.S. Office of Education have not proved that interest inventories have any negative consequences and that "legislative action designed to improve vocational services or to remedy bias appears especially inappropriate" (p. 42). Although Holland calls for more scientific inquiry before any changes are made in vocational assessment devices, Harmon (1973) has pointed out that "although science and scientific method will tell us what the situation is now and even how to change it in a variety of ways, they will not tell us which way we should go. It is a matter of choice" (p. 496).

ACHIEVEMENT TESTS

Diamond (1980) met with five major educational test publishers in order to discuss sex bias in achievement tests. She found that most of the publishers had already given some thought to the issue of sex bias and had prepared guidelines for their item writers. Most of these recommendations concerned what Diamond called "visible" bias, for example, the frequency and degree of stereotyping of male and female representation. Several publishers did report that they analyzed standardization data separately by sex; however, few reported this information in their test manuals. Diamond's survey resulted in several recommendations, summarized below.

1. Guidelines for removing sex bias from the content of tests should be made available by publishers to those who construct tests.
2. Items should be analyzed by sex, and also by sex within ethnic groups.
3. There should be a balance of items biased for and against a particular sex when it is necessary to retain such biased items.
4. Separate norms should be provided for teachers and counselors when sex differences in performance are apparent.
5. Scores should be reported on both sets of norms and should include an explanation of this interpretation.
6. Teachers and counselors should be provided with information about sex differences in performance by the test publisher.

In addition, Diamond suggests further research in order to assess the effects of educational preparation and general ability on sex differences in performance.

CONCLUSIONS

The evolution of interest inventories and achievement tests in response to the urging of professional individuals and groups indicates that educators and psychologists can and do have a great impact on the types of instruments they use with their clients. Having power, they also have responsibility. There must be further research on the psychometric and psychological consequences of sex-biased tests and the results of this research must be communicated to test developers and publishers.

It seems apparent that some value judgments will be needed. We can already predict, with good accuracy and without using any test, what type of occupation a person is likely to enter merely by asking her or him directly what he or she plans to do in the future (Hanson, Prediger, and Schussel, 1977). The question then is, what is the purpose of an interest test? Should it predict according to the status quo or should it suggest an expanded range of options? It is the conclusion of this report that the latter is the more appropriate goal. Since it has been shown (by Prediger, 1978, and others) that tests designed to meet this objective have been devised with considerable success and without a concomitant loss of validity, there seems to be no reason why other measures cannot be modified in the same direction.

Reporting Test Results

Interest inventories typically produce different score patterns for males and females. That is, in general they accurately reflect the world of work. Studies that have reported the scores of males and females on intelligence and ability tests have produced much less consistent results. Jensen (1980) reports that most of the research that has utilized tests and has been published since 1966 has shown insignificant differences between the sexes. (It should be noted that nonsignificant results are often not published.) Those studies that contained significant findings have been tempered by other research suggesting the opposite results. For example, Jensen reviewed 131 studies of verbal ability. Thirty-seven of these studies concluded that females were superior to males. However, 13 suggested that males surpassed their female counterparts in verbal skills. It is apparent that conclusions about actual sex differences cannot be made, at least on the basis of studies reported to date. For a comprehensive review of the literature on sex differences, see Maccoby and Jacklin (1978).

Various explanations have been offered for the sex differences that have been found. Among them are the differential experiences of males and females in our society, the nonrepresentativeness of the samples tested, and biases inherent in the test and/or its administration and interpretation. On the other hand, when tests do not pick up sex differences, this is sometimes attributed to the author's having eliminated or balanced these differences during the test construction stage, as has often been true in the case of intelligence tests, for example, the Stanford-Binet. Jensen points out that test bias can minimize an actual sex difference or can falsely suggest one. Unfortunately, we are not now in a position to be able to tell which, if either, error we are committing.

Whatever the results for any individual on any given test, the way those results are reported may have differential effects on the way a person perceives her or his abilities and status. Although some test authors (such as Holland, 1975) believe that it is advisable to report raw scores, most provide normative data. The real controversy arises between those who favor combined norms and those who prefer that separate-sex norms be reported. Of course, this is not a consideration when males and females perform similarly on a given test. Another question is, if we do provide males and females with information about their relative standing with respect to their own sex, should we also make available cross-sex norms—comparisons of their scores with those of the other sex? Some interest inventory authors claim that cross-sex scores may be the only ones available for particular occupations.

SEPARATE-SEX NORMS—PRO

Wesman (1949) indicates that if a test has not been constructed to assure equal performance of the sexes, we cannot automatically assume, without further investigation, that there are no sex differences on individual items or on total scores. If these differences do exist, Wesman proposes that separate-sex norms be reported. There are two instances, he says, when one might overlook sex differences. If a test has been designed to determine subject mastery and the expectations are the same for both boys and girls, these goals can be decided upon regardless of actual test score distributions. In others words, a decision based on educational, not statistical, concerns is appropriate. Another rationale for ignoring sex differences would be that males and females compete with each other and therefore should be compared with each other. Wesman questions this second justification, saying that in some educational and in many vocational areas males and females will be competing primarily with those of their own sex.

Using as an example the Differential Aptitude Test (DAT), which provides separate-sex norms, Wesman points out that combined norms may sometimes be inappropriate. For example, the Mechanical Reasoning subtest of the DAT substantially favors males. A boy who receives an average score using single-sex norms would receive a much higher score if norms were of the combined type. The combined-norm scoring could be misleading in a counseling situation, Wesman suggests. A boy might be guided into a mechanically oriented career only to find himself average in comparison with most of the competition. On the other hand, a girl who would be only average in mechanical ability when compared with both boys and girls might score extremely well in comparison with members of her own sex. Again, she might be counseled into a field for which, in comparison with the competition, she did not have any special aptitude. Wesman concludes that in order to provide the most meaningful information for each sex, separate-sex norms are necessary. The more sex-segregated the educational or vocational area being considered, the more necessary this is.

For the individual who is considering a course of study or an occupation that is predominantly comprised of members of the opposite sex, Wesman suggests that the person's test scores be compared with opposite-sex norms. However, Johnson (1978), using the Strong-Campbell Interest Inventory, found that employing cross-sex norms reinforced sex stereotyping. For both females and males, scores were high on traditional career choices and low on nontraditional ones when scores were derived by using opposite-sex norms. Johnson concludes that separate-sex norms are essential.

Wesman states that not only should we develop separate norms for the sexes, but we should also provide "separate vocational goal norms, separate curricular norms, separate city norms—in fact, separate norms for every conceivable kind of group with which those who take tests are likely to compete" (p. 228). Jensen (1980) takes a strong stand against such a proposal, claiming that it would only make interpretations more complicated. He suggests that instead of having many sets of norms to compensate for test bias, we would do better to acknowledge whatever test bias may exist against particular groups of individuals.

Herman (1975) defends the DAT against complaints that the use of separate norms labels students according to sex and thus is a "reactionary force tending to maintain the students in outmoded, restrictive sex roles" (p. 2). However, Herman argues, separate-sex norms do just the opposite. Since girls and boys exhibit "large and consistent" sex differences on five of the eight subtests of the DAT, which are probably due to socialization differences, combined-sex norms would reflect the relative superiority of one sex or the other on a particular subtest. In others words, sex differences present in the raw scores would be retained. This would mean that girls "must perform better than boys *relative to their own sex* to score at the median on combined-sex norms for this test" (p. 5).

Herman suggests that separate-sex norms would, therefore, be less sex-restrictive, especially when nontraditional careers are being considered for either sex. On the other hand, he proposes that even if a girl is interested in automotive repair, she should compare her scores on the Mechanical Reasoning Test not only with those of other girls but also with those of boys, her most probable competitors.

Herman concludes that "when boys and girls do equally well on all tests of the DAT or when sex-related curriculum choices and occupational selections are eliminated, combined-sex norms will be more appropriate" (p. 8). He does not advocate separate-sex norms on intelligence tests since few sex differences have been found in the research on these scales. However, he admits that this apparent equality may have been accomplished by design.

Diamond (1978), Lockheed-Katz (1974), and Prediger and Hanson (1976) have all supported separate-sex norms as an interim measure. However, rather than suggesting, as does Herman, that these norms should be used until males and females and/or society change, these authors seem to feel that the tests themselves may have to be changed. They condone the use of separate-sex norms as a compromise, to be used only when it can be demonstrated that they reduce sex bias. One danger noted by Lockheed-Katz is that by reporting separate-sex norms, one may reinforce the expectation that males and females should perform differently. However, she advises that reporting norms separately may make selection procedures more equitable.

Although Diamond advocates changes in the tests themselves, she also makes a case for using separate-sex norms. She, along with the AMEG Commission on Sex Bias in Measurement, suggested to the U.S. Office of Civil Rights that the use of combined-sex norms might limit women's options. Their recommendation advocating separate norms is reflected in the Title IX Regulation of 1975 ("Nondiscrimination on Basis of Sex," 1975).

Further clarifications about the use of separate-sex norms were issued by the U.S. Department of Health, Education and Welfare and have the same effects as Title IX (Schiffer, 1978). Briefly, these guidelines suggest several criteria for determining whether a particular test complies with Title IX. They require that technical materials presented for tests using separate-sex norms explain why this type of reporting is necessary; that the test materials contain a breakdown by sex of the norming group; and that if scales for one sex are to be applied to the other sex, the publisher demonstrate the validity of this procedure. Also, those administering or using tests must be provided with information explaining how one should interpret scores on norms for both sexes.

SEPARATE-SEX NORMS—CON

Holland (1975) suggests that separate sex-norms on interest inventories may be misleading because, although they reduce the effects of differential socialization, they may result in the recommendation of a career for which the testee has little motivation relative to others in that field. He concludes that "interest inventories would do people a disservice if they encouraged people to enter occupations that were grossly inconsistent with their socialization experience" (p. 25). He also points out that some individuals may become upset upon finding that their scores are relatively higher on opposite-sex than on same-sex norms. Holland prefers to report raw scores. Although he finds that using norms on the Self-Directed Search did provide more options to women, he also concludes that the predictive validity of the normed scores dropped. Holland does not see the function of vocational assessment instruments as encouraging change or growth. He indicates that they should "score or note the effects of a lifetime—to fail to do so would lead to invalid assessment" (p. 24).

Cormany (n.d.) also rejects separate-sex norms, for vastly different reasons from Holland's, however. He states that using separate norms reinforces the stereotype that there are different categories of jobs for men and women that have little overlap. He concludes that "what separate norms add to counseling is probably summed up in the put-down 'You did pretty well for a woman' " (p. 4). Cormany feels that tests should be revised so that they are sex-fair and that professional organizations should be involved in helping to encourage such modifications.

Lunneborg and Lunneborg (1978) analyzed predictions made using the Vocational Interest Inventory for 2,175 college graduates who had taken the test as high school juniors and had subsequently graduated in 22 major fields. They found that using separate-sex norms did not increase the accuracy of the predictions. In addition, sex balancing criterion groups artificially was no more effective in producing accurate predictions than was using naturally occurring groups. Finally, they noted that the best predictions were made when all majors were considered, whether or not they were male- or female-dominated. They conclude that it is not advantageous to make predictions on the basis of sex or to balance criterion groups statistically. Nor is it helpful to limit analyses only to those groups in which a particular sex is adequately represented.

Similar conclusions are reached by Campbell (1976). Campbell compared male and female law students on the Strong-Campbell Interest Inventory and found that most of the differences they exhibited were those that typically appear between men and women in any group taking the test. The male and female law students she studied did not respond differently. Campbell discusses the possibility that by retaining separate scales we run the risk of biasing the counseling process in that stereotypes about the world of work may be reinforced.

A slightly different concern is raised by Troll (1976): Should separate scoring criteria be used for males and females? Troll reports that the separate-sex scoring criteria for the Goodenough-Harris figure-drawing test, sometimes used by psychologists to estimate the IQs of schoolchildren, did not seem to be applicable to the sample of 11- to 13-year-old boys and girls she studied and were outdated and stereotyped. Whereas Harris found that many girls in this age range drew sexually mature figures and gave them credit for doing so, Troll found that many in her sample drew more unisex-type figures. Troll noted that males received points for "sketching" or "modeling," whereas girls did not. In addition, free movement was given credit only when shown in a drawing depicting a male. Troll calls for a revision of the scoring procedures on the figure-drawing test.

Another group of researchers object to separate-sex norms because they feel that it is feasible to revise test instruments so that they produce similar scores for males and females. This, of course, would obviate the need for separate norms. For example, on the Unisex Interest Inventory, which was designed to be considerably more sex-balanced than other interest inventories, Rayman (1978) finds that sex balancing results in no loss of internal validity and that his scale has adequate criterion validity.

Hanson, Prediger, and Schussel (1977), having reviewed the literature, conclude that the criterion validity of scores derived from same-sex norms is at least as great as for those derived using combined-sex or opposite-sex norms. They point out, however, that same-sex norms may be considered by some to be biased. In addition, same-sex norms provide the opportunity to compare one's scores with those of the other sex, a practice that the authors feel might not be in the best interests of test takers. Therefore, they too recommend revising tests so that they are sex-balanced. The authors developed such an instrument, the Unisex American College Testing Interest Inventory, and found that they were able to obtain scale distributions for males and females that, on the average, displayed a 92 percent overlap. They report evidence of good reliability and criterion-related validity for their instrument.

CONCLUSIONS AND SUMMARY

Although separate-sex norms may, in some cases, provide more options to a particular individual, it is the conclusion of this study that their use in order to mitigate the effects of sex-biased tests should not be the chosen alternative. Once such an option is condoned, it is all too easy to continue its use while claiming that substantial and significant (and possibly expensive) changes are not currently feasible. It has been pointed out (Hanson et al., 1977) that about half the items in current interest inventories are approximately sex-balanced. Thus, there exists a large pool of items for test authors to draw upon and, as has already been noted, many intelligence tests have been designed to minimize, or at least equalize, the sex differences that show up on test items. Further, there have already been some impressive and successful attempts (Hanson et al., 1977; Rayman, 1978) to create new instruments that are both sex-balanced and valid.

Despite the fact that using same-sex norms for a test in which there are substantial sex differences may result in less restrictive reporting than using combined-sex norms, we can only guess at the psychological effects of telling a person that his or her scores are good (or bad) only with respect to those of his or her own sex. If we choose this one variable on which to separate people, we are making a case for its importance rather than diminishing its effects. There is no way that we can communicate only the benefits of same-sex scores to clients. Whereas those who are sophisticated in tests and measurements can certainly make a case for efficacy of separate scores, the person receiving them may not understand their meaning. The U.S. Department of Health, Education and Welfare's addendum to Title IX requires that those receiving same-sex norms also receive information about how their scores compare to those of members of the other sex, information likely to wipe out much of what same-sex norms were designed to accomplish. Therefore, it seems more beneficial not to rely on stopgap measures such as justifying same-sex and opposite-sex norms in order to comply with the law, but rather to begin to review and revise the instruments that, in many cases, have suggested unwarranted limitations to men and women for several decades.

As the review of the research on sex bias in testing suggests, there are still many areas that require further study. Considering the amount of test use and the importance of test results in the average person's school and vocational life, it seems that there has been relatively little attention paid to determining the factors that affect test outcomes. Several educators and test and measurement specialists have proposed areas for further inquiry (such as Diamond, 1972; Tittle, 1978a). In addition, many sets of guidelines have been generated to assist psychologists, educators, and guidance and employment personnel in evaluating existing instruments; to alert test authors and publishers to areas of concern; and to guide policymakers and administrators in their use and selection of test instruments and programs. One recent volume by Tittle, *Sex Bias in Testing: A Review with Policy Recommendations* (1978b), provides not only a comprehensive look at the issue of test bias but also specific recommendations that should be useful to all those concerned with testing. The reader is also referred to the review articles and guidelines presented by Cook (1978); Datta (1977); Diamond (1975, 1980); Lockheed-Katz (1974); Prediger (1978); Schiffer (1978); and Wild and Dwyer (1977).

APPENDIX A

Sexism Rating Scale

SEXISM RATING SCALE

NAME OF TEST _____

FORM   _____

LEVEL   _____

EVALUATOR   _____

DATE   _____

INSTRUCTIONS: Review all tests questions, instructions, and sample
                responses given by the publishers and the test manual.
                Refer to "Criteria for Evaluation" for definitions
                of the terms used in the rating scale.

ILLUSTRATIONS

1. HOW MANY ILLUSTRATIONS ARE THERE OF ADULT MALES AND FEMALES?*

    ADULT MALES_____ (MAJOR CHAR._____ MINOR CHAR._____)

    ADULT FEMALES_____ (MAJOR CHAR._____ MINOR CHAR._____)

      TOTALS: ADULT MALES_____ (MAJOR CHAR._____ MINOR CHAR._____)

            ADULT FEM._____ (MAJOR CHAR._____ MINOR CHAR._____)

2. HOW MANY ILLUSTRATIONS ARE THERE OF CHILDREN?*

    GIRLS_____ (MAJOR CHAR._____ MINOR CHAR._____)

    BOYS_____ (MAJOR CHAR._____ MINOR CHAR._____)

      TOTALS: GIRLS_____ (MAJOR CHAR._____ MINOR CHAR._____)

            BOYS _____ (MAJOR CHAR._____ MINOR CHAR._____)

3. HOW MANY ILLUSTRATIONS ARE THERE OF MALE OR FEMALE ANIMALS?*

    MALE ANIMALS_____ (MAJOR CHAR._____ MINOR CHAR._____)

    FEMALE ANIMALS_____ (MAJOR CHAR._____ MINOR CHAR._____)

      TOTALS: MALE AN._____ (MAJOR CHAR._____ MINOR CHAR._____)

            FEMALE AN.____ (MAJOR CHAR._____ MINOR CHAR._____)

---

*Count same sex anonymous groups of three or more people as one character. Where sex is indeterminate or the number of people of each sex is approximately equal (as in large groups), do not count illustration. Animals which are clearly sex typed and inanimate objects (e.g., toys) which resemble people or animals should be included.

4. ARE WOMEN OR GIRLS ONLY SHOWN WEARING DRESSES OR SKIRTS?

      YES_____   NO_____

CONTENT

5. HOW MANY ADULT MALES AND FEMALES ARE FEATURED IN QUESTIONS AND STORIES?[*]

| SUBTEST | QUES. | PAGE | ADULT MALES | | ADULT FEMALES | |
			MAJOR CHAR.	MINOR CHAR.	MAJOR CHAR.	MINOR CHAR.

    TOTALS: ADULT MALES_____   (MAJOR CHAR._____   MINOR CHAR._____)

             ADULT FEMALES_____   (MAJOR CHAR._____   MINOR CHAR._____)

---

[*]Count references to a group of men or women, boys or girls as one character; e.g., in "The boys in his class helped Sam with his arithmetic,"
"boys" counts as one character.

6. HOW MANY FEMALE AND MALE CHILDREN ARE FEATURED IN QUESTIONS AND STORIES?[*]

| | | | GIRLS | | BOYS | |
SUBTEST	QUES.	PAGE	MAJOR CHAR.	MINOR CHAR.	MAJOR CHAR.	MINOR CHAR.

TOTALS: GIRLS_____   (MAJOR CHAR._____   MINOR CHAR._____)

BOYS_____   (MAJOR CHAR._____   MINOR CHAR._____)

7. HOW MANY FEMALE AND MALE ANIMALS ARE FEATURED IN QUESTIONS AND STORIES?[*]

| | | | FEMALE ANIMALS | | MALE ANIMALS | |
SUBTEST	QUES.	PAGE	MAJOR CHAR.	MINOR CHAR.	MAJOR CHAR.	MINOR CHAR.

TOTALS: FEMALE ANIMALS_____   (MAJOR CHAR._____   MINOR CHAR._____)

MALE ANIMALS_____   (MAJOR CHAR._____   MINOR CHAR._____)

---

[*]Count references to a group of men or women, boys or girls, as one character; e.g., in "The boys in his class helped Sam with his arithmetic," boys counts as one character.

8. ARE THERE ANY QUESTIONS (OR STATEMENTS) WHICH DEMEAN OR STEREOTYPE
    FEMALES OR MALES, E.G., "SHE'S ONLY A GIRL," "ALL BOYS ARE MEAN"?

           YES_____   NO_____

| | | | DEMEANING REFERENCES TO | |
SUBTEST	QUES.	PAGE	FEMALES	MALES

9. ARE THE EMOTIONS EXPRESSED EITHER VERBALLY OR NONVERBALLY BY MALES
    OR FEMALES SEX STEREOTYPED?

           YES_____   NO_____

| | | | EMOTIONS | |
SUBTEST	QUES.	PAGE	FEMALES	MALES

10. ARE THE NONOCCUPATIONAL ACTIVITIES IN WHICH FEMALES AND MALES ARE ENGAGED SEX STEREOTYPED?

SUBTEST	QUES.	PAGE	FEMALES' ACTIVITIES	STEREO. YES	NO	MALES' ACTIVITIES	STEREO. YES	NO

11. ARE THE OCCUPATIONAL ACTIVITIES IN WHICH FEMALES AND MALES ARE ENGAGED SEX STEREOTYPED? (COUNT "HOMEMAKER" AS AN OCCUPATION.)

SUBTEST	QUES.	PAGE	FEMALES' OCCUPATIONS	STEREO. YES	NO	MALES' OCCUPATIONS	STEREO. YES	NO

TOTALS: FEMALES_____   STEREO._____   NONSTEREO._____

MALES_____   STEREO._____   NONSTEREO._____

12. HOW MANY DIFFERENT OCCUPATIONS ARE DEPICTED FOR EACH SEX?   (INCLUDE ILLUSTRATIONS, QUESTIONS, AND STORIES.)

      TOTALS: FEMALES_____   MALES_____

13. COMPARE THE NUMBER OF MALES AND FEMALES IN QUESTIONS, STATEMENTS, OR STORIES WHO ARE/WERE FIGURES IN HISTORY OR CURRENT EVENTS, OR WHO HAVE MADE ACHIEVEMENTS IN ART, SCIENCE, LITERATURE, ETC.

MALES_____

FEMALES_____

      TOTALS: MALES_____   FEMALES_____

14. DOES THE LANGUAGE OF THE TEST TEND TO EXCLUDE FEMALES? NOTE INSTANCES WHEN SEXUALLY NEUTRAL LANGUAGE, FOR EXAMPLE, "PEOPLE," "MEN AND WOMEN," OR "THEY," COULD BE SUBSTITUTED WITHOUT CHANGING THE INTENDED MEANING.

      YES_____   NO_____

SUBTEST	QUES.	PAGE	FEMALE EXCLUSION

15. ARE THERE SEPARATE FORMS OF THIS TEST FOR MALES AND FEMALES?

      YES_____   NO_____

IF YES, WHAT DOES THE AUTHOR OFFER AS A RATIONALE FOR SEPARATE TESTS? (CITE SOURCE AND PAGES.)

_____

_____

_____

16. ARE THERE SEPARATE NORMS ON THIS TEST FOR FEMALES AND MALES?

    YES_____   NO_____

    IF "YES," WHAT DOES THE AUTHOR OFFER AS A RATIONALE FOR SEPARATE NORMS?
    (CITE SOURCE AND PAGES.)

    _____

    _____

    _____

    _____

    _____

    _____

17. IF EITHER OF THE ABOVE STATEMENTS IS ANSWERED "YES," NOTE DIFFERENCES
    BETWEEN ITEMS AND/OR FORMS. FOR FORMS NOTE ESPECIALLY: CONTENT,
    ILLUSTRATIONS, INSTRUCTIONS FOR ADMINISTRATION, INSTRUCTIONS FOR
    INTERPRETATION OF RESULTS.

    _____

    _____

    _____

    _____

    _____

    _____

18. ARE THERE ANY OTHER INSTANCES OF SEXISM WHICH YOU HAVE NOTICED?

    _____

    _____

    _____

    _____

    _____

    _____

APPENDIX B

Criteria for Evaluation

CRITERIA FOR EVALUATION*

In order to encourage the individual development and self-esteem of each
person regardless of gender, test materials, when they portray people (or
animals having identifiable human attributes), shall portray women and men,
girls and boys, in a wide variety of occupational, emotional, and behavioral
situations, presenting both sexes in the full range of their human potential.

1.   Descriptions, depictions, labels, or retorts that tend to demean,
     stereotype, or be patronizing toward females must not appear.

     (Do references to women indicate that their talents, intelligence,
     or activities are inferior to those of men, or that they are in-
     capable of handling a situation without a man's assistance? For
     example, there should be no labels such as "old maids," "fishwives,"
     "henpeckers," or "woman driver," or retorts such as "She's only a
     girl" or "What do you expect from a girl?" Such references consti-
     tute adverse reflections.)

2.   Instructional materials containing references to, or illustrations
     of, people should refer to or illustrate males and females approxi-
     mately evenly, in both number and importance, except as limited by
     accuracy or special purpose.

     (This criterion is largely self-explanatory. It applies to any
     materials in which the gender of persons is referred to or illus-
     trated, whether incidental to the purpose of the material or not.)

3.   Even though the portrayals of males and females may be approximately
     even in number, the aspect of importance or impact of those portray-
     als is a qualitative judgment. For example, a single illustration
     of one or more females is quantitatively overbalanced by a ten-
     page story of one or more male characters.

4.   Mentally and physically active, creative, problem-solving roles
     and success and failure in those roles should be uniformly distrib-
     uted between male and female characters.

     (It is important to look for instances in which females, both girls
     and women, are involved in mentally and physically active, creative,
     problem-solving roles--conducting a science experiment, participating
     in sports, repairing a broken object, building a bookcase--that are

---

*Adapted from Guidelines for Evaluation of Instructional Materials with Re-
spect to Social Content (Sacramento: California State Department of
Education, 1978).

all too often depicted as male oriented, and to determine whether
such instances occur in a fair proportion to those involving
males.)

5. The consequences of activity undertaken by males and females must
be observed. Positive or negative results can come from the undertaking of any task. A pattern of positive or negative results,
perhaps most simply defined as success or failure, should not emerge
as correlated with sex. It is not suggested that all characters
succeed at all times. However, the ratio of success to failure
must be approximately the same for female characters as for male
characters.

6. Emotions--fear, anger, aggression, excitement, or tenderness--
should occur randomly among characters, regardless of gender.

(All people are capable of, and susceptible to, all emotions, and
the idea that only females cry and only males fight is an inaccu-
rate projection of reality. This is not to say that instructional
materials must consistently depict males and females in reversed
emotional roles. Evaluators should, however, be aware of the tendency to stereotype emotions. If any pattern appears, such as only
females expressing fear or tenderness, or only males expressing
anger, the material does not meet this criterion.)

7. Traditional activities engaged in by characters of one sex should
be balanced by the presentation of nontraditional activities for
characters of that sex.

("Traditional" in this criterion refers to activities that are
generally considered appropriate for persons of one sex, for instance, women cooking, sewing, or cleaning; men working in employment outside the home; boys playing baseball; or girls playing
with dolls. The materials certainly need not exclude such activities. They should balance such portrayals with their opposites--
nontraditional activities for such persons. Examples might be a
boy reading or at quiet play, a man seeking help solving a problem. Adults of both sexes should be portrayed in domestic chores,
recreational activities, and creative endeavors whenever these
activities are portrayed in the materials. Balance is achieved
when instances of traditional activity can be shown in fair proportion to instances of nontraditional activities. The evaluator
should make a qualitative judgment about the competing portrayals.)

8. If professional or executive roles, or vocations, trades, or other
gainful occupations are portrayed, men and women should be represented in approximately equal numbers.

(This criterion is relatively self-explanatory. Its purpose is to
expand the portrayal of male and female occupational roles and en-
able children to identify with all fields of enterprise, regardless
of sex.

Evaluators should ensure that materials indicate an equally wide variety of vocational choices for men and women, measured by the number of vocations in which women are depicted compared to the number in which men are depicted. Disproportionate numbers of women portrayed in a particular vocation should indicate that the material requires careful scrutiny for compliance.

Many professions (for example, medicine, law, engineering, and banking) are typically portrayed as male dominated. Evaluators should ensure that women are depicted in such professional roles approximately as often as men. Whether such equality is achieved can most easily be ascertained by a simple head count comparison of male and female main and background characters portrayed in professional roles. Women should also be presented in executive positions--as business executives, officials, and administrators, for example--as often as men are. Similarly, women should be presented in skilled occupations such as building and other technical trades.)

9. Males and females should both be shown engaging in a variety of occupational and recreational activities that are not stereotyped according to sex.

10. When life-style choices are discussed, boys and girls should be offered an equally wide range of such aspirations and choices.

    (Various occupations and various life-styles--marriage, remaining single, raising children or not doing so--should also be cast in an affirmative light. A child should not learn that although women can and do work outside the home, they are unhappy, tired, or too busy to enjoy life if they do so. Fantasies and dreams of children for their own futures should not be sex stereotyped.)

11. Whenever material presents developments in history or current events, or achievements in art, science, or any other field, the contributions of women should be included and discussed when they are historically accurate.

    (This criterion is designed to prevent a continuation of the common practice in test materials of failure to give sufficient attention to the achievements of women in all fields of endeavor that are discussed. In the development of any field, the contributions of women can, in most cases, be accurately included. Because of the bias in our culture, women have generally been less esteemed and less recognized, no matter what their field, than men who have made comparable contributions.

    The criterion does not demand specific requirements. However, if biographies are included in the material, those of women should also be presented. Evaluators will find that materials that simply ignore half the population of any nation are not acceptable.)

12. In general, sexually neutral language ("people," "persons," "men and women," "pioneers," "they") should be used.

(The standard here is basically objective and easy to measure: Does the material indulge in male references so as to exclude females as participants in society? It is left to the evaluator's discretion to determine when there are extenuating circumstances, such as adherence to grammatical rules or the requirement to convey the author's intended meaning.)

APPENDIX C

Letter to Publishers

Project T.E.S.T.

Project for the Elimination of Sexism in Testing

Dear

Project T.E.S.T. is a program designed to assess sex bias in measurement instruments. Recently we have completed an evaluation of the major psychological, intellectual and diagnostic tests in order to determine the extent of unequal representation and treatment of males and females in test items. (A description of the research is enclosed.)

Since you are a publisher and/or distributor of one or more of the tests we have studied, we thought you would be interested in our results. We would very much appreciate it if you would look them over and provide us with your comments on the enclosed form.

Although the psychometric effects of sex biased test items are still under study, there is some evidence to suggest that the context in which test items are embedded does affect performance. At the very least, biased, derogatory or stereotypical references contained in tests are assimilated by testees. Many of those examined are young children who cannot yet think critically or individuals who may accept such messages, inferring that they are authorized by the institution in which the test is administered. We believe that it is the responsibility of psychologists, educators and publishers to eliminate all types of bias, whether they occur in educational or assessment materials.

It is our hope to be able to provide psychologists, educators, and others who use tests for evaluative purposes with our findings along with some suggestions which will minimize the differential treatment of males and females without affecting the integrity of a test's results. Since you as the publisher (or his or her representative) are the only one in a position to make such recommendations, we are hopeful that you will consider doing so.

For example, as one publisher has suggested, for some items it is conceivable that a change from masculine to feminine names and/or pronouns might equalize the distribution of male and female oriented questions without compromising the test validity. Additionally, words which exclude females such as "frontiersmen" or "firemen" might be changed to neutral terms such as "pioneers" or "firefighters." In some cases where separate norms have been published for males and females, combined norms may now be available and could be provided to examiners.

Due to publication deadlines, we are requesting that you return the enclosed response form by April 15, 1980. A self-addressed enveloped has been provided for your convenience.

Thank you for your assistance.

Sincerely,

Paula Selkow, Ph.D.
Project Director

Project Director: Paula Selkow, Ph.D., Psychology Department, The William Paterson College of New Jersey, 300 Pompton Road, Wayne, New Jersey 07470 (201) 595-2471, 595-2148

Sponsored by a grant from the Women's Educational Equity Act Program, U.S. Department of Health, Education and Welfare

APPENDIX D

Publishers' Response Form

PROJECT T.E.S.T.
RESPONSE FORM

NAME OF TEST _____

Form(s)_____

Level(s)_____

1. Can the proper nouns and pronouns in the test be changed by the examiner to equalize the representation of males and females without altering the validity of the test?

                    yes_____   no_____

    Can this be changed at the discretion of the examiner?
                    yes_____   no_____

    If not please state specifically what can be changed (and/or what should not be changed).

2. Can language which excludes females be changed to language which is sex neutral?
                    yes_____   no_____

    Can this be changed at the discretion of the examiner?
                    yes_____   no_____

    If not please state specifically what can be changed (and/or what should not be changed).

3. Can demeaning or stereotypical statements about males or females be revised or replaced?
                    yes_____   no_____

    Can this be changed at the discretion of the examiner?
                    yes_____   no_____

    If not please state specifically what can be changed (and/or what should not be changed).

4. Can items where emotions are sex stereotyped be revised?
   yes_____   no_____

   Can this be changed at the discretion of the examiner?
   yes_____   no_____

   If not please state specifically what can be changed (and/or what should not be changed).

5. Can questions or stories which depict either sex in a preponderance of highly stereotypical occupational or nonoccupational roles be changed to reflect less stereotypical roles?
   yes_____   no_____

   Can this be changed at the discretion of the examiner?
   yes_____   no_____

   If not please state specifically what can be changed (and/or what should not be changed).

6. What suggestions do you have about equalizing the number of famous men and women referred to in test items?

7. Where separate forms are provided for males and females, can the forms be used interchageably--that is, can females be given the male version of the test and vice versa?
   yes_____   no_____

8. If the test has separate norms, are combined norms available?
   yes_____   no_____

   If so, how can they be obtained by examiners?

9. Is this test in the process of being revised?
   yes_____   no_____

   What is the expected date of publication?_____

   What changes will be made with regard to representation of the sexes and/or stereotypical or demeaning depictions of females and males?

How will the standardization sample or norming procedures be changed?

10. Other suggestions or comments.

APPENDIX E
Tests Listed in Alphabetical Order

TESTS LISTED IN ALPHABETICAL ORDER

Analysis of Learning Potential - Lower Primary 1 (1970)
Analysis of Learning Potential - Primary 2 (1970)
Analysis of Learning Potential - Elementary (1970)
Analysis of Learning Potential - Advanced 1 (1970)
Analysis of Learning Potential - Advanced 2 (1970)
Analysis of Skills in Reading - Level 12 (1974)
Analysis of Skills in Reading - Level 34 (1974)
Analysis of Skills in Reading - Level 56 (1974)
Analysis of Skills in Reading - Level 78 (1974)
Assessment of Children's Language Comprehension (1973)
Bernreuter Personality Inventory (1959)
California Psychological Inventory (1956)
California Test of Personality - Form AA (1953)
Classroom Reading Inventory - All Forms (1976)
Cognitive Abilities Test - Lower Primary 1 (1978)
Cognitive Abilities Test - Lower Primary 2 (1978)
Cognitive Abilities Test - Multilevel (1978)
Comprehensive Tests of Basic Skills - Form S, Level A (1975)
Comprehensive Tests of Basic Skills - Form S, Level B (1975)
Comprehensive Tests of Basic Skills - Form S, Level C (1975)
Comprehensive Tests of Basic Skills - Form S, Level 1 (1975)
Comprehensive Tests of Basic Skills - Form S, Level 3 (1975)
Comrey Personality Scales (1970)
Cooperative Preschool Inventory (1970)
Detroit Test of Learning Aptitude - Form 1 (1958)
Diagnostic Reading Scales (1972)
Diagnostic Skills Battery - Form A, Level 12 (1976)
Diagnostic Skills Battery - Form A, Level 34 (1976)
Diagnostic Skills Battery - Form A, Level 56 (1976)
Diagnostic Skills Battery - Form A, Level 78 (1976)
Diagnostic Skills Battery - Form B, Level 12 (1976)
Diagnostic Skills Battery - Form B, Level 34 (1976)
Diagnostic Skills Battery - Form B, Level 56 (1976)
Diagnostic Skills Battery - Form B, Level 78 (1976)
Differential Aptitude Test - Form S (1972)
Differential Aptitude Test - Form T (1972)
Durrell Analysis of Reading Difficulty (1955)
Durrell Listening-Reading Series - Primary (1970)
Durrell Listening-Reading Series - Intermediate (1969)
Durrell Listening-Reading Series - Advanced (1970)
Education Apperception Test (1973)
First Grade Screening Test - Boy's (1966)
First Grade Screening Test - Girl's (1966)
Gates MacGinitie Reading Tests - Form 1, Basic R (1978)
Gates MacGinitie Reading Tests - Form 2, Basic R (1978)

Geist Picture Interest Inventory - Revised (1975)
Gilmore Oral Reading Test (1968)
Gray Oral Reading Tests - Form A (1963)
Gray Oral Reading Tests - Form B (1963)
Gray Oral Reading Tests - Form C (1963)
Gray Oral Reading Tests - Form D (1963)
Gray Standardized Oral Reading Check Tests (1963)
Gray Standardized Oral Reading Paragraphs (1955)
Henmon-Nelson Tests of Mental Ability - Form 1, Grades K-2 (1973)
Henmon-Nelson Tests of Mental Ability - Form 1, Grades 3-6 (1973)
Henmon-Nelson Tests of Mental Ability - Form 1, Grades 6-9 (1973)
Henmon-Nelson Tests of Mental Ability - Form 1, Grades 9-12 (1973)
Illinois Test of Psycholinguistic Abilities (1968)
Inpatient Multidimensional Psychiatric Scale (1966)
Junior & Senior High School Personality Questionnaire - Form A (1960)
Junior & Senior High School Personality Questionnaire - Form B (1960)
Kuhlmann-Anderson Tests - Booklet D (1960)
Kuhlmann-Anderson Tests - Booklets E & F (1960)
Kuhlmann-Anderson Tests - Booklet G (1960)
Kuhlmann-Anderson Tests - Booklet H (1960)
Lee-Clark Reading Readiness Test (1962)
Lorge-Thorndike Intelligence Test - Form 1 (1964)
Lorge-Thorndike Intelligence Test - Form 2 (1964)
Macmillan Reading Readiness Test (1970)
McCarthy Scales (1972)
Metropolitan Achievement Tests - Math - Form JI, Primer (1978)
Metropolitan Achievement Tests - Math - Form JI, Primary 1 (1978)
Metropolitan Achievement Tests - Math - Form JI, Primary 2 (1978)
Metropolitan Achievement Tests - Math - Form JI, Elementary (1978)
Metropolitan Achievement Tests - Math - Form JI, Intermediate (1978)
Metropolitan Achievement Tests - Math - Form JI, Advanced 1 (1978)
Metropolitan Readiness Test - Form P, Level I (1974)
Metropolitan Readiness Test - Form P, Level II (1974)
Minnesota Multiphasic Personality Inventory (1966)
Minnesota Scholastic Aptitude Test - Form A (1969)
Ohio State University Psychological Test (1959)
Oral Reading Criterion Test (1971)
Otis-Lennon Mental Ability Test - Form J, Primary II Level (1967)
Peabody Individual Achievement Test - Vol. I (1970)
Peabody Individual Achievement Test - Vol. II (1970)
Peabody Picture Vocabulary Test (1959)
Personal Orientation Inventory (1963)
Personal Values Abstract (1970)
Picture Story Language Test (1965)
Pintner-Cunningham Primary Test - Form A (1964)
Pre-assessment Tests, Post-assessment Tests - Level 1 (1975)
Pre-assessment Tests, Post-assessment Tests - Level 2 (1975)
Pre-assessment Tests, Post-assessment Tests - Level 3 (1975)
Pre-reading Screening Procedures (1977)
Prescriptive Reading Inventory - Level A (1972)
Prescriptive Reading Inventory - Level B (1972)
Prescriptive Reading Inventory - Level C (1972)

Prescriptive Reading Inventory - Level D (1972)
Prescriptive Reading Inventory - Level I (1976)
Prescriptive Reading Inventory - Level II (1976)
Primary Mental Abilities - Grades K-1 (1962)
Primary Mental Abilities - Grades 2-4 (1962)
Primary Mental Abilities - Grades 4-6 (1962)
Primary Reading Profiles - Level I (1957)
Primary Reading Profiles - Level II (1957)
Primary Survey Test Battery - Initial Survey Test (1973)
Primary Survey Test Battery - Early Primary Survey Test (1973)
Primary Survey Test Battery - Late Primary Survey Test (1973)
Primary Survey Test Battery - Vocabulary Survey Test (1973)
School and College Ability Tests - Form X, Elementary Level (1979)
School and College Ability Tests - Form X, Intermediate Level (1979)
School and College Ability Tests - Form X, Advanced Level (1978)
School Apperception Method (1968)
School Readiness Survey (1969)
School Readiness Test (1974)
Screening Test of Academic Readiness (1966)
Short Form Test of Academic Aptitude - Level 1 (1970)
Short Form Test of Academic Aptitude - Level 2 (1970)
Short Form Test of Academic Aptitude - Level 3 (1970)
Short Form Test of Academic Aptitude - Level 4 (1970)
Short Form Test of Academic Aptitude - Level 5 (1970)
Sixteen Personality Factor Questionnaire (1956)
Slingerland Screening Tests - Form A (1970)
Slingerland Screening Tests - Form B (1970)
Slingerland Screening Tests - Form C (1970)
Slingerland Screening Tests - Form D (1974)
Slosson Intelligence Test (1963)
Standard Reading Inventory - Form A (1966)
Standard Reading Inventory - Form B (1966)
Stanford Achievement Test - Form A, Primary Level I (1972)
Stanford Achievement Test - Form A, Primary Level II (1972)
Stanford Achievement Test - Form A, Primary Level III (1972)
Stanford Achievement Test - Form A, Intermediate I (1972)
Stanford Achievement Test - Form A, Intermediate II (1972)
Stanford Achievement Test - Form A, Advanced (1972)
Stanford-Binet (1973)
Stanford Diagnostic Mathematics Test - Form A, Blue Level (1976)
Stanford Diagnostic Mathematics Test - Form A, Brown Level (1976)
Stanford Diagnostic Mathematics Test - Form A, Green Level (1976)
Stanford Diagnostic Mathematics Test - Form A, Red Level (1976)
Stanford Diagnostic Reading Test - Form A, Blue Level (1974)
Stanford Diagnostic Reading Test - Form A, Brown Level (1976)
Stanford Diagnostic Reading Test - Form A, Green Level (1976)
Stanford Diagnostic Reading Test - Form A, Red Level (1976)
Test for Auditory Comprehension of Language (1973)
Thematic Apperception Test (1943)
Wechsler Adult Intelligence Scale (1955)
Wechsler Intelligence Scale for Children - Revised (1974)
Wechsler Preschool and Primary Scale of Intelligence (1962)
Wide Range Intelligence Personality Test (1978)
Woodcock Reading Mastery Test (1973)

APPENDIX F
Tests Listed by Publisher

TESTS LISTED BY PUBLISHER

ADDISON-WESLEY PUBLISHING CO.:   SEE EDUCATIONAL TESTING SERVICE

AMERICAN GUIDANCE SERVICE

First Grade Screening Test
Peabody Individual Achievement Test
Peabody Picture Vocabulary Test
Woodcock Reading Mastery Test

BOBBS MERRILL CO., INC.

Detroit Test of Learning Aptitude
Gray Oral Reading Tests
Gray Standardized Oral Reading Check Tests
Gray Standardized Oral Reading Paragraphs
Junior & Senior High School Personality Questionnaire

WILLIAM C. BROWN

Classroom Reading Inventory

CONSULTING PSYCHOLOGISTS PRESS

Assessment of Children's Language Comprehension
Bernreuter Personality Inventory
California Psychological Inventory
Inpatient Multidimensional Psychiatric Scale
Personal Values Abstract
School Readiness Survey

CTB/McGRAW-HILL

California Test of Personality
Comprehensive Tests of Basic Skills
Diagnostic Reading Scales
Lee-Clark Reading Readiness Test
Prescriptive Reading Inventory
Short Form Test of Academic Aptitude

DRIER PUBLISHING CO.:   SEE JAMESTOWN

EDUCATIONAL & INDUSTRIAL TESTING SERVICES

Comrey Personality Scales
Personal Orientation Inventory

EDUCATORS PUBLISHING SERVICE

Pre-reading Screening Procedures
Slingerland Screening Tests

EDUCATIONAL TESTING SERVICE   (DISTRIBUTOR: ADDISON-WESLEY PUBLISHING CO.)

Cooperative Preschool Inventory
School and College Ability Tests

HARCOURT, BRACE, JAVONOVICH: SEE PSYCHOLOGICAL CORPORATION

HARVARD UNIVERSITY

Thematic Apperception Test

HOUGHTON MIFFLIN

Cognitive Abilities Test
Gates MacGinitie Reading Tests
Henmon-Nelson Tests of Mental Ability
Lorge-Thorndike Intelligence Test
Primary Reading Profiles
Stanford Binet

INDUSTRIAL PSYCHOLOGY

Sixteen Personality Factor Questionnaire

JAMESTOWN PUBLISHERS   (FORMERLY DRIER)

Oral Reading Criterion Test

JASTAK ASSOCIATES, INC.   (DISTRIBUTOR: WESTERN PSYCHOLOGICAL SERVICES)

Wide Range Intelligence Personality Test

KLAMATH

Standard Reading Inventory

MACMILLAN PUBLISHING CO.

Macmillan Reading Readiness Test
Pre-assessment Tests, Post-assessment Tests

PRIORITY INNOVATIONS

Screening Test of Academic Readiness

PSYCHOLOGICAL CORPORATION

Analysis of Learning Potential
Differential Aptitude Test
Durrell Analysis of Reading Difficulty
Durrell Listening-Reading Series
Gilmore Oral Reading Test
McCarthy Scales
Metropolitan Achievement Tests - Math
Metropolitan Readiness Test
Minnesota Multiphasic Personality Inventory
Otis-Lennon Mental Ability Test
Pintner-Cunningham Primary Test
Stanford Achievement Test
Stanford Diagnostic Mathematics Test
Stanford Diagnostic Reading Test
Wechsler Adult Intelligence Scale
Wechsler Intelligence Scale for Children - Revised
Wechsler Preschool and Primary Scale of Intelligence

SCHOLASTIC TESTING SERVICE

Analysis of Skills in Reading
Diagnostic Skills Battery
Kuhlmann-Anderson Tests
School Readiness Test

SCIENCE RESEARCH ASSOCIATES

Primary Mental Abilities

SCOTT, FORESMAN & CO.

Primary Survey Test Battery

SLOSSON EDUCATIONAL PUBLICATIONS, INC.   (DISTRIBUTOR: WESTERN PSYCHOLOGICAL
                                                          SERVICES)

Slosson Intelligence Test

SPRINGER PUBLISHING CO.

School Apperception Method

TEACHING RESOURCES

Test for Auditory Comprehension of Language

UNIVERSITY OF ILLINOIS PRESS   (DISTRIBUTOR: WESTERN PSYCHOLOGICAL SERVICES)

Illinois Test of Psycholinguistic Abilities

WESTERN PSYCHOLOGICAL SERVICES

Education Apperception Test
Geist Picture Interest Inventory - Revised
Picture Story Language Test

WILBUR LAYTON

Minnesota Scholastic Aptitude Test
Ohio State University Psychological Test

APPENDIX G

Tests Listed by Category

TESTS LISTED BY CATEGORY

INTELLIGENCE

Analysis of Learning Potential - Lower Primary 1
Analysis of Learning Potential - Primary 2
Analysis of Learning Potential - Elementary
Analysis of Learning Potential - Advanced 1
Analysis of Learning Potential - Advanced 2
Cognitive Abilities Test - Multilevel
Cognitive Abilities Test - Lower Primary 1
Cognitive Abilities Test - Lower Primary 2
Detroit Test of Learning Aptitude - Form 1
Differential Aptitude Test - Form S
Differential Aptitude Test - Form T
Henmon-Nelson Tests of Mental Ability - Form 1, Grades K-2
Henmon-Nelson Tests of Mental Ability - Form 1, Grades 3-6
Henmon-Nelson Tests of Mental Ability - Form 1, Grades 6-9
Henmon-Nelson Tests of Mental Ability - Form 1, Grades 9-12
Kuhlmann-Anderson Tests - Booklet D
Kuhlmann-Anderson Tests - Booklets E & F
Kuhlmann-Anderson Tests - Booklet G
Kuhlmann-Anderson Tests - Booklet H
Lorge-Thorndike Intelligence Test - Form 1
Lorge-Thorndike Intelligence Test - Form 2
McCarthy Scales
Minnesota Scholastic Aptitude Test - Form A
Ohio State University Psychological Test
Otis-Lennon Mental Ability Test - Form J, Primary II Level
Peabody Individual Achievement Test - Vol. I
Peabody Individual Achievement Test - Vol. II
Peabody Picture Vocabulary Test
Pintner-Cunningham Primary Test - Form A
Primary Mental Abilities - Grades K-1
Primary Mental Abilities - Grades 2-4
Primary Mental Abilities - Grades 4-6
School and College Ability Tests - Form X, Elementary Level
School and College Ability Tests - Form X, Intermediate Level
School and College Ability Tests - Form X, Advanced Level
Short Form Test of Academic Aptitude - Level 1
Short Form Test of Academic Aptitude - Level 2
Short Form Test of Academic Aptitude - Level 3
Short Form Test of Academic Aptitude - Level 4
Short Form Test of Academic Aptitude - Level 5
Slosson Intelligence Test
Stanford-Binet

Wechsler Adult Intelligence Scale
Wechsler Intelligence Scale for Children - Revised
Wechsler Preschool and Primary Scale of Intelligence
Wide Range Intelligence Personality Test

PERSONALITY

Bernreuter Personality Inventory
California Psychological Inventory
California Test of Personality - Form AA
Comrey Personality Scales
Education Apperception Test
Inpatient Multidimensional Psychiatric Scale
Junior & Senior High School Personality Questionnaire - Form A
Junior & Senior High School Personality Questionnaire - Form B
Minnesota Multiphasic Personality Inventory
Personal Orientation Inventory
Personal Values Abstract
School Apperception Method
Sixteen Personality Factor Questionnaire
Thematic Apperception Test

READINESS

Cooperative Preschool Inventory
First Grade Screening Test - Boy's
First Grade Screening Test - Girl's
Lee-Clark Reading Readiness Test
Macmillan Reading Readiness Test
Metropolitan Readiness Test - Form P, Level I
Metropolitan Readiness Test - Form P, Level II
Pre-reading Screening Procedures
School Readiness Survey
School Readiness Test
Screening Test of Academic Readiness

DIAGNOSTIC & ACHIEVEMENT: READING

Analysis of Skills in Reading - Level 12
Analysis of Skills in Reading - Level 34
Analysis of Skills in Reading - Level 56
Analysis of Skills in Reading - Level 78
Classroom Reading Inventory - All Forms
Comprehensive Tests of Basic Skills - Form S, Level A
Comprehensive Tests of Basic Skills - Form S, Level B
Comprehensive Tests of Basic Skills - Form S, Level C
Comprehensive Tests of Basic Skills - Form S, Level 1
Comprehensive Tests of Basic Skills - Form S, Level 3
Diagnostic Reading Scales
Diagnostic Skills Battery - Form A, Level 12
Diagnostic Skills Battery - Form A, Level 34

Diagnostic Skills Battery - Form A, Level 56
Diagnostic Skills Battery - Form A, Level 78
Diagnostic Skills Battery - Form B, Level 12
Diagnostic Skills Battery - Form B, Level 34
Diagnostic Skills Battery - Form B, Level 56
Diagnostic Skills Battery - Form B, Level 78
Durrell Analysis of Reading Difficulty
Durrell Listening-Reading Series - Primary
Durrell Listening-Reading Series - Intermediate
Durrell Listening-Reading Series - Advanced
Gates MacGinitie Reading Tests - Form 1, Basic R
Gates MacGinitie Reading Tests - Form 2, Basic R
Gilmore Oral Reading Test
Gray Oral Reading Tests - Form A
Gray Oral Reading Tests - Form B
Gray Oral Reading Tests - Form C
Gray Oral Reading Tests - Form D
Gray Standardized Oral Reading Check Tests
Gray Standardized Oral Reading Paragraphs
Oral Reading Criterion Test
Pre-assessment Tests, Post-assessment Tests - Level 1
Pre-assessment Tests, Post-assessment Tests - Level 2
Pre-assessment Tests, Post-assessment Tests - Level 3
Prescriptive Reading Inventory - Level A
Prescriptive Reading Inventory - Level B
Prescriptive Reading Inventory - Level C
Prescriptive Reading Inventory - Level D
Prescriptive Reading Inventory - Level I
Prescriptive Reading Inventory - Level II
Primary Reading Profiles - Level 1
Primary Reading Profiles - Level 2
Primary Survey Test Battery - Early Primary Survey Test
Primary Survey Test Battery - Initial Primary Survey Test
Primary Survey Test Battery - Late Primary Survey Test
Primary Survey Test Battery - Vocabulary Survey Test
Standard Reading Inventory - Form A
Standard Reading Inventory - Form B
Stanford Achievement Test - Form A, Primary Level I
Stanford Achievement Test - Form A, Primary Level II
Stanford Achievement Test - Form A, Primary Level III
Stanford Achievement Test - Form A, Intermediate I
Stanford Achievement Test - Form A, Intermediate II
Stanford Achievement Test - Form A, Advanced
Stanford Diagnostic Reading Test - Form A, Blue Level
Stanford Diagnostic Reading Test - Form A, Brown Level
Stanford Diagnostic Reading Test - Form A, Green Level
Stanford Diagnostic Reading Test - Form A, Red Level
Woodcock Reading Mastery Test

DIAGNOSTIC AND ACHIEVEMENT: MATH

Comprehensive Tests of Basic Skills - Form S, Level A
Comprehensive Tests of Basic Skills - Form S, Level B
Comprehensive Tests of Basic Skills - Form S, Level C
Comprehensive Tests of Basic Skills - Form S, Level 1
Comprehensive Tests of Basic Skills - Form S, Level 3
Metropolitan Achievement Tests - Math - Form JI, Primer
Metropolitan Achievement Tests - Math - Form JI, Primary 1
Metropolitan Achievement Tests - Math - Form JI, Primary 2
Metropolitan Achievement Tests - Math - Form JI, Elementary
Metropolitan Achievement Tests - Math - Form JI, Intermediate
Metropolitan Achievement Tests - Math - Form JI, Advanced 1
Primary Survey Test Battery - Primary Survey Test
Primary Survey Test Battery - Initial Survey Test
Primary Survey Test Battery - Late Primary Survey Test
Stanford Diagnostic Mathematics Test - Form A, Blue Level
Stanford Diagnostic Mathematics Test - Form A, Brown Level
Stanford Diagnostic Mathematics Test - Form A, Green Level
Stanford Diagnostic Mathematics Test - Form A, Red Level

LANGUAGE

Assessment of Children's Language Comprehension
Illinois Test of Psycholinguistic Abilities
Picture Story Language Test
Slingerland Screening Tests - Form A
Slingerland Screening Tests - Form B
Slingerland Screening Tests - Form C
Slingerland Screening Tests - Form D
Test for Auditory Comprehension of Language

OTHER

Geist Picture Interest Inventory - Revised

APPENDIX H

Test Evaluations

ANALYSIS OF LEARNING POTENTIAL - LOWER PRIMARY 1

	MEAN	STANDARD DEVIATION
ILLUSTRATIONS-NUMBER OF MALE ADULTS	17.00	11.53
ILLUSTRATIONS-NUMBER OF FEMALE ADULTS	20.66	15.04
ILLUSTRATIONS-NUMBER OF MALE CHILDREN	86.66	76.07
ILLUSTRATIONS-NUMBER OF FEMALE CHILDREN	43.66	33.70
ILLUSTRATIONS-NUMBER OF MALE ANIMALS	0.00	0.00
ILLUSTRATIONS-NUMBER OF FEMALE ANIMALS	0.00	0.00
CONTENT-NUMBER OF MALE ADULTS	5.33	1.15
CONTENT-NUMBER OF FEMALE ADULTS	6.66	1.52
CONTENT-NUMBER OF MALE CHILDREN	10.00	3.60
CONTENT-NUMBER OF FEMALE CHILDREN	6.00	2.00
CONTENT-NUMBER OF MALE ANIMALS	0.50	0.57
CONTENT-NUMBER OF FEMALE ANIMALS	0.00	0.00
MALES IN STERO. NONOCC. ROLES	8.00	4.08
FEMALES IN STERO. NONOCC. ROLES	3.00	2.58
TOTAL MALES IN NONOCC. ROLES	8.00	4.08
TOTAL FEMALES IN NONOCC. ROLES	3.25	2.21
MALES IN STERO. OCCUPATIONAL ROLES	1.25	0.50
FEMALES IN STERO. OCCUPATIONAL ROLES	3.00	4.08
TOTAL MALES IN OCCUPATIONAL ROLES	1.25	0.50
TOTAL FEMALES IN OCCUPATIONAL ROLES	3.00	4.08
TOTAL OCCUPATIONS DEPICTED FOR MALES	0.50	0.57
TOTAL OCCUPATIONS DEPICTED FOR FEMALES	0.75	0.95
NUMBER OF FAMOUS MEN	0.00	0.00
NUMBER OF FAMOUS WOMEN	0.00	0.00

FEMALES DRESSED ONLY IN SKIRTS	YES
DEMEANING OR STERO. STATEMENTS	NO
STERO. EMOTIONAL RESPONSES	NO
LANGUAGE EXCLUDING WOMEN	NO
SEPARATE FORMS	NO
SEPARATE NORMS	NO

ANALYSIS OF LEARNING POTENTIAL - LOWER PRIMARY 2

	MEAN	STANDARD DEVIATION
ILLUSTRATIONS-NUMBER OF MALE ADULTS	7.75	4.99
ILLUSTRATIONS-NUMBER OF FEMALE ADULTS	13.00	9.96
ILLUSTRATIONS-NUMBER OF MALE CHILDREN	40.00	34.34
ILLUSTRATIONS-NUMBER OF FEMALE CHILDREN	19.00	16.10
ILLUSTRATIONS-NUMBER OF MALE ANIMALS	0.00	0.00
ILLUSTRATIONS-NUMBER OF FEMALE ANIMALS	0.00	0.00
CONTENT-NUMBER OF MALE ADULTS	3.00	0.00
CONTENT-NUMBER OF FEMALE ADULTS	2.00	0.00
CONTENT-NUMBER OF MALE CHILDREN	1.50	0.70
CONTENT-NUMBER OF FEMALE CHILDREN	1.50	0.70
CONTENT-NUMBER OF MALE ANIMALS	0.00	0.00
CONTENT-NUMBER OF FEMALE ANIMALS	0.00	0.00
MALES IN STERO. NONOCC. ROLES	7.33	2.30
FEMALES IN STERO. NONOCC. ROLES	1.33	0.57
TOTAL MALES IN NONOCC. ROLES	8.00	2.00
TOTAL FEMALES IN NONOCC. ROLES	1.66	1.15
MALES IN STERO. OCCUPATIONAL ROLES	1.50	1.29
FEMALES IN STERO. OCCUPATIONAL ROLES	1.75	1.70
TOTAL MALES IN OCCUPATIONAL ROLES	1.50	1.29
TOTAL FEMALES IN OCCUPATIONAL ROLES	1.75	1.70
TOTAL OCCUPATIONS DEPICTED FOR MALES	2.33	1.52
TOTAL OCCUPATIONS DEPICTED FOR FEMALES	1.00	1.00
NUMBER OF FAMOUS MEN	0.00	0.00
NUMBER OF FAMOUS WOMEN	0.00	0.00

FEMALES DRESSED ONLY IN SKIRTS	YES
DEMEANING OR STERO. STATEMENTS	NO
STERO. EMOTIONAL RESPONSES	NO
LANGUAGE EXCLUDING WOMEN	NO
SEPARATE FORMS	NO
SEPARATE NORMS	NO

ANALYSIS OF LEARNING POTENTIAL - ELEMENTARY

	MEAN	STANDARD DEVIATION
ILLUSTRATIONS-NUMBER OF MALE ADULTS	.	.
ILLUSTRATIONS-NUMBER OF FEMALE ADULTS	.	.
ILLUSTRATIONS-NUMBER OF MALE CHILDREN	.	.
ILLUSTRATIONS-NUMBER OF FEMALE CHILDREN	.	.
ILLUSTRATIONS-NUMBER OF MALE ANIMALS	.	.
ILLUSTRATIONS-NUMBER OF FEMALE ANIMALS	.	.
CONTENT-NUMBER OF MALE ADULTS	6.00	.
CONTENT-NUMBER OF FEMALE ADULTS	3.00	.
CONTENT-NUMBER OF MALE CHILDREN	6.25	4.11
CONTENT-NUMBER OF FEMALE CHILDREN	4.00	2.94
CONTENT-NUMBER OF MALE ANIMALS	0.75	0.95
CONTENT-NUMBER OF FEMALE ANIMALS	0.25	0.50
MALES IN STERO. NONOCC. ROLES	0.25	0.50
FEMALES IN STERO. NONOCC. ROLES	0.00	0.00
TOTAL MALES IN NONOCC. ROLES	0.50	0.57
TOTAL FEMALES IN NONOCC. ROLES	0.00	0.00
MALES IN STERO. OCCUPATIONAL ROLES	0.25	0.50
FEMALES IN STERO. OCCUPATIONAL ROLES	0.00	0.00
TOTAL MALES IN OCCUPATIONAL ROLES	0.25	0.50
TOTAL FEMALES IN OCCUPATIONAL ROLES	0.00	0.00
TOTAL OCCUPATIONS DEPICTED FOR MALES	0.25	0.50
TOTAL OCCUPATIONS DEPICTED FOR FEMALES	0.00	0.00
NUMBER OF FAMOUS MEN	0.00	0.00
NUMBER OF FAMOUS WOMEN	0.00	0.00

FEMALES DRESSED ONLY IN SKIRTS	NA
DEMEANING OR STERO. STATEMENTS	NO
STERO. EMOTIONAL RESPONSES	NO
LANGUAGE EXCLUDING WOMEN	NO
SEPARATE FORMS	NO
SEPARATE NORMS	NO

ANALYSIS OF LEARNING POTENTIAL - ADVANCED 1

	MEAN	STANDARD DEVIATION
ILLUSTRATIONS-NUMBER OF MALE ADULTS	0.00	0.00
ILLUSTRATIONS-NUMBER OF FEMALE ADULTS	0.00	0.00
ILLUSTRATIONS-NUMBER OF MALE CHILDREN	0.00	0.00
ILLUSTRATIONS-NUMBER OF FEMALE CHILDREN	0.00	0.00
ILLUSTRATIONS-NUMBER OF MALE ANIMALS	0.00	0.00
ILLUSTRATIONS-NUMBER OF FEMALE ANIMALS	0.00	0.00
CONTENT-NUMBER OF MALE ADULTS	6.50	6.36
CONTENT-NUMBER OF FEMALE ADULTS	0.50	0.70
CONTENT-NUMBER OF MALE CHILDREN	3.33	4.16
CONTENT-NUMBER OF FEMALE CHILDREN	2.66	2.08
CONTENT-NUMBER OF MALE ANIMALS	0.00	0.00
CONTENT-NUMBER OF FEMALE ANIMALS	0.00	0.00
MALES IN STERO. NONOCC. ROLES	0.33	0.57
FEMALES IN STERO. NONOCC. ROLES	0.00	0.00
TOTAL MALES IN NONOCC. ROLES	0.66	0.57
TOTAL FEMALES IN NONOCC. ROLES	0.00	0.00
MALES IN STERO. OCCUPATIONAL ROLES	1.33	1.52
FEMALES IN STERO. OCCUPATIONAL ROLES	0.00	0.00
TOTAL MALES IN OCCUPATIONAL ROLES	1.33	1.52
TOTAL FEMALES IN OCCUPATIONAL ROLES	0.00	0.00
TOTAL OCCUPATIONS DEPICTED FOR MALES	1.50	0.70
TOTAL OCCUPATIONS DEPICTED FOR FEMALES	0.00	0.00
NUMBER OF FAMOUS MEN	0.00	0.00
NUMBER OF FAMOUS WOMEN	0.00	0.00

FEMALES DRESSED ONLY IN SKIRTS	NO
DEMEANING OR STERO. STATEMENTS	NO
STERO. EMOTIONAL RESPONSES	NO
LANGUAGE EXCLUDING WOMEN	NO
SEPARATE FORMS	NO
SEPARATE NORMS	NO

ANALYSIS OF LEARNING POTENTIAL - ADVANCED 2

	MEAN	STANDARD DEVIATION
ILLUSTRATIONS-NUMBER OF MALE ADULTS	0.00	0.00
ILLUSTRATIONS-NUMBER OF FEMALE ADULTS	0.00	0.00
ILLUSTRATIONS-NUMBER OF MALE CHILDREN	0.00	0.00
ILLUSTRATIONS-NUMBER OF FEMALE CHILDREN	0.00	0.00
ILLUSTRATIONS-NUMBER OF MALE ANIMALS	0.00	0.00
ILLUSTRATIONS-NUMBER OF FEMALE ANIMALS	0.00	0.00
CONTENT-NUMBER OF MALE ADULTS	8.33	4.04
CONTENT-NUMBER OF FEMALE ADULTS	0.66	1.15
CONTENT-NUMBER OF MALE CHILDREN	3.66	3.51
CONTENT-NUMBER OF FEMALE CHILDREN	0.33	0.57
CONTENT-NUMBER OF MALE ANIMALS	0.00	0.00
CONTENT-NUMBER OF FEMALE ANIMALS	0.00	0.00
MALES IN STERO. NONOCC. ROLES	0.66	1.15
FEMALES IN STERO. NONOCC. ROLES	0.00	0.00
TOTAL MALES IN NONOCC. ROLES	0.66	1.15
TOTAL FEMALES IN NONOCC. ROLES	0.00	0.00
MALES IN STERO. OCCUPATIONAL ROLES	1.33	0.57
FEMALES IN STERO. OCCUPATIONAL ROLES	0.00	0.00
TOTAL MALES IN OCCUPATIONAL ROLES	1.33	0.57
TOTAL FEMALES IN OCCUPATIONAL ROLES	0.00	0.00
TOTAL OCCUPATIONS DEPICTED FOR MALES	0.66	0.57
TOTAL OCCUPATIONS DEPICTED FOR FEMALES	0.00	0.00
NUMBER OF FAMOUS MEN	1.00	0.00
NUMBER OF FAMOUS WOMEN	0.00	0.00

FEMALES DRESSED ONLY IN SKIRTS	NO
DEMEANING OR STERO. STATEMENTS	NO
STERO. EMOTIONAL RESPONSES	NO
LANGUAGE EXCLUDING WOMEN	NO
SEPARATE FORMS	NO
SEPARATE NORMS	NO

ANALYSIS OF SKILLS IN READING - LEVEL 12

	MEAN	STANDARD DEVIATION
ILLUSTRATIONS-NUMBER OF MALE ADULTS	6.00	1.73
ILLUSTRATIONS-NUMBER OF FEMALE ADULTS	0.66	0.57
ILLUSTRATIONS-NUMBER OF MALE CHILDREN	4.33	0.57
ILLUSTRATIONS-NUMBER OF FEMALE CHILDREN	2.00	0.00
ILLUSTRATIONS-NUMBER OF MALE ANIMALS	0.00	0.00
ILLUSTRATIONS-NUMBER OF FEMALE ANIMALS	0.66	1.15
CONTENT-NUMBER OF MALE ADULTS	4.66	2.30
CONTENT-NUMBER CF FEMALE ADULTS	3.33	1.15
CONTENT-NUMBER OF MALE CHILDREN	12.66	2.30
CONTENT-NUMBER OF FEMALE CHILDREN	10.66	2.30
CONTENT-NUMBER CF MALE ANIMALS	1.66	0.57
CONTENT-NUMBER OF FEMALE ANIMALS	2.00	.
MALES IN STERO. NONOCC. ROLES	3.00	.
FEMALES IN STERO. NONOCC. ROLES	0.00	.
TOTAL MALES IN NONOCC. ROLES	3.00	.
TOTAL FEMALES IN NONOCC. ROLES	1.00	.
MALES IN STERO. OCCUPATIONAL ROLES	0.66	1.15
FEMALES IN STERO. OCCUPATIONAL ROLES	0.00	0.00
TOTAL MALES IN OCCUPATIONAL ROLES	0.66	1.15
TOTAL FEMALES IN OCCUPATIONAL ROLES	0.00	0.00
TOTAL OCCUPATIONS DEPICTED FOR MALES	0.66	1.15
TOTAL OCCUPATIONS DEPICTED FOR FEMALES	0.00	0.00
NUMBER OF FAMOUS MEN	0.00	0.00
NUMBER OF FAMOUS WOMEN	0.00	0.00

FEMALES DRESSED ONLY IN SKIRTS	NO
DEMEANING OR STERO. STATEMENTS	NA
STERO. EMOTIONAL RESPONSES	NO
LANGUAGE EXCLUDING WOMEN	YES
SEPARATE FORMS	NO
SEPARATE NORMS	NO

ANALYSIS OF SKILLS IN READING - LEVEL 34

	MEAN	STANDARD DEVIATION
ILLUSTRATIONS-NUMBER OF MALE ADULTS	.	.
ILLUSTRATIONS-NUMBER OF FEMALE ADULTS	.	.
ILLUSTRATIONS-NUMBER OF MALE CHILDREN	.	.
ILLUSTRATIONS-NUMBER OF FEMALE CHILDREN	.	.
ILLUSTRATIONS-NUMBER OF MALE ANIMALS	.	.
ILLUSTRATIONS-NUMBER OF FEMALE ANIMALS	.	.
CONTENT-NUMBER OF MALE ADULTS	6.33	2.51
CONTENT-NUMBER OF FEMALE ADULTS	4.33	1.15
CONTENT-NUMBER OF MALE CHILDREN	5.33	0.57
CONTENT-NUMBER OF FEMALE CHILDREN	4.33	1.52
CONTENT-NUMBER OF MALE ANIMALS	2.00	1.00
CONTENT-NUMBER OF FEMALE ANIMALS	0.00	0.00
MALES IN STERO. NONOCC. ROLES	0.00	0.00
FEMALES IN STERO. NONOCC. ROLES	0.00	0.00
TOTAL MALES IN NONOCC. ROLES	0.00	0.00
TOTAL FEMALES IN NONOCC. ROLES	0.00	0.00
MALES IN STERO. OCCUPATIONAL ROLES	0.00	0.00
FEMALES IN STERO. OCCUPATIONAL ROLES	0.00	0.00
TOTAL MALES IN OCCUPATIONAL ROLES	0.00	0.00
TOTAL FEMALES IN OCCUPATIONAL ROLES	0.33	0.57
TOTAL OCCUPATIONS DEPICTED FOR MALES	0.00	0.00
TOTAL OCCUPATIONS DEPICTED FOR FEMALES	0.33	0.57
NUMBER OF FAMOUS MEN	1.00	0.00
NUMBER OF FAMOUS WOMEN	0.66	0.57

FEMALES DRESSED ONLY IN SKIRTS	NA
DEMEANING OR STERO. STATEMENTS	NO
STERO. EMOTIONAL RESPONSES	NO
LANGUAGE EXCLUDING WOMEN	NO
SEPARATE FORMS	NO
SEPARATE NORMS	NO

ANALYSIS OF SKILLS IN READING - LEVEL 56

	MEAN	STANDARD DEVIATION
ILLUSTRATIONS-NUMBER OF MALE ADULTS	.	.
ILLUSTRATIONS-NUMBER OF FEMALE ADULTS	.	.
ILLUSTRATIONS-NUMBER OF MALE CHILDREN	.	.
ILLUSTRATIONS-NUMBER OF FEMALE CHILDREN	.	.
ILLUSTRATIONS-NUMBER OF MALE ANIMALS	.	.
ILLUSTRATIONS-NUMBER OF FEMALE ANIMALS	.	.
CONTENT-NUMBER OF MALE ADULTS	6.66	3.78
CONTENT-NUMBER OF FEMALE ADULTS	3.66	3.05
CONTENT-NUMBER OF MALE CHILDREN	9.33	1.52
CONTENT-NUMBER OF FEMALE CHILDREN	3.66	2.08
CONTENT-NUMBER OF MALE ANIMALS	1.33	0.57
CONTENT-NUMBER OF FEMALE ANIMALS	0.00	0.00
MALES IN STERO. NONOCC. ROLES	0.00	0.00
FEMALES IN STERO. NONOCC. ROLES	0.00	0.00
TOTAL MALES IN NONOCC. ROLES	0.00	0.00
TOTAL FEMALES IN NONOCC. ROLES	0.33	0.57
MALES IN STERO. OCCUPATIONAL ROLES	0.00	0.00
FEMALES IN STERO. OCCUPATIONAL ROLES	0.00	0.00
TOTAL MALES IN OCCUPATIONAL ROLES	0.00	0.00
TOTAL FEMALES IN OCCUPATIONAL ROLES	0.00	0.00
TOTAL OCCUPATIONS DEPICTED FOR MALES	0.00	0.00
TOTAL OCCUPATIONS DEPICTED FOR FEMALES	0.00	0.00
NUMBER OF FAMOUS MEN	0.33	0.57
NUMBER OF FAMOUS WOMEN	0.00	0.00

FEMALES DRESSED ONLY IN SKIRTS	NA
DEMEANING OR STERO. STATEMENTS	NO
STERO. EMOTIONAL RESPONSES	NO
LANGUAGE EXCLUDING WOMEN	NO
SEPARATE FORMS	NO
SEPARATE NORMS	NO

ANALYSIS OF SKILLS IN READING - LEVEL 78

	MEAN	STANDARD DEVIATION
ILLUSTRATIONS-NUMBER OF MALE ADULTS	0.00	0.00
ILLUSTRATIONS-NUMBER OF FEMALE ADULTS	0.00	0.00
ILLUSTRATIONS-NUMBER OF MALE CHILDREN	0.00	0.00
ILLUSTRATIONS-NUMBER OF FEMALE CHILDREN	0.00	0.00
ILLUSTRATIONS-NUMBER OF MALE ANIMALS	.	.
ILLUSTRATIONS-NUMBER OF FEMALE ANIMALS	.	.
CONTENT-NUMBER OF MALE ADULTS	7.66	0.57
CONTENT-NUMBER OF FEMALE ADULTS	5.33	0.57
CONTENT-NUMBER OF MALE CHILDREN	7.00	1.73
CONTENT-NUMBER OF FEMALE CHILDREN	3.00	0.00
CONTENT-NUMBER OF MALE ANIMALS	0.00	0.00
CONTENT-NUMBER OF FEMALE ANIMALS	0.00	0.00
MALES IN STERO. NONOCC. ROLES	0.00	0.00
FEMALES IN STERO. NONOCC. ROLES	0.00	0.00
TOTAL MALES IN NONOCC. ROLES	0.00	0.00
TOTAL FEMALES IN NONOCC. ROLES	0.00	0.00
MALES IN STERO. OCCUPATIONAL ROLES	1.00	1.00
FEMALES IN STERO. OCCUPATIONAL ROLES	0.33	0.57
TOTAL MALES IN OCCUPATIONAL ROLES	1.00	1.00
TOTAL FEMALES IN OCCUPATIONAL ROLES	0.33	0.57
TOTAL OCCUPATIONS DEPICTED FOR MALES	0.33	0.57
TOTAL OCCUPATIONS DEPICTED FOR FEMALES	0.00	0.00
NUMBER OF FAMOUS MEN	1.00	1.00
NUMBER OF FAMOUS WOMEN	0.00	0.00

FEMALES DRESSED ONLY IN SKIRTS	NA
DEMEANING OR STERO. STATEMENTS	NO
STERO. EMOTIONAL RESPONSES	NO
LANGUAGE EXCLUDING WOMEN	NO
SEPARATE FORMS	NO
SEPARATE NORMS	NO

ASSESSMENT OF CHILDRENS LANGUAGE COMPREHENSION

	MEAN	STANDARD DEVIATION
ILLUSTRATIONS-NUMBER OF MALE ADULTS	2.25	0.50
ILLUSTRATIONS-NUMBER OF FEMALE ADULTS	7.75	3.50
ILLUSTRATIONS-NUMBER OF MALE CHILDREN	15.25	7.41
ILLUSTRATIONS-NUMBER OF FEMALE CHILDREN	6.25	2.06
ILLUSTRATIONS-NUMBER OF MALE ANIMALS	0.00	0.00
ILLUSTRATIONS-NUMBER OF FEMALE ANIMALS	0.00	0.00
CONTENT-NUMBER OF MALE ADULTS	1.66	0.57
CONTENT-NUMBER OF FEMALE ADULTS	5.00	1.73
CONTENT-NUMBER OF MALE CHILDREN	7.00	3.46
CONTENT-NUMBER OF FEMALE CHILDREN	2.33	1.15
CONTENT-NUMBER OF MALE ANIMALS	0.00	0.00
CONTENT-NUMBER OF FEMALE ANIMALS	0.00	0.00
MALES IN STERO. NONOCC. ROLES	0.00	0.00
FEMALES IN STERO. NONOCC. ROLES	0.00	0.00
TOTAL MALES IN NONOCC. ROLES	0.00	0.00
TOTAL FEMALES IN NONOCC. ROLES	0.00	0.00
MALES IN STERO. OCCUPATIONAL ROLES	0.00	0.00
FEMALES IN STERO. OCCUPATIONAL ROLES	0.00	0.00
TOTAL MALES IN OCCUPATIONAL ROLES	0.00	0.00
TOTAL FEMALES IN OCCUPATIONAL ROLES	0.00	0.00
TOTAL OCCUPATIONS DEPICTED FOR MALES	0.00	0.00
TOTAL OCCUPATIONS DEPICTED FOR FEMALES	0.00	0.00
NUMBER OF FAMOUS MEN	0.00	0.00
NUMBER OF FAMOUS WOMEN	0.00	0.00

FEMALES DRESSED ONLY IN SKIRTS	NO
DEMEANING OR STERO. STATEMENTS	NO
STERO. EMOTIONAL RESPONSES	NO
LANGUAGE EXCLUDING WOMEN	NO
SEPARATE FORMS	NO
SEPARATE NORMS	NO

BERNREUTER PERSONALITY INVENTORY

	MEAN	STANDARD DEVIATION
ILLUSTRATIONS-NUMBER OF MALE ADULTS	•	•
ILLUSTRATIONS-NUMBER OF FEMALE ADULTS	•	•
ILLUSTRATIONS-NUMBER OF MALE CHILDREN	•	•
ILLUSTRATIONS-NUMBER OF FEMALE CHILDREN	•	•
ILLUSTRATIONS-NUMBER OF MALE ANIMALS	•	•
ILLUSTRATIONS-NUMBER OF FEMALE ANIMALS	•	•
CONTENT-NUMBER OF MALE ADULTS	5.50	0.70
CONTENT-NUMBER OF FEMALE ADULTS	0.00	0.00
CONTENT-NUMBER OF MALE CHILDREN	0.00	0.00
CONTENT-NUMBER OF FEMALE CHILDREN	0.00	0.00
CONTENT-NUMBER OF MALE ANIMALS	0.00	0.00
CONTENT-NUMBER OF FEMALE ANIMALS	0.00	0.00
MALES IN STERO. NONOCC. ROLES	0.00	0.00
FEMALES IN STERO. NONOCC. ROLES	0.00	0.00
TOTAL MALES IN NONOCC. ROLES	0.00	0.00
TOTAL FEMALES IN NONOCC. ROLES	0.00	0.00
MALES IN STERO. OCCUPATIONAL ROLES	5.00	•
FEMALES IN STERO. OCCUPATIONAL ROLES	0.00	•
TOTAL MALES IN OCCUPATIONAL ROLES	5.00	•
TOTAL FEMALES IN OCCUPATIONAL ROLES	0.00	•
TOTAL OCCUPATIONS DEPICTED FOR MALES	0.00	0.00
TOTAL OCCUPATIONS DEPICTED FOR FEMALES	0.00	0.00
NUMBER OF FAMOUS MEN	0.00	0.00
NUMBER OF FAMOUS WOMEN	0.00	0.00

FEMALES DRESSED ONLY IN SKIRTS	NA
DEMEANING OR STERO. STATEMENTS	YES
STERO. EMOTIONAL RESPONSES	NA
LANGUAGE EXCLUDING WOMEN	YES
SEPARATE FORMS	NO
SEPARATE NORMS	YES

CALIFORNIA PSYCHOLOGICAL INVENTORY

	MEAN	STANDARD DEVIATION
ILLUSTRATIONS—NUMBER OF MALE ADULTS	.	.
ILLUSTRATIONS—NUMBER OF FEMALE ADULTS	.	.
ILLUSTRATIONS—NUMBER OF MALE CHILDREN	.	.
ILLUSTRATIONS—NUMBER OF FEMALE CHILDREN	.	.
ILLUSTRATIONS—NUMBER OF MALE ANIMALS	.	.
ILLUSTRATIONS—NUMBER OF FEMALE ANIMALS	.	.
CONTENT—NUMBER OF MALE ADULTS	9.66	6.65
CONTENT—NUMBER OF FEMALE ADULTS	5.33	2.88
CONTENT—NUMBER OF MALE CHILDREN	.	.
CONTENT—NUMBER OF FEMALE CHILDREN	1.00	0.00
CONTENT—NUMBER OF MALE ANIMALS	0.00	0.00
CONTENT—NUMBER OF FEMALE ANIMALS	0.00	0.00
MALES IN STERO. NONOCC. ROLES	0.00	0.00
FEMALES IN STERO. NONOCC. ROLES	0.00	0.00
TOTAL MALES IN NONOCC. ROLES	0.00	0.00
TOTAL FEMALES IN NONOCC. ROLES	0.00	0.00
MALES IN STERO. OCCUPATIONAL ROLES	0.00	0.00
FEMALES IN STERO. OCCUPATIONAL ROLES	0.00	0.00
TOTAL MALES IN OCCUPATIONAL ROLES	0.00	0.00
TOTAL FEMALES IN OCCUPATIONAL ROLES	0.00	0.00
TOTAL OCCUPATIONS DEPICTED FOR MALES	0.00	0.00
TOTAL OCCUPATIONS DEPICTED FOR FEMALES	0.00	0.00
NUMBER OF FAMOUS MEN	2.66	0.57
NUMBER OF FAMOUS WOMEN	0.00	0.00

FEMALES DRESSED ONLY IN SKIRTS	NA
DEMEANING OR STERO. STATEMENTS	NO
STERO. EMOTIONAL RESPONSES	NO
LANGUAGE EXCLUDING WOMEN	YES
SEPARATE FORMS	NO
SEPARATE NORMS	NO

CALIFORNIA TEST OF PERSONALITY - FORM AA

	MEAN	STANDARD DEVIATION
ILLUSTRATIONS-NUMBER OF MALE ADULTS	•	•
ILLUSTRATIONS-NUMBER OF FEMALE ADULTS	•	•
ILLUSTRATIONS-NUMBER OF MALE CHILDREN	•	•
ILLUSTRATIONS-NUMBER OF FEMALE CHILDREN	•	•
ILLUSTRATIONS-NUMBER OF MALE ANIMALS	•	•
ILLUSTRATIONS-NUMBER OF FEMALE ANIMALS	•	•
CONTENT-NUMBER OF MALE ADULTS	•	•
CONTENT-NUMBER OF FEMALE ADULTS	•	•
CONTENT-NUMBER OF MALE CHILDREN	•	•
CONTENT-NUMBER OF FEMALE CHILDREN	•	•
CONTENT-NUMBER OF MALE ANIMALS	•	•
CONTENT-NUMBER OF FEMALE ANIMALS	•	•
MALES IN STERO. NONOCC. ROLES	•	•
FEMALES IN STERO. NONOCC. ROLES	•	•
TOTAL MALES IN NONOCC. ROLES	•	•
TOTAL FEMALES IN NONOCC. ROLES	•	•
MALES IN STERO. OCCUPATIONAL ROLES	•	•
FEMALES IN STERO. OCCUPATIONAL ROLES	•	•
TOTAL MALES IN OCCUPATIONAL ROLES	•	•
TOTAL FEMALES IN OCCUPATIONAL ROLES	•	•
TOTAL OCCUPATIONS DEPICTED FOR MALES	•	•
TOTAL OCCUPATIONS DEPICTED FOR FEMALES	•	•
NUMBER OF FAMOUS MEN	•	•
NUMBER OF FAMOUS WOMEN	•	•

FEMALES DRESSED ONLY IN SKIRTS	NA
DEMEANING OR STERO. STATEMENTS	NA
STERO. EMOTIONAL RESPONSES	NA
LANGUAGE EXCLUDING WOMEN	NA
SEPARATE FORMS	NA
SEPARATE NORMS	NA

CLASSROOM READING INVENTORY - ALL FORMS

	MEAN	STANDARD DEVIATION
ILLUSTRATIONS-NUMBER OF MALE ADULTS	5.66	3.51
ILLUSTRATIONS-NUMBER OF FEMALE ADULTS	1.66	0.57
ILLUSTRATIONS-NUMBER OF MALE CHILDREN	7.50	2.12
ILLUSTRATIONS-NUMBER OF FEMALE CHILDREN	3.00	1.00
ILLUSTRATIONS-NUMBER OF MALE ANIMALS	1.00	1.00
ILLUSTRATIONS-NUMBER OF FEMALE ANIMALS	0.00	0.00
CONTENT-NUMBER OF MALE ADULTS	8.66	4.16
CONTENT-NUMBER OF FEMALE ADULTS	5.00	2.64
CONTENT-NUMBER OF MALE CHILDREN	7.66	2.08
CONTENT-NUMBER CF FEMALE CHILDREN	3.33	0.57
CONTENT-NUMBER OF MALE ANIMALS	1.66	1.15
CONTENT-NUMBER CF FEMALE ANIMALS	0.00	0.00
MALES IN STERO. NONOCC. ROLES	1.33	1.15
FEMALES IN STERO. NONOCC. ROLES	0.33	0.57
TOTAL MALES IN NONOCC. ROLES	1.66	1.52
TOTAL FEMALES IN NONOCC. ROLES	0.66	1.15
MALES IN STERO. OCCUPATIONAL ROLES	1.33	1.52
FEMALES IN STERO. OCCUPATIONAL ROLES	1.33	2.30
TOTAL MALES IN CCCUPATICNAL ROLES	1.33	1.52
TOTAL FEMALES IN OCCUPATIONAL ROLES	1.33	2.30
TOTAL OCCUPATIONS DEPICTED FOR MALES	2.66	1.52
TOTAL OCCUPATIONS DEPICTED FOR FEMALES	0.00	0.00
NUMBER OF FAMOUS MEN	1.66	0.57
NUMBER OF FAMCUS WOMEN	1.00	0.00

FEMALES DRESSED ONLY IN SKIRTS	NO
DEMEANING OR STERO. STATEMENTS	NO
STERO. EMOTIONAL RESPONSES	NO
LANGUAGE EXCLUDING WOMEN	NO
SEPARATE FORMS	NO
SEPARATE NORMS	NO

COGNITIVE ABILITIES TEST - LOWER PRIMARY 1

	MEAN	STANDARD DEVIATION
ILLUSTRATIONS-NUMBER OF MALE ADULTS	20.25	1.50
ILLUSTRATIONS-NUMBER OF FEMALE ADULTS	5.50	1.00
ILLUSTRATIONS-NUMBER OF MALE CHILDREN	14.50	1.73
ILLUSTRATIONS-NUMBER OF FEMALE CHILDREN	27.75	6.65
ILLUSTRATIONS-NUMBER OF MALE ANIMALS	0.00	0.00
ILLUSTRATIONS-NUMBER OF FEMALE ANIMALS	0.00	0.00
CONTENT-NUMBER OF MALE ADULTS	1.00	0.00
CONTENT-NUMBER OF FEMALE ADULTS	0.00	0.00
CONTENT-NUMBER OF MALE CHILDREN	2.00	1.41
CONTENT-NUMBER OF FEMALE CHILDREN	4.50	0.70
CONTENT-NUMBER OF MALE ANIMALS	0.00	0.00
CONTENT-NUMBER OF FEMALE ANIMALS	0.00	0.00
MALES IN STERO. NONOCC. ROLES	7.25	4.50
FEMALES IN STERO. NONOCC. ROLES	1.25	0.95
TOTAL MALES IN NONOCC. ROLES	10.00	2.44
TOTAL FEMALES IN NONOCC. ROLES	1.75	1.50
MALES IN STERO. OCCUPATIONAL ROLES	5.00	1.63
FEMALES IN STERO. OCCUPATIONAL ROLES	0.00	0.00
TOTAL MALES IN OCCUPATIONAL ROLES	5.00	1.63
TOTAL FEMALES IN OCCUPATIONAL ROLES	0.00	0.00
TOTAL OCCUPATIONS DEPICTED FOR MALES	4.00	1.15
TOTAL OCCUPATIONS DEPICTED FOR FEMALES	0.00	0.00
NUMBER OF FAMOUS MEN	0.00	0.00
NUMBER OF FAMOUS WOMEN	0.00	0.00

FEMALES DRESSED ONLY IN SKIRTS	NO
DEMEANING OR STERO. STATEMENTS	NO
STERO. EMOTIONAL RESPONSES	NO
LANGUAGE EXCLUDING WOMEN	NO
SEPARATE FORMS	NO
SEPARATE NORMS	NO

COGNITIVE ABILITIES TEST - LOWER PRIMARY 2

	MEAN	STANDARD DEVIATION
ILLUSTRATIONS-NUMBER OF MALE ADULTS	23.00	3.91
ILLUSTRATIONS-NUMBER OF FEMALE ADULTS	4.25	0.95
ILLUSTRATIONS-NUMBER OF MALE CHILDREN	28.75	7.58
ILLUSTRATIONS-NUMBER OF FEMALE CHILDREN	8.50	2.64
ILLUSTRATIONS-NUMBER OF MALE ANIMALS	0.00	0.00
ILLUSTRATIONS-NUMBER OF FEMALE ANIMALS	0.00	0.00
CONTENT-NUMBER OF MALE ADULTS	0.00	.
CONTENT-NUMBER OF FEMALE ADULTS	1.00	.
CONTENT-NUMBER OF MALE CHILDREN	0.75	0.95
CONTENT-NUMBER OF FEMALE CHILDREN	1.00	0.81
CONTENT-NUMBER OF MALE ANIMALS	0.00	0.00
CONTENT-NUMBER OF FEMALE ANIMALS	0.00	0.00
MALES IN STERO. NONOCC. ROLES	8.25	6.55
FEMALES IN STERO. NONOCC. ROLES	0.75	0.50
TOTAL MALES IN NONOCC. ROLES	11.50	4.79
TOTAL FEMALES IN NONOCC. ROLES	1.00	0.81
MALES IN STERO. OCCUPATIONAL ROLES	8.75	5.73
FEMALES IN STERO. OCCUPATIONAL ROLES	0.00	0.00
TOTAL MALES IN OCCUPATIONAL ROLES	8.75	5.73
TOTAL FEMALES IN OCCUPATIONAL ROLES	0.00	0.00
TOTAL OCCUPATIONS DEPICTED FOR MALES	7.33	1.52
TOTAL OCCUPATIONS DEPICTED FOR FEMALES	0.00	0.00
NUMBER OF FAMOUS MEN	0.00	0.00
NUMBER OF FAMOUS WOMEN	0.00	0.00

FEMALES DRESSED ONLY IN SKIRTS	NO
DEMEANING OR STERO. STATEMENTS	NO
STERO. EMOTIONAL RESPONSES	NO
LANGUAGE EXCLUDING WOMEN	NO
SEPARATE FORMS	NO
SEPARATE NORMS	NO

COGNITIVE ABILITIES TEST - MULTILEVEL

	MEAN	STANDARD DEVIATION
ILLUSTRATIONS-NUMBER OF MALE ADULTS	0.00	0.00
ILLUSTRATIONS-NUMBER OF FEMALE ADULTS	0.00	0.00
ILLUSTRATIONS-NUMBER OF MALE CHILDREN	0.00	0.00
ILLUSTRATIONS-NUMBER OF FEMALE CHILDREN	0.00	0.00
ILLUSTRATIONS-NUMBER OF MALE ANIMALS	0.00	0.00
ILLUSTRATIONS-NUMBER OF FEMALE ANIMALS	0.00	0.00
CONTENT-NUMBER OF MALE ADULTS	6.33	1.15
CONTENT-NUMBER OF FEMALE ADULTS	4.66	3.05
CONTENT-NUMBER OF MALE CHILDREN	2.00	0.00
CONTENT-NUMBER OF FEMALE CHILDREN	5.50	0.70
CONTENT-NUMBER OF MALE ANIMALS	0.00	.
CONTENT-NUMBER OF FEMALE ANIMALS	1.00	.
MALES IN STERO. NONOCC. ROLES	0.33	0.57
FEMALES IN STERO. NONOCC. ROLES	0.00	0.00
TOTAL MALES IN NONOCC. ROLES	0.33	0.57
TOTAL FEMALES IN NONOCC. ROLES	0.00	0.00
MALES IN STERO. OCCUPATIONAL ROLES	1.33	1.15
FEMALES IN STERO. OCCUPATIONAL ROLES	0.00	0.00
TOTAL MALES IN OCCUPATIONAL ROLES	2.00	2.00
TOTAL FEMALES IN OCCUPATIONAL ROLES	0.00	0.00
TOTAL OCCUPATIONS DEPICTED FOR MALES	4.00	.
TOTAL OCCUPATIONS DEPICTED FOR FEMALES	1.00	.
NUMBER OF FAMOUS MEN	1.00	0.00
NUMBER OF FAMOUS WOMEN	0.00	0.00

FEMALES DRESSED ONLY IN SKIRTS	NO
DEMEANING OR STERO. STATEMENTS	NO
STERO. EMOTIONAL RESPONSES	YES
LANGUAGE EXCLUDING WOMEN	YES
SEPARATE FORMS	NO
SEPARATE NORMS	NO

COMPREHENSIVE TESTS OF BASIC SKILLS - FORM S, LEVEL A

	MEAN	STANDARD DEVIATION
ILLUSTRATIONS-NUMBER OF MALE ADULTS	1.66	0.57
ILLUSTRATIONS-NUMBER OF FEMALE ADULTS	2.00	0.00
ILLUSTRATIONS-NUMBER OF MALE CHILDREN	17.66	7.50
ILLUSTRATIONS-NUMBER OF FEMALE CHILDREN	9.66	2.30
ILLUSTRATIONS-NUMBER OF MALE ANIMALS	0.00	0.00
ILLUSTRATIONS-NUMBER OF FEMALE ANIMALS	0.00	0.00
CONTENT-NUMBER OF MALE ADULTS	0.00	0.00
CONTENT-NUMBER OF FEMALE ADULTS	0.00	0.00
CONTENT-NUMBER OF MALE CHILDREN	0.00	0.00
CONTENT-NUMBER OF FEMALE CHILDREN	0.00	0.00
CONTENT-NUMBER OF MALE ANIMALS	0.00	0.00
CONTENT-NUMBER OF FEMALE ANIMALS	0.00	0.00
MALES IN STERO. NONOCC. ROLES	1.33	1.15
FEMALES IN STERO. NONOCC. ROLES	1.33	1.15
TOTAL MALES IN NONOCC. ROLES	1.33	1.15
TOTAL FEMALES IN NONOCC. ROLES	1.33	1.15
MALES IN STERO. OCCUPATIONAL ROLES	0.66	0.57
FEMALES IN STERO. OCCUPATIONAL ROLES	0.66	0.57
TOTAL MALES IN OCCUPATIONAL ROLES	0.66	0.57
TOTAL FEMALES IN OCCUPATIONAL ROLES	0.66	0.57
TOTAL OCCUPATIONS DEPICTED FOR MALES	0.66	0.57
TOTAL OCCUPATIONS DEPICTED FOR FEMALES	0.66	0.57
NUMBER OF FAMOUS MEN	0.66	0.57
NUMBER OF FAMOUS WOMEN	0.00	0.00

FEMALES DRESSED ONLY IN SKIRTS	YES
DEMEANING OR STERO. STATEMENTS	NO
STERO. EMOTIONAL RESPONSES	NO
LANGUAGE EXCLUDING WOMEN	NO
SEPARATE FORMS	NO
SEPARATE NORMS	NA

COMPREHENSIVE TESTS OF BASIC SKILLS - FORM S, LEVEL B

	MEAN	STANDARD DEVIATION
ILLUSTRATIONS-NUMBER OF MALE ADULTS	7.00	0.00
ILLUSTRATIONS-NUMBER OF FEMALE ADULTS	6.33	4.04
ILLUSTRATIONS-NUMBER OF MALE CHILDREN	32.00	0.00
ILLUSTRATIONS-NUMBER OF FEMALE CHILDREN	34.00	0.00
ILLUSTRATIONS-NUMBER OF MALE ANIMALS	0.00	0.00
ILLUSTRATIONS-NUMBER OF FEMALE ANIMALS	0.00	0.00
CONTENT-NUMBER OF MALE ADULTS	3.00	0.00
CONTENT-NUMBER OF FEMALE ADULTS	3.00	0.00
CONTENT-NUMBER OF MALE CHILDREN	5.00	0.00
CONTENT-NUMBER OF FEMALE CHILDREN	8.00	0.00
CONTENT-NUMBER CF MALE ANIMALS	0.00	0.00
CONTENT-NUMBER OF FEMALE ANIMALS	0.00	0.00
MALES IN STERO. NONOCC. ROLES	2.00	0.00
FEMALES IN STERO. NONOCC. ROLES	3.33	0.57
TOTAL MALES IN NONOCC. ROLES	2.00	0.00
TOTAL FEMALES IN NONOCC. ROLES	5.00	0.00
MALES IN STERO. OCCUPATIONAL ROLES	0.00	0.00
FEMALES IN STERO. OCCUPATIONAL ROLES	0.00	0.00
TOTAL MALES IN OCCUPATIONAL ROLES	0.00	0.00
TOTAL FEMALES IN OCCUPATIONAL ROLES	0.00	0.00
TOTAL OCCUPATIONS DEPICTED FOR MALES	0.00	0.00
TOTAL OCCUPATIONS DEPICTED FOR FEMALES	0.00	0.00
NUMBER OF FAMOUS MEN	0.00	0.00
NUMBER OF FAMOUS WOMEN	0.00	0.00

FEMALES DRESSED ONLY IN SKIRTS	NO
DEMEANING OR STERO. STATEMENTS	NO
STERO. EMOTIONAL RESPONSES	NO
LANGUAGE EXCLUDING WOMEN	NO
SEPARATE FORMS	NO
SEPARATE NORMS	NO

COMPREHENSIVE TEST OF BASIC SKILLS - FORM S, LEVEL C

	MEAN	STANDARD DEVIATION
ILLUSTRATIONS-NUMBER OF MALE ADULTS	37.00	1.41
ILLUSTRATIONS-NUMBER OF FEMALE ADULTS	6.50	0.70
ILLUSTRATIONS-NUMBER OF MALE CHILDREN	21.50	0.70
ILLUSTRATIONS-NUMBER OF FEMALE CHILDREN	15.00	0.00
ILLUSTRATIONS-NUMBER OF MALE ANIMALS	0.00	0.00
ILLUSTRATIONS-NUMBER OF FEMALE ANIMALS	0.00	0.00
CONTENT-NUMBER OF MALE ADULTS	10.00	5.65
CONTENT-NUMBER OF FEMALE ADULTS	11.50	4.94
CONTENT-NUMBER OF MALE CHILDREN	16.00	8.48
CONTENT-NUMBER OF FEMALE CHILDREN	11.00	1.41
CONTENT-NUMBER OF MALE ANIMALS	2.50	0.70
CONTENT-NUMBER OF FEMALE ANIMALS	0.00	0.00
MALES IN STERO. NONOCC. ROLES	0.50	0.70
FEMALES IN STERO. NONOCC. ROLES	0.00	0.00
TOTAL MALES IN NONOCC. ROLES	0.50	0.70
TOTAL FEMALES IN NONOCC. ROLES	0.00	0.00
MALES IN STERO. OCCUPATIONAL ROLES	0.50	0.70
FEMALES IN STERO. OCCUPATIONAL ROLES	0.00	0.00
TOTAL MALES IN OCCUPATIONAL ROLES	0.50	0.70
TOTAL FEMALES IN OCCUPATIONAL ROLES	0.00	0.00
TOTAL OCCUPATIONS DEPICTED FOR MALES	0.00	0.00
TOTAL OCCUPATIONS DEPICTED FOR FEMALES	0.00	0.00
NUMBER OF FAMOUS MEN	0.50	0.70
NUMBER OF FAMOUS WOMEN	0.00	0.00

FEMALES DRESSED ONLY IN SKIRTS	NO
DEMEANING OR STERO. STATEMENTS	NO
STERO. EMOTIONAL RESPONSES	NO
LANGUAGE EXCLUDING WOMEN	NO
SEPARATE FORMS	NO
SEPARATE NORMS	NO

COMPREHENSIVE TESTS OF BASIC SKILLS - FORM S, LEVEL 1

	MEAN	STANDARD DEVIATION
ILLUSTRATIONS-NUMBER OF MALE ADULTS	0.00	0.00
ILLUSTRATIONS-NUMBER OF FEMALE ADULTS	0.00	0.00
ILLUSTRATIONS-NUMBER OF MALE CHILDREN	2.00	0.00
ILLUSTRATIONS-NUMBER OF FEMALE CHILDREN	1.00	0.00
ILLUSTRATIONS-NUMBER OF MALE ANIMALS	0.00	0.00
ILLUSTRATIONS-NUMBER OF FEMALE ANIMALS	0.00	0.00
CONTENT-NUMBER OF MALE ADULTS	6.00	0.00
CONTENT-NUMBER OF FEMALE ADULTS	6.66	0.57
CONTENT-NUMBER OF MALE CHILDREN	23.66	6.42
CONTENT-NUMBER OF FEMALE CHILDREN	15.33	1.52
CONTENT-NUMBER OF MALE ANIMALS	0.00	0.00
CONTENT-NUMBER OF FEMALE ANIMALS	0.00	0.00
MALES IN STERO. NONOCC. ROLES	1.00	0.00
FEMALES IN STERO. NONOCC. ROLES	0.00	0.00
TOTAL MALES IN NONOCC. ROLES	1.00	0.00
TOTAL FEMALES IN NONOCC. ROLES	0.00	0.00
MALES IN STERO. OCCUPATIONAL ROLES	0.00	0.00
FEMALES IN STERO. OCCUPATIONAL ROLES	0.00	0.00
TOTAL MALES IN OCCUPATIONAL ROLES	0.00	0.00
TOTAL FEMALES IN OCCUPATIONAL ROLES	0.00	0.00
TOTAL OCCUPATIONS DEPICTED FOR MALES	0.00	0.00
TOTAL OCCUPATIONS DEPICTED FOR FEMALES	0.00	0.00
NUMBER OF FAMOUS MEN	0.00	0.00
NUMBER OF FAMOUS WOMEN	0.66	0.57

FEMALES DRESSED ONLY IN SKIRTS	NO
DEMEANING OR STERO. STATEMENTS	NO
STERO. EMOTIONAL RESPONSES	NO
LANGUAGE EXCLUDING WOMEN	YES
SEPARATE FORMS	NO
SEPARATE NORMS	NO

COMPREHENSIVE TEST OF BASIC SKILLS - FORM S, LEVEL 3

	MEAN	STANDARD DEVIATION
ILLUSTRATIONS-NUMBER OF MALE ADULTS	•	•
ILLUSTRATIONS-NUMBER OF FEMALE ADULTS	•	•
ILLUSTRATIONS-NUMBER OF MALE CHILDREN	•	•
ILLUSTRATIONS-NUMBER OF FEMALE CHILDREN	•	•
ILLUSTRATIONS-NUMBER OF MALE ANIMALS	•	•
ILLUSTRATIONS-NUMBER OF FEMALE ANIMALS	•	•
CONTENT-NUMBER OF MALE ADULTS	22.00	1.73
CONTENT-NUMBER OF FEMALE ADULTS	17.33	1.15
CONTENT-NUMBER OF MALE CHILDREN	2.66	0.57
CONTENT-NUMBER OF FEMALE CHILDREN	7.33	2.88
CONTENT-NUMBER OF MALE ANIMALS	0.00	0.00
CONTENT-NUMBER OF FEMALE ANIMALS	0.00	0.00
MALES IN STERO. NONOCC. ROLES	0.00	0.00
FEMALES IN STERO. NONOCC. ROLES	0.00	0.00
TOTAL MALES IN NONOCC. ROLES	0.00	0.00
TOTAL FEMALES IN NONOCC. ROLES	0.00	0.00
MALES IN STERO. OCCUPATIONAL ROLES	0.00	0.00
FEMALES IN STERO. OCCUPATIONAL ROLES	0.00	0.00
TOTAL MALES IN OCCUPATIONAL ROLES	0.00	0.00
TOTAL FEMALES IN OCCUPATIONAL ROLES	0.00	0.00
TOTAL OCCUPATIONS DEPICTED FOR MALES	0.00	0.00
TOTAL OCCUPATIONS DEPICTED FOR FEMALES	0.00	0.00
NUMBER OF FAMOUS MEN	0.00	0.00
NUMBER OF FAMOUS WOMEN	0.00	0.00

FEMALES DRESSED ONLY IN SKIRTS	NA
DEMEANING OR STERO. STATEMENTS	NO
STERO. EMOTIONAL RESPONSES	NO
LANGUAGE EXCLUDING WOMEN	NO
SEPARATE FORMS	NO
SEPARATE NORMS	NO

COMREY PERSONALITY SCALES

	MEAN	STANDARD DEVIATION
ILLUSTRATIONS-NUMBER OF MALE ADULTS	.	.
ILLUSTRATIONS-NUMBER OF FEMALE ADULTS	.	.
ILLUSTRATIONS-NUMBER OF MALE CHILDREN	.	.
ILLUSTRATIONS-NUMBER OF FEMALE CHILDREN	.	.
ILLUSTRATIONS-NUMBER OF MALE ANIMALS	.	.
ILLUSTRATIONS-NUMBER OF FEMALE ANIMALS	.	.
CONTENT-NUMBER OF MALE ADULTS	0.25	0.50
CONTENT-NUMBER OF FEMALE ADULTS	0.00	0.00
CONTENT-NUMBER OF MALE CHILDREN	0.75	0.95
CONTENT-NUMBER OF FEMALE CHILDREN	0.00	0.00
CONTENT-NUMBER OF MALE ANIMALS	0.00	0.00
CONTENT-NUMBER OF FEMALE ANIMALS	0.00	0.00
MALES IN STERO. NONOCC. ROLES	0.00	0.00
FEMALES IN STERO. NONOCC. ROLES	0.00	0.00
TOTAL MALES IN NONOCC. ROLES	0.00	0.00
TOTAL FEMALES IN NONOCC. ROLES	0.00	0.00
MALES IN STERO. OCCUPATIONAL ROLES	0.00	0.00
FEMALES IN STERO. OCCUPATIONAL ROLES	0.00	0.00
TOTAL MALES IN OCCUPATIONAL ROLES	0.00	0.00
TOTAL FEMALES IN OCCUPATIONAL ROLES	0.00	0.00
TOTAL OCCUPATIONS DEPICTED FOR MALES	0.00	0.00
TOTAL OCCUPATIONS DEPICTED FOR FEMALES	0.00	0.00
NUMBER OF FAMOUS MEN	0.00	0.00
NUMBER OF FAMOUS WOMEN	0.00	0.00

FEMALES DRESSED ONLY IN SKIRTS	NA
DEMEANING OR STERO. STATEMENTS	NA
STERO. EMOTIONAL RESPONSES	NO
LANGUAGE EXCLUDING WOMEN	NO
SEPARATE FORMS	NO
SEPARATE NORMS	NO

COOPERATIVE PRESCHOOL INVENTORY

	MEAN	STANDARD DEVIATION
ILLUSTRATIONS-NUMBER OF MALE ADULTS	.	.
ILLUSTRATIONS-NUMBER OF FEMALE ADULTS	.	.
ILLUSTRATIONS-NUMBER OF MALE CHILDREN	.	.
ILLUSTRATIONS-NUMBER OF FEMALE CHILDREN	.	.
ILLUSTRATIONS-NUMBER OF MALE ANIMALS	.	.
ILLUSTRATIONS-NUMBER OF FEMALE ANIMALS	.	.
CONTENT-NUMBER OF MALE ADULTS	0.50	1.00
CONTENT-NUMBER OF FEMALE ADULTS	1.00	1.41
CONTENT-NUMBER OF MALE CHILDREN	0.75	1.50
CONTENT-NUMBER OF FEMALE CHILDREN	0.00	0.00
CONTENT-NUMBER OF MALE ANIMALS	0.00	0.00
CONTENT-NUMBER OF FEMALE ANIMALS	0.00	0.00
MALES IN STERO. NONOCC. ROLES	3.25	3.94
FEMALES IN STERO. NONOCC. ROLES	0.00	0.00
TOTAL MALES IN NONOCC. ROLES	3.25	3.94
TOTAL FEMALES IN NONOCC. ROLES	0.00	0.00
MALES IN STERO. OCCUPATIONAL ROLES	0.50	1.00
FEMALES IN STERO. OCCUPATIONAL ROLES	0.25	0.50
TOTAL MALES IN OCCUPATIONAL ROLES	0.50	1.00
TOTAL FEMALES IN OCCUPATIONAL ROLES	0.25	0.50
TOTAL OCCUPATIONS DEPICTED FOR MALES	0.50	1.00
TOTAL OCCUPATIONS DEPICTED FOR FEMALES	0.25	0.50
NUMBER OF FAMOUS MEN	0.00	0.00
NUMBER OF FAMOUS WOMEN	0.00	0.00

FEMALES DRESSED ONLY IN SKIRTS	NA
DEMEANING OR STERO. STATEMENTS	NO
STERO. EMOTIONAL RESPONSES	NO
LANGUAGE EXCLUDING WOMEN	NO
SEPARATE FORMS	NO
SEPARATE NORMS	NO

DETROIT TEST OF LEARNING APTITUDE - FORM 1

	MEAN	STANDARD DEVIATION
ILLUSTRATIONS-NUMBER OF MALE ADULTS	7.75	0.50
ILLUSTRATIONS-NUMBER OF FEMALE ADULTS	3.75	1.50
ILLUSTRATIONS-NUMBER OF MALE CHILDREN	12.50	3.00
ILLUSTRATIONS-NUMBER OF FEMALE CHILDREN	7.75	2.06
ILLUSTRATIONS-NUMBER OF MALE ANIMALS	0.25	0.50
ILLUSTRATIONS-NUMBER OF FEMALE ANIMALS	0.50	1.00
CONTENT-NUMBER OF MALE ADULTS	16.25	4.11
CONTENT-NUMBER OF FEMALE ADULTS	5.00	2.16
CONTENT-NUMBER OF MALE CHILDREN	8.50	4.35
CONTENT-NUMBER OF FEMALE CHILDREN	4.50	1.29
CONTENT-NUMBER OF MALE ANIMALS	0.00	0.00
CONTENT-NUMBER OF FEMALE ANIMALS	0.00	0.00
MALES IN STERO. NONOCC. ROLES	2.00	0.81
FEMALES IN STERO. NONOCC. ROLES	1.50	1.73
TOTAL MALES IN NONOCC. ROLES	2.75	1.50
TOTAL FEMALES IN NONOCC. ROLES	2.00	2.30
MALES IN STERO. OCCUPATIONAL ROLES	5.00	1.63
FEMALES IN STERO. OCCUPATIONAL ROLES	0.50	0.57
TOTAL MALES IN OCCUPATIONAL ROLES	5.00	1.63
TOTAL FEMALES IN OCCUPATIONAL ROLES	0.50	0.57
TOTAL OCCUPATIONS DEPICTED FOR MALES	4.75	1.25
TOTAL OCCUPATIONS DEPICTED FOR FEMALES	0.50	0.57
NUMBER OF FAMOUS MEN	0.00	0.00
NUMBER OF FAMOUS WOMEN	0.00	0.00

FEMALES DRESSED ONLY IN SKIRTS	NO
DEMEANING OR STERO. STATEMENTS	NO
STERO. EMOTIONAL RESPONSES	NO
LANGUAGE EXCLUDING WOMEN	YES
SEPARATE FORMS	NO
SEPARATE NORMS	NO

DIAGNOSTIC READING SCALES

	MEAN	STANDARD DEVIATION
ILLUSTRATIONS-NUMBER OF MALE ADULTS	.	.
ILLUSTRATIONS-NUMBER OF FEMALE ADULTS	.	.
ILLUSTRATIONS-NUMBER OF MALE CHILDREN	.	.
ILLUSTRATIONS-NUMBER OF FEMALE CHILDREN	.	.
ILLUSTRATIONS-NUMBER OF MALE ANIMALS	.	.
ILLUSTRATIONS-NUMBER OF FEMALE ANIMALS	.	.
CONTENT-NUMBER OF MALE ADULTS	14.75	6.23
CONTENT-NUMBER OF FEMALE ADULTS	1.00	0.81
CONTENT-NUMBER OF MALE CHILDREN	9.00	1.41
CONTENT-NUMBER OF FEMALE CHILDREN	6.25	0.55
CONTENT-NUMBER OF MALE ANIMALS	1.50	0.57
CONTENT-NUMBER OF FEMALE ANIMALS	1.25	0.50
MALES IN STERO. NONOCC. ROLES	3.00	4.24
FEMALES IN STERO. NONOCC. ROLES	2.00	.
TOTAL MALES IN NONOCC. ROLES	5.00	4.24
TOTAL FEMALES IN NONOCC. ROLES	5.00	.
MALES IN STERO. OCCUPATIONAL ROLES	5.33	1.52
FEMALES IN STERO. OCCUPATIONAL ROLES	1.00	0.00
TOTAL MALES IN OCCUPATIONAL ROLES	6.00	1.73
TOTAL FEMALES IN OCCUPATIONAL ROLES	1.00	0.00
TOTAL OCCUPATIONS DEPICTED FOR MALES	5.33	2.30
TOTAL OCCUPATIONS DEPICTED FOR FEMALES	0.25	0.50
NUMBER OF FAMOUS MEN	4.00	0.81
NUMBER OF FAMOUS WOMEN	0.00	0.00

FEMALES DRESSED ONLY IN SKIRTS	NA
DEMEANING OR STERO. STATEMENTS	NO
STERO. EMOTIONAL RESPONSES	NO
LANGUAGE EXCLUDING WOMEN	NO
SEPARATE FORMS	NO
SEPARATE NORMS	NO

DIAGNOSTIC SKILLS BATTERY - FORM A, LEVEL 12

	MEAN	STANDARD DEVIATION
ILLUSTRATIONS-NUMBER OF MALE ADULTS	4.25	2.06
ILLUSTRATIONS-NUMBER OF FEMALE ADULTS	2.00	1.82
ILLUSTRATIONS-NUMBER OF MALE CHILDREN	7.25	3.09
ILLUSTRATIONS-NUMBER OF FEMALE CHILDREN	1.50	1.00
ILLUSTRATIONS-NUMBER OF MALE ANIMALS	0.50	1.00
ILLUSTRATIONS-NUMBER OF FEMALE ANIMALS	2.00	2.16
CONTENT-NUMBER OF MALE ADULTS	3.75	2.50
CONTENT-NUMBER OF FEMALE ADULTS	4.25	2.87
CONTENT-NUMBER OF MALE CHILDREN	6.00	1.63
CONTENT-NUMBER OF FEMALE CHILDREN	6.00	2.44
CONTENT-NUMBER OF MALE ANIMALS	0.00	0.00
CONTENT-NUMBER OF FEMALE ANIMALS	0.50	1.00
MALES IN STERO. NONOCC. ROLES	1.75	1.50
FEMALES IN STERO. NONOCC. ROLES	0.00	0.00
TOTAL MALES IN NONOCC. ROLES	2.25	1.70
TOTAL FEMALES IN NONOCC. ROLES	0.50	0.57
MALES IN STERO. OCCUPATIONAL ROLES	1.00	0.81
FEMALES IN STERO. OCCUPATIONAL ROLES	0.00	0.00
TOTAL MALES IN OCCUPATIONAL ROLES	1.25	1.25
TOTAL FEMALES IN OCCUPATIONAL ROLES	0.00	0.00
TOTAL OCCUPATIONS DEPICTED FOR MALES	1.75	0.95
TOTAL OCCUPATIONS DEPICTED FOR FEMALES	0.25	0.50
NUMBER OF FAMOUS MEN	1.50	1.73
NUMBER OF FAMOUS WOMEN	1.25	1.50

FEMALES DRESSED ONLY IN SKIRTS	YES
DEMEANING OR STERO. STATEMENTS	NO
STERO. EMOTIONAL RESPONSES	NO
LANGUAGE EXCLUDING WOMEN	YES
SEPARATE FORMS	NO
SEPARATE NORMS	NO

DIAGNOSTIC SKILLS BATTERY - FORM A, LEVEL 34

	MEAN	STANDARD DEVIATION
ILLUSTRATIONS-NUMBER OF MALE ADULTS	.	.
ILLUSTRATIONS-NUMBER OF FEMALE ADULTS	.	.
ILLUSTRATIONS-NUMBER OF MALE CHILDREN	.	.
ILLUSTRATIONS-NUMBER OF FEMALE CHILDREN	.	.
ILLUSTRATIONS-NUMBER OF MALE ANIMALS	.	.
ILLUSTRATIONS-NUMBER OF FEMALE ANIMALS	.	.
CONTENT-NUMBER OF MALE ADULTS	12.66	1.52
CONTENT-NUMBER OF FEMALE ADULTS	7.66	0.57
CONTENT-NUMBER OF MALE CHILDREN	15.33	4.72
CONTENT-NUMBER OF FEMALE CHILDREN	19.66	4.93
CONTENT-NUMBER OF MALE ANIMALS	0.66	0.57
CONTENT-NUMBER OF FEMALE ANIMALS	0.00	0.00
MALES IN STERO. NONOCC. ROLES	0.50	0.70
FEMALES IN STERO. NONOCC. ROLES	0.50	0.70
TOTAL MALES IN NONOCC. ROLES	3.00	2.82
TOTAL FEMALES IN NONOCC. ROLES	3.50	2.12
MALES IN STERO. OCCUPATIONAL ROLES	1.00	0.00
FEMALES IN STERO. OCCUPATIONAL ROLES	0.00	0.00
TOTAL MALES IN OCCUPATIONAL ROLES	1.00	0.00
TOTAL FEMALES IN OCCUPATIONAL ROLES	0.00	0.00
TOTAL OCCUPATIONS DEPICTED FOR MALES	0.66	0.57
TOTAL OCCUPATIONS DEPICTED FOR FEMALES	0.00	0.00
NUMBER OF FAMOUS MEN	0.00	0.00
NUMBER OF FAMOUS WOMEN	0.00	0.00

FEMALES DRESSED ONLY IN SKIRTS	NA
DEMEANING OR STERO. STATEMENTS	NO
STERO. EMOTIONAL RESPONSES	NO
LANGUAGE EXCLUDING WOMEN	YES
SEPARATE FORMS	NO
SEPARATE NORMS	NO

DIAGNOSTIC SKILLS BATTERY - FORM A, LEVEL 56

	MEAN	STANDARD DEVIATION
ILLUSTRATIONS-NUMBER OF MALE ADULTS	.	.
ILLUSTRATIONS-NUMBER OF FEMALE ADULTS	.	.
ILLUSTRATIONS-NUMBER OF MALE CHILDREN	.	.
ILLUSTRATIONS-NUMBER OF FEMALE CHILDREN	.	.
ILLUSTRATIONS-NUMBER OF MALE ANIMALS	.	.
ILLUSTRATIONS-NUMBER OF FEMALE ANIMALS	.	.
CONTENT-NUMBER OF MALE ADULTS	11.25	3.86
CONTENT-NUMBER OF FEMALE ADULTS	8.75	3.20
CONTENT-NUMBER OF MALE CHILDREN	13.25	6.55
CONTENT-NUMBER OF FEMALE CHILDREN	9.75	6.70
CONTENT-NUMBER OF MALE ANIMALS	0.25	0.50
CONTENT-NUMBER OF FEMALE ANIMALS	1.00	0.81
MALES IN STERO. NONOCC. ROLES	3.00	1.00
FEMALES IN STERO. NONOCC. ROLES	0.33	0.57
TOTAL MALES IN NONOCC. ROLES	5.66	1.52
TOTAL FEMALES IN NONOCC. ROLES	2.00	2.00
MALES IN STERO. OCCUPATIONAL ROLES	3.66	1.15
FEMALES IN STERO. OCCUPATIONAL ROLES	0.66	1.15
TOTAL MALES IN OCCUPATIONAL ROLES	3.66	1.15
TOTAL FEMALES IN OCCUPATIONAL ROLES	0.66	1.15
TOTAL OCCUPATIONS DEPICTED FOR MALES	4.25	0.95
TOTAL OCCUPATIONS DEPICTED FOR FEMALES	0.50	1.00
NUMBER OF FAMOUS MEN	1.00	1.00
NUMBER OF FAMOUS WOMEN	0.00	0.00

FEMALES DRESSED ONLY IN SKIRTS	NA
DEMEANING OR STERO. STATEMENTS	NO
STERO. EMOTIONAL RESPONSES	NO
LANGUAGE EXCLUDING WOMEN	YES
SEPARATE FORMS	NO
SEPARATE NORMS	NO

DIAGNOSTIC SKILLS BATTERY - FORM A, LEVEL 78

	MEAN	STANDARD DEVIATION
ILLUSTRATIONS-NUMBER OF MALE ADULTS	.	.
ILLUSTRATIONS-NUMBER OF FEMALE ADULTS	.	.
ILLUSTRATIONS-NUMBER OF MALE CHILDREN	.	.
ILLUSTRATIONS-NUMBER OF FEMALE CHILDREN	.	.
ILLUSTRATIONS-NUMBER OF MALE ANIMALS	.	.
ILLUSTRATIONS-NUMBER OF FEMALE ANIMALS	.	.
CONTENT-NUMBER OF MALE ADULTS	17.50	0.70
CONTENT-NUMBER OF FEMALE ADULTS	11.50	3.53
CONTENT-NUMBER OF MALE CHILDREN	10.50	6.36
CONTENT-NUMBER OF FEMALE CHILDREN	12.00	8.48
CONTENT-NUMBER OF MALE ANIMALS	0.00	0.00
CONTENT-NUMBER OF FEMALE ANIMALS	0.00	0.00
MALES IN STERO. NONOCC. ROLES	5.00	.
FEMALES IN STERO. NONOCC. ROLES	5.00	.
TOTAL MALES IN NONOCC. ROLES	5.00	.
TOTAL FEMALES IN NONOCC. ROLES	7.00	.
MALES IN STERO. OCCUPATIONAL ROLES	1.50	2.12
FEMALES IN STERO. OCCUPATIONAL ROLES	0.00	0.00
TOTAL MALES IN OCCUPATIONAL ROLES	2.00	2.82
TOTAL FEMALES IN OCCUPATIONAL ROLES	0.50	0.70
TOTAL OCCUPATIONS DEPICTED FOR MALES	3.00	1.41
TOTAL OCCUPATIONS DEPICTED FOR FEMALES	0.50	0.70
NUMBER OF FAMOUS MEN	1.50	0.70
NUMBER OF FAMOUS WOMEN	0.00	0.00

FEMALES DRESSED ONLY IN SKIRTS	NA
DEMEANING OR STERO. STATEMENTS	NO
STERO. EMOTIONAL RESPONSES	NO
LANGUAGE EXCLUDING WOMEN	NO
SEPARATE FORMS	NO
SEPARATE NORMS	NO

DIAGNOSTIC SKILLS BATTERY - FORM B, LEVEL 12

	MEAN	STANDARD DEVIATION
ILLUSTRATIONS-NUMBER OF MALE ADULTS	1.66	0.57
ILLUSTRATIONS-NUMBER OF FEMALE ADULTS	1.00	0.00
ILLUSTRATIONS-NUMBER OF MALE CHILDREN	7.33	2.88
ILLUSTRATIONS-NUMBER OF FEMALE CHILDREN	5.00	1.00
ILLUSTRATIONS-NUMBER OF MALE ANIMALS	0.00	0.00
ILLUSTRATIONS-NUMBER OF FEMALE ANIMALS	1.00	0.00
CONTENT-NUMBER OF MALE ADULTS	3.33	3.21
CONTENT-NUMBER OF FEMALE ADULTS	3.00	3.46
CONTENT-NUMBER OF MALE CHILDREN	6.33	0.57
CONTENT-NUMBER OF FEMALE CHILDREN	6.66	1.15
CONTENT-NUMBER OF MALE ANIMALS	0.66	0.57
CONTENT-NUMBER OF FEMALE ANIMALS	0.66	0.57
MALES IN STERO. NONOCC. ROLES	1.00	1.00
FEMALES IN STERO. NONOCC. ROLES	1.00	1.00
TOTAL MALES IN NONOCC. ROLES	2.00	1.00
TOTAL FEMALES IN NONOCC. ROLES	1.66	0.57
MALES IN STERO. OCCUPATIONAL ROLES	2.33	1.15
FEMALES IN STERO. OCCUPATIONAL ROLES	0.00	0.00
TOTAL MALES IN OCCUPATIONAL ROLES	2.33	1.15
TOTAL FEMALES IN OCCUPATIONAL ROLES	0.00	0.00
TOTAL OCCUPATIONS DEPICTED FOR MALES	1.50	2.12
TOTAL OCCUPATIONS DEPICTED FOR FEMALES	0.50	0.70
NUMBER OF FAMOUS MEN	0.00	.
NUMBER OF FAMOUS WOMEN	.	.

FEMALES DRESSED ONLY IN SKIRTS	YES
DEMEANING OR STERO. STATEMENTS	NO
STERO. EMOTIONAL RESPONSES	NO
LANGUAGE EXCLUDING WOMEN	YES
SEPARATE FORMS	NO
SEPARATE NORMS	NO

DIAGNOSTIC SKILLS BATTERY - FORM B, LEVEL 34

	MEAN	STANDARD DEVIATION
ILLUSTRATIONS-NUMBER OF MALE ADULTS	0.00	0.00
ILLUSTRATIONS-NUMBER OF FEMALE ADULTS	0.00	0.00
ILLUSTRATIONS-NUMBER OF MALE CHILDREN	0.00	0.00
ILLUSTRATIONS-NUMBER OF FEMALE CHILDREN	1.00	0.00
ILLUSTRATIONS-NUMBER OF MALE ANIMALS	0.00	0.00
ILLUSTRATIONS-NUMBER OF FEMALE ANIMALS	0.50	0.70
CONTENT-NUMBER OF MALE ADULTS	16.00	2.82
CONTENT-NUMBER OF FEMALE ADULTS	10.50	2.12
CONTENT-NUMBER OF MALE CHILDREN	21.00	2.82
CONTENT-NUMBER OF FEMALE CHILDREN	21.00	2.82
CONTENT-NUMBER OF MALE ANIMALS	0.00	0.00
CONTENT-NUMBER OF FEMALE ANIMALS	0.00	0.00
MALES IN STERO. NONOCC. ROLES	1.50	2.12
FEMALES IN STERO. NONOCC. ROLES	2.50	2.12
TOTAL MALES IN NONOCC. ROLES	1.50	2.12
TOTAL FEMALES IN NONOCC. ROLES	2.50	2.12
MALES IN STERO. OCCUPATIONAL ROLES	0.50	0.70
FEMALES IN STERO. OCCUPATIONAL ROLES	1.00	1.41
TOTAL MALES IN OCCUPATIONAL ROLES	1.00	0.00
TOTAL FEMALES IN OCCUPATIONAL ROLES	1.00	1.41
TOTAL OCCUPATIONS DEPICTED FOR MALES	2.00	1.41
TOTAL OCCUPATIONS DEPICTED FOR FEMALES	1.00	1.41
NUMBER OF FAMOUS MEN	3.00	0.00
NUMBER OF FAMOUS WOMEN	0.00	0.00

FEMALES DRESSED ONLY IN SKIRTS	YES
DEMEANING OR STERO. STATEMENTS	NO
STERO. EMOTIONAL RESPONSES	NO
LANGUAGE EXCLUDING WOMEN	YES
SEPARATE FORMS	NO
SEPARATE NORMS	NO

DIAGNOSTIC SKILLS BATTERY - FORM B, LEVEL 56

	MEAN	STANDARD DEVIATION
ILLUSTRATIONS-NUMBER OF MALE ADULTS	.	.
ILLUSTRATIONS-NUMBER OF FEMALE ADULTS	.	.
ILLUSTRATIONS-NUMBER OF MALE CHILDREN	.	.
ILLUSTRATIONS-NUMBER OF FEMALE CHILDREN	.	.
ILLUSTRATIONS-NUMBER OF MALE ANIMALS	.	.
ILLUSTRATIONS-NUMBER OF FEMALE ANIMALS	.	.
CONTENT-NUMBER OF MALE ADULTS	14.00	2.82
CONTENT-NUMBER OF FEMALE ADULTS	16.00	0.00
CONTENT-NUMBER OF MALE CHILDREN	24.00	1.41
CONTENT-NUMBER OF FEMALE CHILDREN	27.00	1.41
CONTENT-NUMBER OF MALE ANIMALS	.	.
CONTENT-NUMBER OF FEMALE ANIMALS	.	.
MALES IN STERO. NONOCC. ROLES	2.50	0.70
FEMALES IN STERO. NONOCC. ROLES	4.50	0.70
TOTAL MALES IN NONOCC. ROLES	4.50	0.70
TOTAL FEMALES IN NONOCC. ROLES	7.00	1.41
MALES IN STERO. OCCUPATIONAL ROLES	2.50	0.70
FEMALES IN STERO. OCCUPATIONAL ROLES	0.00	0.00
TOTAL MALES IN OCCUPATIONAL ROLES	3.00	1.41
TOTAL FEMALES IN OCCUPATIONAL ROLES	0.50	0.70
TOTAL OCCUPATIONS DEPICTED FOR MALES	5.00	1.41
TOTAL OCCUPATIONS DEPICTED FOR FEMALES	0.50	0.70
NUMBER OF FAMOUS MEN	6.00	0.00
NUMBER OF FAMOUS WOMEN	0.00	0.00

FEMALES DRESSED ONLY IN SKIRTS	NA
DEMEANING OR STERO. STATEMENTS	NA
STERO. EMOTIONAL RESPONSES	YES
LANGUAGE EXCLUDING WOMEN	YES
SEPARATE FORMS	NO
SEPARATE NORMS	NO

DIAGNOSTIC SKILLS BATTERY - FORM B, LEVEL 78

	MEAN	STANDARD DEVIATION
ILLUSTRATIONS-NUMBER OF MALE ADULTS	.	.
ILLUSTRATIONS-NUMBER OF FEMALE ADULTS	.	.
ILLUSTRATIONS-NUMBER OF MALE CHILDREN	.	.
ILLUSTRATIONS-NUMBER OF FEMALE CHILDREN	.	.
ILLUSTRATIONS-NUMBER OF MALE ANIMALS	.	.
ILLUSTRATIONS-NUMBER OF FEMALE ANIMALS	.	.
CONTENT-NUMBER OF MALE ADULTS	21.50	3.53
CONTENT-NUMBER OF FEMALE ADULTS	11.50	2.12
CONTENT-NUMBER OF MALE CHILDREN	20.00	7.07
CONTENT-NUMBER OF FEMALE CHILDREN	22.50	7.77
CONTENT-NUMBER OF MALE ANIMALS	0.00	0.00
CONTENT-NUMBER OF FEMALE ANIMALS	1.00	0.00
MALES IN STERO. NONOCC. ROLES	5.00	4.24
FEMALES IN STERO. NONOCC. ROLES	2.00	0.00
TOTAL MALES IN NONOCC. ROLES	6.00	4.24
TOTAL FEMALES IN NONOCC. ROLES	3.00	0.00
MALES IN STERO. OCCUPATIONAL ROLES	3.00	2.82
FEMALES IN STERO. OCCUPATIONAL ROLES	0.00	.
TOTAL MALES IN OCCUPATIONAL ROLES	3.50	2.12
TOTAL FEMALES IN OCCUPATIONAL ROLES	1.00	.
TOTAL OCCUPATIONS DEPICTED FOR MALES	1.00	1.41
TOTAL OCCUPATIONS DEPICTED FOR FEMALES	3.00	2.82
NUMBER OF FAMOUS MEN	5.00	0.00
NUMBER OF FAMOUS WOMEN	0.00	0.00

FEMALES DRESSED ONLY IN SKIRTS	NA
DEMEANING OR STERO. STATEMENTS	NA
STERO. EMOTIONAL RESPONSES	NO
LANGUAGE EXCLUDING WOMEN	YES
SEPARATE FORMS	NO
SEPARATE NORMS	NO

DIFFERENTIAL APTITUDE TEST - FORM S

	MEAN	STANDARD DEVIATION
ILLUSTRATIONS-NUMBER OF MALE ADULTS	15.00	3.46
ILLUSTRATIONS-NUMBER OF FEMALE ADULTS	1.66	1.15
TLLUSTRATIONS-NUMBER OF MALE CHILDREN	1.00	0.00
ILLUSTRATIONS-NUMBER OF FEMALE CHILDREN	.50	.70
ILLUSTRATIONS-NUMBER OF MALE ANIMALS	0.00	0.00
ILLUSTRATIONS-NUMBER OF FEMALE ANIMALS	0.00	0.00
CONTENT-NUMBER OF MALE ADULTS	31.33	17.92
CONTENT-NUMBER OF FEMALE ADULTS	8.33	6.65
CONTENT-NUMBER OF MALE CHILDREN	15.00	16.46
CONTENT-NUMBER OF FEMALE CHILDREN	7.33	5.13
CONTENT-NUMBER OF MALE ANIMALS	0.00	0.00
CONTENT-NUMBER OF FEMALE ANIMALS	0.00	0.00
MALES IN STERO. NONOCC. ROLES	2.50	3.53
FEMALES IN STERO. NONOCC. ROLES	0.00	0.00
TOTAL MALES IN NONOCC. ROLES	2.50	3.53
TOTAL FEMALES IN NONOCC. ROLES	0.00	0.00
MALES IN STERO. OCCUPATIONAL ROLES	3.66	2.30
FEMALES IN STERO. OCCUPATIONAL ROLES	0.33	0.57
TOTAL MALES IN OCCUPATIONAL ROLES	3.66	2.30
TOTAL FEMALES IN OCCUPATIONAL ROLES	0.66	0.57
TOTAL OCCUPATIONS DEPICTED FOR MALES	2.00	2.64
TOTAL OCCUPATIONS DEPICTED FOR FEMALES	3.00	4.35
NUMBER OF FAMOUS MEN	5.00	4.24
NUMBER OF FAMOUS WOMEN	.	.

FEMALES DRESSED ONLY IN SKIRTS	YES
DEMEANING OR STERO. STATEMENTS	NA
STERO. EMOTIONAL RESPONSES	NO
LANGUAGE EXCLUDING WOMEN	YES
SEPARATE FORMS	NO
SEPARATE NORMS	NO

DIFFERENTIAL APTITUDE TEST - FORM T

	MEAN	STANDARD DEVIATION
ILLUSTRATIONS-NUMBER OF MALE ADULTS	9.75	2.06
ILLUSTRATIONS-NUMBER OF FEMALE ADULTS	2.00	0.81
ILLUSTRATIONS-NUMBER OF MALE CHILDREN	5.50	2.38
ILLUSTRATIONS-NUMBER OF FEMALE CHILDREN	0.25	0.50
ILLUSTRATIONS-NUMBER OF MALE ANIMALS	0.00	0.00
ILLUSTRATIONS-NUMBER OF FEMALE ANIMALS	0.00	0.00
CONTENT-NUMBER OF MALE ADULTS	19.00	6.97
CONTENT-NUMBER OF FEMALE ADULTS	6.00	2.00
CONTENT-NUMBER OF MALE CHILDREN	9.75	8.57
CONTENT-NUMBER OF FEMALE CHILDREN	2.00	2.16
CONTENT-NUMBER OF MALE ANIMALS	0.00	0.00
CONTENT-NUMBER OF FEMALE ANIMALS	0.00	0.00
MALES IN STERO. NONOCC. ROLES	0.50	0.70
FEMALES IN STERO. NONOCC. ROLES	1.00	0.00
TOTAL MALES IN NONOCC. ROLES	0.50	0.70
TOTAL FEMALES IN NONOCC. ROLES	1.00	0.00
MALES IN STERO. OCCUPATIONAL ROLES	1.50	1.73
FEMALES IN STERO. OCCUPATIONAL ROLES	0.00	0.00
TOTAL MALES IN OCCUPATIONAL ROLES	1.50	1.73
TOTAL FEMALES IN OCCUPATIONAL ROLES	0.00	0.00
TOTAL OCCUPATIONS DEPICTED FOR MALES	1.50	1.73
TOTAL OCCUPATIONS DEPICTED FOR FEMALES	0.00	0.00
NUMBER OF FAMOUS MEN	0.00	0.00
NUMBER OF FAMOUS WOMEN	0.00	0.00

FEMALES DRESSED ONLY IN SKIRTS	YES
DEMEANING OR STERO. STATEMENTS	NO
STERO. EMOTIONAL RESPONSES	NO
LANGUAGE EXCLUDING WOMEN	NO
SEPARATE FORMS	NO
SEPARATE NORMS	NO

DURRELL ANALYSIS OF READING DIFFICULTY

	MEAN	STANDARD DEVIATION
ILLUSTRATIONS-NUMBER OF MALE ADULTS	.	.
ILLUSTRATIONS-NUMBER OF FEMALE ADULTS	.	.
ILLUSTRATIONS-NUMBER OF MALE CHILDREN	.	.
ILLUSTRATIONS-NUMBER OF FEMALE CHILDREN	.	.
ILLUSTRATIONS-NUMBER OF MALE ANIMALS	.	.
ILLUSTRATIONS-NUMBER OF FEMALE ANIMALS	.	.
CONTENT-NUMBER OF MALE ADULTS	6.00	0.00
CONTENT-NUMBER OF FEMALE ADULTS	1.00	0.00
CONTENT-NUMBER OF MALE CHILDREN	4.00	0.00
CONTENT-NUMBER OF FEMALE CHILDREN	1.00	0.00
CONTENT-NUMBER OF MALE ANIMALS	3.00	0.00
CONTENT-NUMBER OF FEMALE ANIMALS	2.00	0.00
MALES IN STERO. NONOCC. ROLES	1.00	0.00
FEMALES IN STERO. NONOCC. ROLES	0.00	0.00
TOTAL MALES IN NONOCC. ROLES	1.00	0.00
TOTAL FEMALES IN NONOCC. ROLES	0.00	0.00
MALES IN STERO. OCCUPATIONAL ROLES	0.00	0.00
FEMALES IN STERO. OCCUPATIONAL ROLES	0.00	0.00
TOTAL MALES IN OCCUPATIONAL ROLES	0.00	0.00
TOTAL FEMALES IN OCCUPATIONAL ROLES	0.00	0.00
TOTAL OCCUPATIONS DEPICTED FOR MALES	0.00	0.00
TOTAL OCCUPATIONS DEPICTED FOR FEMALES	0.00	0.00
NUMBER OF FAMOUS MEN	0.00	0.00
NUMBER OF FAMOUS WOMEN	0.00	0.00

FEMALES DRESSED ONLY IN SKIRTS   NA

DEMEANING OR STERO. STATEMENTS   YES

STERO. EMOTIONAL RESPONSES   NO

LANGUAGE EXCLUDING WOMEN   NO

SEPARATE FORMS   NO

SEPARATE NORMS   NO

DURRELL LISTENING-READING SERIES - PRIMARY

	MEAN	STANDARD DEVIATION
ILLUSTRATIONS-NUMBER OF MALE ADULTS	4.00	0.00
ILLUSTRATIONS-NUMBER OF FEMALE ADULTS	3.00	0.00
ILLUSTRATIONS-NUMBER OF MALE CHILDREN	10.66	0.57
ILLUSTRATIONS-NUMBER OF FEMALE CHILDREN	2.00	0.00
ILLUSTRATIONS-NUMBER OF MALE ANIMALS	0.00	0.00
ILLUSTRATIONS-NUMBER OF FEMALE ANIMALS	0.00	0.00
CONTENT-NUMBER OF MALE ADULTS	7.00	3.60
CONTENT-NUMBER OF FEMALE ADULTS	2.33	1.15
CONTENT-NUMBER OF MALE CHILDREN	11.00	2.64
CONTENT-NUMBER OF FEMALE CHILDREN	5.33	1.15
CONTENT-NUMBER OF MALE ANIMALS	4.66	0.57
CONTENT-NUMBER OF FEMALE ANIMALS	0.00	0.00
MALES IN STERO. NONOCC. ROLES	2.00	1.41
FEMALES IN STERO. NONOCC. ROLES	2.00	1.41
TOTAL MALES IN NONOCC. ROLES	2.50	0.70
TOTAL FEMALES IN NONOCC. ROLES	2.00	1.41
MALES IN STERO. OCCUPATIONAL ROLES	3.33	1.52
FEMALES IN STERO. OCCUPATIONAL ROLES	0.00	0.00
TOTAL MALES IN OCCUPATIONAL ROLES	3.33	1.52
TOTAL FEMALES IN OCCUPATIONAL ROLES	0.00	0.00
TOTAL OCCUPATIONS DEPICTED FOR MALES	4.33	1.15
TOTAL OCCUPATIONS DEPICTED FOR FEMALES	0.00	0.00
NUMBER OF FAMOUS MEN	0.00	0.00
NUMBER OF FAMOUS WOMEN	0.00	0.00

FEMALES DRESSED ONLY IN SKIRTS	YES
DEMEANING OR STERO. STATEMENTS	NA
STERO. EMOTIONAL RESPONSES	NO
LANGUAGE EXCLUDING WOMEN	YES
SEPARATE FORMS	NO
SEPARATE NORMS	NO

DURRELL LISTENING READING SERIES - INTERMEDIATE

	MEAN	STANDARD DEVIATION
ILLUSTRATIONS-NUMBER OF MALE ADULTS	22.00	0.00
ILLUSTRATIONS-NUMBER OF FEMALE ADULTS	4.00	0.00
ILLUSTRATIONS-NUMBER OF MALE CHILDREN	10.33	0.57
ILLUSTRATIONS-NUMBER OF FEMALE CHILDREN	2.00	0.00
ILLUSTRATIONS-NUMBER OF MALE ANIMALS	0.00	0.00
ILLUSTRATIONS-NUMBER OF FEMALE ANIMALS	0.00	0.00
CONTENT-NUMBER OF MALE ADULTS	5.66	2.08
CONTENT-NUMBER OF FEMALE ADULTS	1.00	.
CONTENT-NUMBER OF MALE CHILDREN	3.50	3.53
CONTENT-NUMBER OF FEMALE CHILDREN	0.00	0.00
CONTENT-NUMBER OF MALE ANIMALS	3.50	2.12
CONTENT-NUMBER OF FEMALE ANIMALS	1.00	.
MALES IN STERO. NONOCC. ROLES	3.00	1.41
FEMALES IN STERO. NONOCC. ROLES	.	.
TOTAL MALES IN NONOCC. ROLES	3.50	2.12
TOTAL FEMALES IN NONOCC. ROLES	.	.
MALES IN STERO. OCCUPATIONAL ROLES	3.00	0.00
FEMALES IN STERO. OCCUPATIONAL ROLES	.	.
TOTAL MALES IN OCCUPATIONAL ROLES	3.00	0.00
TOTAL FEMALES IN OCCUPATIONAL ROLES	.	.
TOTAL OCCUPATIONS DEPICTED FOR MALES	4.33	2.88
TOTAL OCCUPATIONS DEPICTED FOR FEMALES	0.66	0.57
NUMBER OF FAMOUS MEN	3.50	0.70
NUMBER OF FAMOUS WOMEN	0.00	0.00

FEMALES DRESSED ONLY IN SKIRTS	YES
DEMEANING OR STERO. STATEMENTS	NA
STERO. EMOTIONAL RESPONSES	NO
LANGUAGE EXCLUDING WOMEN	YES
SEPARATE FORMS	NO
SEPARATE NORMS	NO

DURRELL LISTENING READING SERIES - ADVANCED

	MEAN	STANDARD DEVIATION
ILLUSTRATIONS-NUMBER OF MALE ADULTS	.	.
ILLUSTRATIONS-NUMBER OF FEMALE ADULTS	.	.
ILLUSTRATIONS-NUMBER OF MALE CHILDREN	.	.
ILLUSTRATIONS-NUMBER OF FEMALE CHILDREN	.	.
ILLUSTRATIONS-NUMBER OF MALE ANIMALS	.	.
ILLUSTRATIONS-NUMBER OF FEMALE ANIMALS	.	.
CONTENT-NUMBER OF MALE ADULTS	5.66	1.15
CONTENT-NUMBER OF FEMALE ADULTS	2.50	0.70
CONTENT-NUMBER OF MALE CHILDREN	0.50	0.70
CONTENT-NUMBER OF FEMALE CHILDREN	0.00	0.00
CONTENT-NUMBER OF MALE ANIMALS	3.00	0.00
CONTENT-NUMBER OF FEMALE ANIMALS	0.00	0.00
MALES IN STERO. NONOCC. ROLES	2.00	.
FEMALES IN STERO. NONOCC. ROLES	1.00	.
TOTAL MALES IN NONOCC. ROLES	2.00	.
TOTAL FEMALES IN NONOCC. ROLES	1.00	.
MALES IN STERO. OCCUPATIONAL ROLES	3.50	0.70
FEMALES IN STERO. OCCUPATIONAL ROLES	.	.
TOTAL MALES IN OCCUPATIONAL ROLES	3.50	0.70
TOTAL FEMALES IN OCCUPATIONAL ROLES	.	.
TOTAL OCCUPATIONS DEPICTED FOR MALES	2.00	1.41
TOTAL OCCUPATIONS DEPICTED FOR FEMALES	0.00	0.00
NUMBER OF FAMOUS MEN	2.50	0.70
NUMBER OF FAMOUS WOMEN	1.00	0.00

FEMALES DRESSED ONLY IN SKIRTS	NA
DEMEANING OR STERO. STATEMENTS	NA
STERO. EMOTIONAL RESPONSES	YES
LANGUAGE EXCLUDING WOMEN	YES
SEPARATE FORMS	NO
SEPARATE NORMS	NO

EDUCATION APPERCEPTION TEST

	MEAN	STANDARD DEVIATION
ILLUSTRATIONS-NUMBER OF MALE ADULTS	4.25	0.50
ILLUSTRATIONS-NUMBER OF FEMALE ADULTS	7.00	0.00
ILLUSTRATIONS-NUMBER OF MALE CHILDREN	12.75	3.77
ILLUSTRATIONS-NUMBER OF FEMALE CHILDREN	10.50	1.73
ILLUSTRATIONS-NUMBER OF MALE ANIMALS	0.00	0.00
ILLUSTRATIONS-NUMBER OF FEMALE ANIMALS	0.00	0.00
CONTENT-NUMBER OF MALE ADULTS	4.00	0.00
CONTENT-NUMBER OF FEMALE ADULTS	6.00	1.41
CONTENT-NUMBER OF MALE CHILDREN	13.50	6.36
CONTENT-NUMBER OF FEMALE CHILDREN	10.50	2.12
CONTENT-NUMBER OF MALE ANIMALS	0.00	0.00
CONTENT-NUMBER OF FEMALE ANIMALS	0.00	0.00
MALES IN STERO. NONOCC. ROLES	2.50	0.70
FEMALES IN STERO. NONOCC. ROLES	2.00	1.41
TOTAL MALES IN NONOCC. ROLES	2.50	0.70
TOTAL FEMALES IN NONOCC. ROLES	2.00	1.41
MALES IN STERO. OCCUPATIONAL ROLES	4.00	.
FEMALES IN STERO. OCCUPATIONAL ROLES	8.00	.
TOTAL MALES IN OCCUPATIONAL ROLES	4.00	.
TOTAL FEMALES IN OCCUPATIONAL ROLES	8.00	.
TOTAL OCCUPATIONS DEPICTED FOR MALES	0.50	0.70
TOTAL OCCUPATIONS DEPICTED FOR FEMALES	1.50	0.70
NUMBER OF FAMOUS MEN	0.00	0.00
NUMBER OF FAMOUS WOMEN	0.00	0.00

FEMALES DRESSED ONLY IN SKIRTS	YES
DEMEANING OR STERO. STATEMENTS	NA
STERO. EMOTIONAL RESPONSES	NO
LANGUAGE EXCLUDING WOMEN	NA
SEPARATE FORMS	YES
SEPARATE NORMS	NO

FIRST GRADE SCREENING TEST - BOY'S

	MEAN	STANDARD DEVIATION
ILLUSTRATIONS-NUMBER OF MALE ADULTS	5.25	2.87
ILLUSTRATIONS-NUMBER OF FEMALE ADULTS	6.75	4.92
ILLUSTRATIONS-NUMBER OF MALE CHILDREN	10.75	0.50
ILLUSTRATIONS-NUMBER OF FEMALE CHILDREN	0.00	0.00
ILLUSTRATIONS-NUMBER OF MALE ANIMALS	0.00	0.00
ILLUSTRATIONS-NUMBER OF FEMALE ANIMALS	0.00	0.00
CONTENT-NUMBER OF MALE ADULTS	3.50	3.53
CONTENT-NUMBER OF FEMALE ADULTS	5.00	1.41
CONTENT-NUMBER OF MALE CHILDREN	7.50	4.94
CONTENT-NUMBER OF FEMALE CHILDREN	0.00	0.00
CONTENT-NUMBER OF MALE ANIMALS	0.00	0.00
CONTENT-NUMBER OF FEMALE ANIMALS	0.00	0.00
MALES IN STERO. NONOCC. ROLES	1.50	2.38
FEMALES IN STERO. NONOCC. ROLES	0.25	0.50
TOTAL MALES IN NONOCC. ROLES	1.75	2.87
TOTAL FEMALES IN NONOCC. ROLES	0.25	0.50
MALES IN STERO. OCCUPATIONAL ROLES	5.00	1.15
FEMALES IN STERO. OCCUPATIONAL ROLES	2.25	0.95
TOTAL MALES IN OCCUPATIONAL ROLES	5.50	0.57
TOTAL FEMALES IN OCCUPATIONAL ROLES	2.25	0.95
TOTAL OCCUPATIONS DEPICTED FOR MALES	5.50	0.70
TOTAL OCCUPATIONS DEPICTED FOR FEMALES	2.50	0.70
NUMBER OF FAMOUS MEN	0.00	0.00
NUMBER OF FAMOUS WOMEN	0.00	0.00

FEMALES DRESSED ONLY IN SKIRTS	YES
DEMEANING OR STERO. STATEMENTS	YES
STERO. EMOTIONAL RESPONSES	NO
LANGUAGE EXCLUDING WOMEN	NA
SEPARATE FORMS	YES
SEPARATE NORMS	NO

FIRST GRADE SCREENING TEST - GIRL'S

	MEAN	STANDARD DEVIATION
ILLUSTRATIONS-NUMBER OF MALE ADULTS	5.25	2.87
ILLUSTRATIONS-NUMBER OF FEMALE ADULTS	6.25	4.99
ILLUSTRATIONS-NUMBER OF MALE CHILDREN	2.50	5.00
ILLUSTRATIONS-NUMBER OF FEMALE CHILDREN	10.75	0.50
ILLUSTRATIONS-NUMBER OF MALE ANIMALS	0.00	0.00
ILLUSTRATIONS-NUMBER OF FEMALE ANIMALS	0.00	0.00
CONTENT-NUMBER OF MALE ADULTS	3.50	3.53
CONTENT-NUMBER OF FEMALE ADULTS	5.00	1.41
CONTENT-NUMBER OF MALE CHILDREN	0.00	0.00
CONTENT-NUMBER OF FEMALE CHILDREN	7.50	4.94
CONTENT-NUMBER OF MALE ANIMALS	0.00	0.00
CONTENT-NUMBER OF FEMALE ANIMALS	0.00	0.00
MALES IN STERO. NONOCC. ROLES	0.25	0.50
FEMALES IN STERO. NONOCC. ROLES	1.00	1.41
TOTAL MALES IN NONOCC. ROLES	0.25	0.50
TOTAL FEMALES IN NONOCC. ROLES	1.75	2.87
MALES IN STERO. OCCUPATIONAL ROLES	5.00	1.15
FEMALES IN STERO. OCCUPATIONAL ROLES	2.25	0.95
TOTAL MALES IN OCCUPATIONAL ROLES	5.50	0.57
TOTAL FEMALES IN OCCUPATIONAL ROLES	2.25	0.95
TOTAL OCCUPATIONS DEPICTED FOR MALES	5.50	0.70
TOTAL OCCUPATIONS DEPICTED FOR FEMALES	2.00	0.81
NUMBER OF FAMOUS MEN	0.00	0.00
NUMBER OF FAMOUS WOMEN	0.00	0.00

FEMALES DRESSED ONLY IN SKIRTS	YES
DEMEANING OR STERO. STATEMENTS	NO
STERO. EMOTIONAL RESPONSES	NO
LANGUAGE EXCLUDING WOMEN	NO
SEPARATE FORMS	YES
SEPARATE NORMS	NO

GATES MACGINITIE READING TEST - FORM 1, BASIC R

	MEAN	STANDARD DEVIATION
ILLUSTRATIONS-NUMBER OF MALE ADULTS	3.00	0.00
ILLUSTRATIONS-NUMBER OF FEMALE ADULTS	1.00	0.00
ILLUSTRATIONS-NUMBER OF MALE CHILDREN	5.00	1.41
ILLUSTRATIONS-NUMBER OF FEMALE CHILDREN	3.50	0.70
ILLUSTRATIONS-NUMBER OF MALE ANIMALS	.	.
ILLUSTRATIONS-NUMBER OF FEMALE ANIMALS	.	.
CONTENT-NUMBER OF MALE ADULTS	0.33	0.57
CONTENT-NUMBER OF FEMALE ADULTS	0.00	0.00
CONTENT-NUMBER OF MALE CHILDREN	2.00	0.00
CONTENT-NUMBER OF FEMALE CHILDREN	1.66	0.57
CONTENT-NUMBER OF MALE ANIMALS	0.00	0.00
CONTENT-NUMBER OF FEMALE ANIMALS	0.00	0.00
MALES IN STERO. NONOCC. ROLES	1.33	1.15
FEMALES IN STERO. NONOCC. ROLES	1.00	0.00
TOTAL MALES IN NONOCC. ROLES	2.33	2.51
TOTAL FEMALES IN NONOCC. ROLES	1.33	0.57
MALES IN STERO. OCCUPATIONAL ROLES	0.66	0.57
FEMALES IN STERO. OCCUPATIONAL ROLES	0.00	0.00
TOTAL MALES IN OCCUPATIONAL ROLES	0.66	0.57
TOTAL FEMALES IN OCCUPATIONAL ROLES	0.00	0.00
TOTAL OCCUPATIONS DEPICTED FOR MALES	0.66	0.57
TOTAL OCCUPATIONS DEPICTED FOR FEMALES	0.00	0.00
NUMBER OF FAMOUS MEN	0.00	0.00
NUMBER OF FAMOUS WOMEN	0.00	0.00

FEMALES DRESSED ONLY IN SKIRTS	NO
DEMEANING OR STERO. STATEMENTS	NA
STERO. EMOTIONAL RESPONSES	NO
LANGUAGE EXCLUDING WOMEN	NO
SEPARATE FORMS	NO
SEPARATE NORMS	NO

GATES MACGINITIE READING TESTS - FORM 2, BASIC R

	MEAN	STANDARD DEVIATION
ILLUSTRATIONS-NUMBER OF MALE ADULTS	7.50	3.53
ILLUSTRATIONS-NUMBER OF FEMALE ADULTS	1.00	0.00
ILLUSTRATIONS-NUMBER OF MALE CHILDREN	8.50	4.94
ILLUSTRATIONS-NUMBER OF FEMALE CHILDREN	7.00	2.82
ILLUSTRATIONS-NUMBER OF MALE ANIMALS	0.00	0.00
ILLUSTRATIONS-NUMBER OF FEMALE ANIMALS	0.00	0.00
CONTENT-NUMBER OF MALE ADULTS	2.33	0.57
CONTENT-NUMBER OF FEMALE ADULTS	0.00	0.00
CONTENT-NUMBER CF MALE CHILDREN	2.66	0.57
CONTENT-NUMBER OF FEMALE CHILDREN	2.00	0.00
CONTENT-NUMBER OF MALE ANIMALS	0.00	0.00
CONTENT-NUMBER CF FEMALE ANIMALS	0.00	0.00
MALES IN STERO. NONOCC. ROLES	1.33	1.52
FEMALES IN STERO. NONOCC. ROLES	1.00	0.00
TOTAL MALES IN NONOCC. ROLES	1.33	1.52
TOTAL FEMALES IN NONOCC. ROLES	2.33	1.52
MALES IN STERO. OCCUPATIONAL ROLES	2.00	1.00
FEMALES IN STERO. OCCUPATIONAL ROLES	0.00	0.00
TOTAL MALES IN OCCUPATIONAL ROLES	2.00	1.00
TOTAL FEMALES IN OCCUPATIONAL ROLES	0.00	0.00
TOTAL OCCUPATIONS DEPICTED FOR MALES	0.33	0.57
TOTAL OCCUPATIONS DEPICTED FOR FEMALES	0.00	0.00
NUMBER OF FAMOUS MEN	0.00	0.00
NUMBER OF FAMOUS WOMEN	0.00	0.00

FEMALES DRESSED ONLY IN SKIRTS	NO
DEMEANING OR STERO. STATEMENTS	NA
STERO. EMOTIONAL RESPONSES	NO
LANGUAGE EXCLUDING WOMEN	NO
SEPARATE FORMS	NO
SEPARATE NORMS	NO

GEIST PICTURE INTEREST INVENTORY - REVISED

	MEAN	STANDARD DEVIATION
ILLUSTRATIONS-NUMBER OF MALE ADULTS	113.00	0.00
ILLUSTRATIONS-NUMBER OF FEMALE ADULTS	68.00	0.00
ILLUSTRATIONS-NUMBER OF MALE CHILDREN	2.33	4.04
ILLUSTRATIONS-NUMBER OF FEMALE CHILDREN	0.33	0.57
ILLUSTRATIONS-NUMBER OF MALE ANIMALS	0.00	0.00
ILLUSTRATIONS-NUMBER OF FEMALE ANIMALS	0.00	0.00
CONTENT-NUMBER OF MALE ADULTS	46.33	57.73
CONTENT-NUMBER OF FEMALE ADULTS	68.00	0.00
CONTENT-NUMBER OF MALE CHILDREN	0.00	0.00
CONTENT-NUMBER OF FEMALE CHILDREN	0.00	0.00
CONTENT-NUMBER OF MALE ANIMALS	0.00	0.00
CONTENT-NUMBER OF FEMALE ANIMALS	0.00	0.00
MALES IN STERO. NONOCC. ROLES	0.00	0.00
FEMALES IN STERO. NONOCC. ROLES	0.00	0.00
TOTAL FEMALES IN NONOCC. ROLES	0.00	0.00
TOTAL MALES IN NONOCC. ROLES	0.00	0.00
MALES IN STERO. OCCUPATIONAL ROLES	89.00	19.46
FEMALES IN STERO. OCCUPATIONAL ROLES	35.00	4.00
TOTAL MALES IN OCCUPATIONAL ROLES	124.00	9.53
TOTAL FEMALES IN OCCUPATIONAL ROLES	74.00	5.29
TOTAL OCCUPATIONS DEPICTED FOR MALES	122.00	0.00
TOTAL OCCUPATIONS DEPICTED FOR FEMALES	77.00	0.00
NUMBER OF FAMOUS MEN	0.00	0.00
NUMBER OF FAMOUS WOMEN	0.00	0.00

FEMALES DRESSED ONLY IN SKIRTS	NO
DEMEANING OR STERO. STATEMENTS	NO
STERO. EMOTIONAL RESPONSES	NO
LANGUAGE EXCLUDING WOMEN	NO
SEPARATE FORMS	YES
SEPARATE NORMS	YES

GILMORE ORAL READING TEST

	MEAN	STANDARD DEVIATION
ILLUSTRATIONS-NUMBER OF MALE ADULTS	.	.
ILLUSTRATIONS-NUMBER OF FEMALE ADULTS	.	.
ILLUSTRATIONS-NUMBER OF MALE CHILDREN	.	.
ILLUSTRATIONS-NUMBER OF FEMALE CHILDREN	.	.
ILLUSTRATIONS-NUMBER OF MALE ANIMALS	.	.
ILLUSTRATIONS-NUMBER OF FEMALE ANIMALS	.	.
CONTENT-NUMBER OF MALE ADULTS	3.50	1.91
CONTENT-NUMBER OF FEMALE ADULTS	1.50	1.29
CONTENT-NUMBER OF MALE CHILDREN	5.25	2.21
CONTENT-NUMBER OF FEMALE CHILDREN	6.25	3.30
CONTENT-NUMBER OF MALE ANIMALS	0.25	0.50
CONTENT-NUMBER OF FEMALE ANIMALS	0.25	0.50
MALES IN STERO. NONOCC. ROLES	2.50	1.00
FEMALES IN STERO. NONOCC. ROLES	3.00	1.00
TOTAL MALES IN NONOCC. ROLES	3.25	1.70
TOTAL FEMALES IN NONOCC. ROLES	3.66	1.52
MALES IN STERO. OCCUPATIONAL ROLES	2.00	0.81
FEMALES IN STERO. OCCUPATIONAL ROLES	2.00	1.00
TOTAL MALES IN OCCUPATIONAL ROLES	2.00	0.81
TOTAL FEMALES IN OCCUPATIONAL ROLES	2.00	1.00
TOTAL OCCUPATIONS DEPICTED FOR MALES	0.50	0.57
TOTAL OCCUPATIONS DEPICTED FOR FEMALES	0.75	0.95
NUMBER OF FAMOUS MEN	0.25	0.50
NUMBER OF FAMOUS WOMEN	0.00	0.00

FEMALES DRESSED ONLY IN SKIRTS	NA
DEMEANING OR STERO. STATEMENTS	YES
STERO. EMOTIONAL RESPONSES	NO
LANGUAGE EXCLUDING WOMEN	NO
SEPARATE FORMS	NO
SEPARATE NORMS	NO

GRAY ORAL READING TESTS - FORM A

	MEAN	STANDARD DEVIATION
ILLUSTRATIONS-NUMBER OF MALE ADULTS	0.00	0.00
ILLUSTRATIONS-NUMBER OF FEMALE ADULTS	0.25	0.50
ILLUSTRATIONS-NUMBER OF MALE CHILDREN	0.00	0.00
ILLUSTRATIONS-NUMBER OF FEMALE CHILDREN	0.25	0.50
ILLUSTRATIONS-NUMBER OF MALE ANIMALS	0.00	0.00
ILLUSTRATIONS-NUMBER OF FEMALE ANIMALS	0.00	0.00
CONTENT-NUMBER OF MALE ADULTS	3.00	0.81
CONTENT-NUMBER CF FEMALE ADULTS	1.00	0.00
CONTENT-NUMBER OF MALE CHILDREN	2.75	0.50
CONTENT-NUMBER OF FEMALE CHILDREN	2.00	0.00
CONTENT-NUMBER OF MALE ANIMALS	0.75	0.50
CONTENT-NUMBER OF FEMALE ANIMALS	0.25	0.50
MALES IN STERO. NONOCC. ROLES	0.50	0.57
FEMALES IN STERO. NONOCC. ROLES	0.25	0.50
TOTAL MALES IN NONOCC. ROLES	0.75	0.95
TOTAL FEMALES IN NONOCC. ROLES	0.50	1.00
MALES IN STERO. OCCUPATIONAL ROLES	0.00	0.00
FEMALES IN STERC. OCCUPATIONAL ROLES	0.25	0.50
TOTAL MALES IN OCCUPATIONAL ROLES	0.00	0.00
TOTAL FEMALES IN OCCUPATIONAL ROLES	0.25	0.50
TOTAL OCCUPATIONS DEPICTED FOR MALES	0.25	0.50
TOTAL OCCUPATIONS DEPICTED FOR FEMALES	0.25	0.50
NUMBER OF FAMOUS MEN	1.00	0.00
NUMBER OF FAMOUS WOMEN	0.00	0.00

FEMALES DRESSED ONLY IN SKIRTS	NO
DEMEANING OR STERO. STATEMENTS	NA
STERO. EMOTIONAL RESPONSES	NO
LANGUAGE EXCLUDING WOMEN	NO
SEPARATE FORMS	NO
SEPARATE NORMS	NO

GRAY ORAL READING TESTS - FORM B

	MEAN	STANDARD DEVIATION
ILLUSTRATIONS-NUMBER OF MALE ADULTS	.	.
ILLUSTRATIONS-NUMBER OF FEMALE ADULTS	.	.
ILLUSTRATIONS-NUMBER OF MALE CHILDREN	.	.
ILLUSTRATIONS-NUMBER OF FEMALE CHILDREN	.	.
ILLUSTRATIONS-NUMBER OF MALE ANIMALS	.	.
ILLUSTRATIONS-NUMBER OF FEMALE ANIMALS	.	.
CONTENT-NUMBER OF MALE ADULTS	4.33	0.57
CONTENT-NUMBER OF FEMALE ADULTS	2.33	0.57
CONTENT-NUMBER OF MALE CHILDREN	2.66	0.57
CONTENT-NUMBER OF FEMALE CHILDREN	2.33	0.57
CONTENT-NUMBER OF MALE ANIMALS	0.00	0.00
CONTENT-NUMBER OF FEMALE ANIMALS	0.00	0.00
MALES IN STERO. NONOCC. ROLES	0.00	0.00
FEMALES IN STERO. NONOCC. ROLES	0.00	0.00
TOTAL MALES IN NONOCC. ROLES	0.00	0.00
TOTAL FEMALES IN NONOCC. ROLES	0.00	0.00
MALES IN STERO. OCCUPATIONAL ROLES	2.33	0.57
FEMALES IN STERO. OCCUPATIONAL ROLES	0.00	0.00
TOTAL MALES IN OCCUPATIONAL ROLES	2.66	0.57
TOTAL FEMALES IN OCCUPATIONAL ROLES	0.00	0.00
TOTAL OCCUPATIONS DEPICTED FOR MALES	3.00	0.00
TOTAL OCCUPATIONS DEPICTED FOR FEMALES	0.00	0.00
NUMBER OF FAMOUS MEN	0.00	0.00
NUMBER OF FAMOUS WOMEN	0.00	0.00

FEMALES DRESSED ONLY IN SKIRTS	NA
DEMEANING OR STERO. STATEMENTS	NA
STERO. EMOTIONAL RESPONSES	NO
LANGUAGE EXCLUDING WOMEN	NO
SEPARATE FORMS	NO
SEPARATE NORMS	NO

GRAY ORAL READING TESTS - FORM C

	MEAN	STANDARD DEVIATION
ILLUSTRATIONS-NUMBER OF MALE ADULTS	.	.
ILLUSTRATIONS-NUMBER OF FEMALE ADULTS	.	.
ILLUSTRATIONS-NUMBER OF MALE CHILDREN	.	.
ILLUSTRATIONS-NUMBER OF FEMALE CHILDREN	.	.
ILLUSTRATIONS-NUMBER OF MALE ANIMALS	.	.
ILLUSTRATIONS-NUMBER OF FEMALE ANIMALS	.	.
CONTENT-NUMBER OF MALE ADULTS	7.00	1.73
CONTENT-NUMBER OF FEMALE ADULTS	1.00	0.00
CONTENT-NUMBER OF MALE CHILDREN	3.66	1.15
CONTENT-NUMBER OF FEMALE CHILDREN	3.00	0.00
CONTENT-NUMBER OF MALE ANIMALS	0.33	0.57
CONTENT-NUMBER OF FEMALE ANIMALS	0.00	0.00
MALES IN STERO. NONOCC. ROLES	0.33	0.57
FEMALES IN STERO. NONOCC. ROLES	0.33	0.57
TOTAL MALES IN NONOCC. ROLES	0.33	0.57
TOTAL FEMALES IN NONOCC. ROLES	0.33	0.57
MALES IN STERO. OCCUPATIONAL ROLES	2.50	0.70
FEMALES IN STERO. OCCUPATIONAL ROLES	0.00	0.00
TOTAL MALES IN OCCUPATIONAL ROLES	2.50	0.70
TOTAL FEMALES IN OCCUPATIONAL ROLES	0.00	0.00
TOTAL OCCUPATIONS DEPICTED FOR MALES	2.00	1.73
TOTAL OCCUPATIONS DEPICTED FOR FEMALES	0.00	0.00
NUMBER OF FAMOUS MEN	0.00	0.00
NUMBER OF FAMOUS WOMEN	0.00	0.00

FEMALES DRESSED ONLY IN SKIRTS	NA
DEMEANING OR STERO. STATEMENTS	NO
STERO. EMOTIONAL RESPONSES	NO
LANGUAGE EXCLUDING WOMEN	NO
SEPARATE FORMS	NO
SEPARATE NORMS	NO

GRAY ORAL READING TESTS - FORM D

	MEAN	STANDARD DEVIATION
ILLUSTRATIONS-NUMBER OF MALE ADULTS	•	•
ILLUSTRATIONS-NUMBER OF FEMALE ADULTS	•	•
ILLUSTRATIONS-NUMBER OF MALE CHILDREN	•	•
ILLUSTRATIONS-NUMBER OF FEMALE CHILDREN	•	•
ILLUSTRATIONS-NUMBER OF MALE ANIMALS	•	•
ILLUSTRATIONS-NUMBER OF FEMALE ANIMALS	•	•
CONTENT-NUMBER OF MALE ADULTS	4.66	0.57
CONTENT-NUMBER OF FEMALE ADULTS	2.00	0.00
CONTENT-NUMBER OF MALE CHILDREN	2.66	1.15
CONTENT-NUMBER OF FEMALE CHILDREN	2.00	0.00
CONTENT-NUMBER OF MALE ANIMALS	1.00	0.00
CONTENT-NUMBER OF FEMALE ANIMALS	1.00	0.00
MALES IN STERO. NONOCC. ROLES	0.00	0.00
FEMALES IN STERO. NONOCC. ROLES	0.00	0.00
TOTAL MALES IN NONOCC. ROLES	0.00	0.00
TOTAL FEMALES IN NONOCC. ROLES	0.00	0.00
MALES IN STERO. OCCUPATIONAL ROLES	3.00	1.00
FEMALES IN STERO. OCCUPATIONAL ROLES	0.00	0.00
TOTAL MALES IN OCCUPATIONAL ROLES	4.33	3.21
TOTAL FEMALES IN OCCUPATIONAL ROLES	0.00	0.00
TOTAL OCCUPATIONS DEPICTED FOR MALES	3.00	1.00
TOTAL OCCUPATIONS DEPICTED FOR FEMALES	0.00	0.00
NUMBER OF FAMOUS MEN	0.00	0.00
NUMBER OF FAMOUS WOMEN	0.00	0.00

FEMALES DRESSED ONLY IN SKIRTS   NA

DEMEANING OR STERO. STATEMENTS   NO

STERO. EMOTIONAL RESPONSES   NO

LANGUAGE EXCLUDING WOMEN   NO

SEPARATE FORMS   NO

SEPARATE NORMS   NO

GRAY STANDARDIZED ORAL READING CHECK TESTS

	MEAN	STANDARD DEVIATION
ILLUSTRATIONS-NUMBER OF MALE ADULTS	.	.
ILLUSTRATIONS-NUMBER OF FEMALE ADULTS	.	.
ILLUSTRATIONS-NUMBER OF MALE CHILDREN	.	.
ILLUSTRATIONS-NUMBER OF FEMALE CHILDREN	.	.
ILLUSTRATIONS-NUMBER OF MALE ANIMALS	.	.
ILLUSTRATIONS-NUMBER OF FEMALE ANIMALS	.	.
CONTENT-NUMBER OF MALE ADULTS	6.00	0.00
CONTENT-NUMBER OF FEMALE ADULTS	1.66	0.57
CONTENT-NUMBER OF MALE CHILDREN	2.33	0.57
CONTENT-NUMBER OF FEMALE CHILDREN	1.33	0.57
CONTENT-NUMBER OF MALE ANIMALS	2.66	1.52
CONTENT-NUMBER CF FEMALE ANIMALS	7.00	0.00
MALES IN STERO. NONOCC. ROLES	2.50	0.70
FEMALES IN STERO. NONOCC. ROLES	1.00	0.00
TOTAL MALES IN NONOCC. ROLES	3.00	0.00
TOTAL FEMALES IN NONOCC. ROLES	1.00	0.00
MALES IN STERO. OCCUPATIONAL ROLES	0.00	0.00
FEMALES IN STERO. OCCUPATIONAL ROLES	0.00	0.00
TOTAL MALES IN OCCUPATIONAL ROLES	0.00	0.00
TOTAL FEMALES IN OCCUPATIONAL ROLES	0.00	0.00
TOTAL OCCUPATIONS DEPICTED FOR MALES	0.00	0.00
TOTAL OCCUPATIONS DEPICTED FOR FEMALES	1.00	0.00
NUMBER OF FAMOUS MEN	0.00	0.00
NUMBER OF FAMOUS WOMEN	0.00	0.00

FEMALES DRESSED ONLY IN SKIRTS	NA
DEMEANING OR STERO. STATEMENTS	NO
STERO. EMOTIONAL RESPONSES	NO
LANGUAGE EXCLUDING WOMEN	NO
SEPARATE FORMS	NO
SEPARATE NORMS	NO

GRAY STANDARDIZED ORAL READING PARAGRAPHS

	MEAN	STANDARD DEVIATION
ILLUSTRATIONS-NUMBER OF MALE ADULTS	•	•
ILLUSTRATIONS-NUMBER OF FEMALE ADULTS	•	•
ILLUSTRATIONS-NUMBER OF MALE CHILDREN	•	•
ILLUSTRATIONS-NUMBER OF FEMALE CHILDREN	•	•
ILLUSTRATIONS-NUMBER OF MALE ANIMALS	•	•
ILLUSTRATIONS-NUMBER OF FEMALE ANIMALS	•	•
CONTENT-NUMBER OF MALE ADULTS	4.50	2.12
CONTENT-NUMBER OF FEMALE ADULTS	1.50	0.70
CONTENT-NUMBER OF MALE CHILDREN	1.50	2.12
CONTENT-NUMBER OF FEMALE CHILDREN	1.00	0.00
CONTENT-NUMBER OF MALE ANIMALS	3.00	1.41
MALES IN STERO. NONOCC. ROLES	1.50	0.70
FEMALES IN STERO. NONOCC. ROLES	0.00	0.00
TOTAL MALES IN NONOCC. ROLES	2.50	2.12
TOTAL FEMALES IN NONOCC. ROLES	0.00	0.00
MALES IN STERO. OCCUPATIONAL ROLES	0.00	0.00
FEMALES IN STERO. OCCUPATIONAL ROLES	0.00	0.00
TOTAL MALES IN OCCUPATIONAL ROLES	0.00	0.00
TOTAL FEMALES IN OCCUPATIONAL ROLES	0.00	0.00
TOTAL OCCUPATIONS DEPICTED FOR MALES	0.50	0.70
TOTAL OCCUPATIONS DEPICTED FOR FEMALES	0.50	0.70
NUMBER OF FAMOUS MEN	0.00	0.00
NUMBER OF FAMOUS WOMEN	0.00	0.00

FEMALES DRESSED ONLY IN SKIRTS	NA
DEMEANING OR STERO. STATEMENTS	NO
STERO. EMOTIONAL RESPONSES	NO
LANGUAGE EXCLUDING WOMEN	YES
SEPARATE FORMS	NO
SEPARATE NORMS	NO

HENMON-NELSON TESTS OF MENTAL ABILITY - FORM 1, GRADES K-2

	MEAN	STANDARD DEVIATION
ILLUSTRATIONS-NUMBER OF MALE ADULTS	0.00	0.00
ILLUSTRATIONS-NUMBER OF FEMALE ADULTS	0.00	0.00
ILLUSTRATIONS-NUMBER OF MALE CHILDREN	0.00	0.00
ILLUSTRATIONS-NUMBER OF FEMALE CHILDREN	0.00	0.00
ILLUSTRATIONS-NUMBER OF MALE ANIMALS	0.00	0.00
ILLUSTRATIONS-NUMBER OF FEMALE ANIMALS	0.00	0.00
CONTENT-NUMBER OF MALE ADULTS	1.50	0.70
CONTENT-NUMBER OF FEMALE ADULTS	1.50	0.70
CONTENT-NUMBER OF MALE CHILDREN	4.50	0.70
CONTENT-NUMBER CF FEMALE CHILDREN	1.00	0.00
CONTENT-NUMBER OF MALE ANIMALS	0.00	0.00
CONTENT-NUMBER CF FEMALE ANIMALS	0.00	0.00
MALES IN STERO. NONOCC. ROLES	0.00	0.00
FEMALES IN STERO. NONOCC. ROLES	0.00	0.00
TOTAL MALES IN NONOCC. ROLES	3.50	0.70
TOTAL FEMALES IN NONOCC. ROLES	0.00	0.00
MALES IN STERC. OCCUPATIONAL ROLES	0.00	0.00
FEMALES IN STERO. OCCUPATIONAL ROLES	0.00	0.00
TOTAL MALES IN CCCUPATIONAL ROLES	0.00	0.00
TOTAL FEMALES IN OCCUPATIONAL ROLES	0.00	0.00
TOTAL OCCUPATIONS DEPICTED FOR MALES	0.00	0.00
TOTAL OCCUPATIONS DEPICTED FOR FEMALES	0.00	0.00
NUMBER OF FAMOUS MEN	0.00	0.00
NUMBER OF FAMOUS WOMEN	0.00	0.00

FEMALES DRESSED ONLY IN SKIRTS	NO
DEMEANING OR STERO. STATEMENTS	NA
STERO. EMOTIONAL RESPONSES	NA
LANGUAGE EXCLUDING WOMEN	NA
SEPARATE FORMS	NO
SEPARATE NORMS	NO

HENMON-NELSON TESTS OF MENTAL ABILITY - FORM 1, GRADES 3-6

	MEAN	STANDARD DEVIATION
ILLUSTRATIONS-NUMBER OF MALE ADULTS	0.00	0.00
ILLUSTRATIONS-NUMBER OF FEMALE ADULTS	0.00	0.00
ILLUSTRATIONS-NUMBER OF MALE CHILDREN	0.00	0.00
ILLUSTRATIONS-NUMBER OF FEMALE CHILDREN	0.00	0.00
ILLUSTRATIONS-NUMBER OF MALE ANIMALS	0.00	0.00
ILLUSTRATIONS-NUMBER OF FEMALE ANIMALS	0.00	0.00
CONTENT-NUMBER OF MALE ADULTS	1.50	0.70
CONTENT-NUMBER OF FEMALE ADULTS	1.50	0.70
CONTENT-NUMBER OF MALE CHILDREN	4.00	0.70
CONTENT-NUMBER CF FEMALE CHILDREN	1.00	0.00
CONTENT-NUMBER OF MALE ANIMALS	0.00	0.00
CONTENT-NUMBER CF FEMALE ANIMALS	0.00	0.00
MALES IN STERO. NONOCC. ROLES	0.00	0.00
FEMALES IN STERO. NONOCC. ROLES	0.00	0.00
TOTAL MALES IN NONOCC. ROLES	0.00	0.00
TOTAL FEMALES IN NONOCC. ROLES	0.00	0.00
MALES IN STERO. OCCUPATIONAL ROLES	0.00	0.00
FEMALES IN STERO. OCCUPATIONAL ROLES	0.00	0.00
TOTAL MALES IN CCCUPATIONAL ROLES	0.00	0.00
TOTAL FEMALES IN OCCUPATIONAL ROLES	0.00	0.00
TOTAL OCCUPATIONS DEPICTED FOR MALES	0.00	0.00
TOTAL OCCUPATIONS DEPICTED FOR FEMALES	0.00	0.00
NUMBER OF FAMOUS MEN	0.00	0.00
NUMBER OF FAMOUS WOMEN	0.00	0.00

FEMALES DRESSED ONLY IN SKIRTS	NA
DEMEANING OR STERO. STATEMENTS	NA
STERO. EMOTIONAL RESPONSES	NA
LANGUAGE EXCLUDING WOMEN	NA
SEPARATE FORMS	NO
SEPARATE NORMS	NO

HENMON-NELSON TESTS OF MENTAL ABILITY - FORM 1, GRADES 6-9

	MEAN	STANDARD DEVIATION
ILLUSTRATIONS-NUMBER OF MALE ADULTS	•	•
ILLUSTRATIONS-NUMBER OF FEMALE ADULTS	•	•
ILLUSTRATIONS-NUMBER OF MALE CHILDREN	•	•
ILLUSTRATIONS-NUMBER OF FEMALE CHILDREN	•	•
ILLUSTRATIONS-NUMBER OF MALE ANIMALS	•	•
ILLUSTRATIONS-NUMBER OF FEMALE ANIMALS	•	•
CONTENT-NUMBER OF MALE ADULTS	4.00	•
CONTENT-NUMBER OF FEMALE ADULTS	0.00	•
CONTENT-NUMBER OF MALE CHILDREN	0.00	•
CONTENT-NUMBER OF FEMALE CHILDREN	0.00	•
CONTENT-NUMBER OF MALE ANIMALS	0.00	•
CONTENT-NUMBER OF FEMALE ANIMALS	0.00	•
MALES IN STERO. NONOCC. ROLES	0.00	•
FEMALES IN STERO. NONOCC. ROLES	0.00	•
TOTAL MALES IN NONOCC. ROLES	0.00	•
TOTAL FEMALES IN NONOCC. ROLES	0.00	•
MALES IN STERO. OCCUPATIONAL ROLES	0.00	•
FEMALES IN STERO. OCCUPATIONAL ROLES	0.00	•
TOTAL MALES IN OCCUPATIONAL ROLES	0.00	•
TOTAL FEMALES IN OCCUPATIONAL ROLES	0.00	•
TOTAL OCCUPATIONS DEPICTED FOR MALES	0.00	•
TOTAL OCCUPATIONS DEPICTED FOR FEMALES	0.00	•
NUMBER OF FAMOUS MEN	1.00	•
NUMBER OF FAMOUS WOMEN	0.00	•

FEMALES DRESSED ONLY IN SKIRTS	NA
DEMEANING OR STERO. STATEMENTS	NA
STERO. EMOTIONAL RESPONSES	NA
LANGUAGE EXCLUDING WOMEN	NO
SEPARATE FORMS	NO
SEPARATE NORMS	NO

HENMON-NELSON TESTS OF MENTAL ABILITY - FORM 1, GRADES 9-12

	MEAN	STANDARD DEVIATION
ILLUSTRATIONS-NUMBER OF MALE ADULTS	1.25	0.50
ILLUSTRATIONS-NUMBER OF FEMALE ADULTS	1.25	0.95
ILLUSTRATIONS-NUMBER OF MALE CHILDREN	3.33	1.15
ILLUSTRATIONS-NUMBER OF FEMALE CHILDREN	2.00	1.00
ILLUSTRATIONS-NUMBER OF MALE ANIMALS	0.00	0.00
ILLUSTRATIONS-NUMBER OF FEMALE ANIMALS	0.00	0.00
CONTENT-NUMBER OF MALE ADULTS	0.75	0.50
CONTENT-NUMBER OF FEMALE ADULTS	0.25	0.50
CONTENT-NUMBER OF MALE CHILDREN	14.66	0.57
CONTENT-NUMBER OF FEMALE CHILDREN	11.66	1.15
CONTENT-NUMBER OF MALE ANIMALS	.	.
CONTENT-NUMBER OF FEMALE ANIMALS	.	.
MALES IN STERO. NONOCC. ROLES	.	.
FEMALES IN STERO. NONOCC. ROLES	.	.
TOTAL MALES IN NONOCC. ROLES	.	.
TOTAL FEMALES IN NONOCC. ROLES	.	.
MALES IN STERO. OCCUPATIONAL ROLES	1.00	0.00
FEMALES IN STERO. OCCUPATIONAL ROLES	0.00	0.00
TOTAL MALES IN OCCUPATIONAL ROLES	2.00	0.00
TOTAL FEMALES IN OCCUPATIONAL ROLES	0.00	0.00
TOTAL OCCUPATIONS DEPICTED FOR MALES	1.00	.
TOTAL OCCUPATIONS DEPICTED FOR FEMALES	0.00	.
NUMBER OF FAMOUS MEN	.	.
NUMBER OF FAMOUS WOMEN	.	.

FEMALES DRESSED ONLY IN SKIRTS	YES
DEMEANING OR STERO. STATEMENTS	NO
STERO. EMOTIONAL RESPONSES	NO
LANGUAGE EXCLUDING WOMEN	NO
SEPARATE FORMS	NO
SEPARATE NORMS	NO

ILLINOIS TEST OF PSYCHOLINGUISTIC ABILITIES

	MEAN	STANDARD DEVIATION
ILLUSTRATIONS-NUMBER OF MALE ADULTS	20.00	0.00
ILLUSTRATIONS-NUMBER OF FEMALE ADULTS	11.66	0.57
ILLUSTRATIONS-NUMBER OF MALE CHILDREN	18.00	0.00
ILLUSTRATIONS-NUMBER OF FEMALE CHILDREN	42.66	0.57
ILLUSTRATIONS-NUMBER OF MALE ANIMALS	0.00	0.00
ILLUSTRATIONS-NUMBER OF FEMALE ANIMALS	0.00	0.00
CONTENT-NUMBER OF MALE ADULTS	3.00	0.00
CONTENT-NUMBER OF FEMALE ADULTS	1.33	0.57
CONTENT-NUMBER OF MALE CHILDREN	1.00	0.00
CONTENT-NUMBER OF FEMALE CHILDREN	0.00	0.00
CONTENT-NUMBER OF MALE ANIMALS	0.00	0.00
CONTENT-NUMBER OF FEMALE ANIMALS	0.00	0.00
MALES IN STERO. NONOCC. ROLES	2.66	0.57
FEMALES IN STERO. NONOCC. ROLES	5.00	0.00
TOTAL MALES IN NONOCC. ROLES	2.66	0.57
TOTAL FEMALES IN NONOCC. ROLES	6.00	0.00
MALES IN STERO. OCCUPATIONAL ROLES	5.00	0.00
FEMALES IN STERO. OCCUPATIONAL ROLES	0.00	0.00
TOTAL MALES IN OCCUPATIONAL ROLES	5.00	0.00
TOTAL FEMALES IN OCCUPATIONAL ROLES	0.00	0.00
TOTAL OCCUPATIONS DEPICTED FOR MALES	2.66	0.57
TOTAL OCCUPATIONS DEPICTED FOR FEMALES	0.00	0.00
NUMBER OF FAMOUS MEN	0.00	0.00
NUMBER OF FAMOUS WOMEN	0.00	0.00

FEMALES DRESSED ONLY IN SKIRTS	YES
DEMEANING OR STERO. STATEMENTS	NO
STERO. EMOTIONAL RESPONSES	NO
LANGUAGE EXCLUDING WOMEN	NO
SEPARATE FORMS	NO
SEPARATE NORMS	NO

INPATIENT MULTIDIMENSIONAL PSYCHIATRIC SCALE

	MEAN	STANDARD DEVIATION
ILLUSTRATIONS-NUMBER OF MALE ADULTS	•	•
ILLUSTRATIONS-NUMBER OF FEMALE ADULTS	•	•
ILLUSTRATIONS-NUMBER OF MALE CHILDREN	•	•
ILLUSTRATIONS-NUMBER OF FEMALE CHILDREN	•	•
ILLUSTRATIONS-NUMBER OF MALE ANIMALS	•	•
ILLUSTRATIONS-NUMBER OF FEMALE ANIMALS	•	•
CONTENT-NUMBER OF MALE ADULTS	•	•
CONTENT-NUMBER OF FEMALE ADULTS	•	•
CONTENT-NUMBER OF MALE CHILDREN	•	•
CONTENT-NUMBER OF FEMALE CHILDREN	•	•
CONTENT-NUMBER OF MALE ANIMALS	•	•
CONTENT-NUMBER OF FEMALE ANIMALS	•	•
MALES IN STERO. NONOCC. ROLES	•	•
FEMALES IN STERO. NONOCC. ROLES	•	•
TOTAL MALES IN NONOCC. ROLES	•	•
TOTAL FEMALES IN NONOCC. ROLES	•	•
MALES IN STERO. OCCUPATIONAL ROLES	•	•
FEMALES IN STERO. OCCUPATIONAL ROLES	•	•
TOTAL MALES IN OCCUPATIONAL ROLES	•	•
TOTAL FEMALES IN OCCUPATIONAL ROLES	•	•
TOTAL OCCUPATIONS DEPICTED FOR MALES	•	•
TOTAL OCCUPATIONS DEPICTED FOR FEMALES	•	•
NUMBER OF FAMOUS MEN	•	•
NUMBER OF FAMOUS WOMEN	•	•

FEMALES DRESSED ONLY IN SKIRTS	NA
DEMEANING OR STERO. STATEMENTS	NA
STERO. EMOTIONAL RESPONSES	NA
LANGUAGE EXCLUDING WOMEN	NA
SEPARATE FORMS	NA
SEPARATE NORMS	YES

JUNIOR AND SENIOR HIGH SCHOOL PERSONALITY QUESTIONNAIRE - FORM A

	MEAN	STANDARD DEVIATION
ILLUSTRATIONS-NUMBER OF MALE ADULTS	.	.
ILLUSTRATIONS-NUMBER OF FEMALE ADULTS	.	.
ILLUSTRATIONS-NUMBER OF MALE CHILDREN	.	.
ILLUSTRATIONS-NUMBER OF FEMALE CHILDREN	.	.
ILLUSTRATIONS-NUMBER OF MALE ANIMALS	.	.
ILLUSTRATIONS-NUMBER OF FEMALE ANIMALS	.	.
CONTENT-NUMBER OF MALE ADULTS	0.00	0.00
CONTENT-NUMBER OF FEMALE ADULTS	0.00	0.00
CONTENT-NUMBER OF MALE CHILDREN	2.00	0.00
CONTENT-NUMBER OF FEMALE CHILDREN	2.00	0.00
CONTENT-NUMBER OF MALE ANIMALS	0.00	0.00
CONTENT-NUMBER OF FEMALE ANIMALS	0.00	0.00
MALES IN STERO. NONOCC. ROLES	0.00	0.00
FEMALES IN STERO. NONOCC. ROLES	0.00	0.00
TOTAL MALES IN NONOCC. ROLES	0.00	0.00
TOTAL FEMALES IN NONOCC. ROLES	0.00	0.00
MALES IN STERO. OCCUPATIONAL ROLES	0.66	0.57
FEMALES IN STERO. OCCUPATIONAL ROLES	0.00	0.00
TOTAL MALES IN OCCUPATIONAL ROLES	0.66	0.57
TOTAL FEMALES IN OCCUPATIONAL ROLES	0.00	0.00
TOTAL OCCUPATIONS DEPICTED FOR MALES	0.00	0.00
TOTAL OCCUPATIONS DEPICTED FOR FEMALES	0.00	0.00
NUMBER OF FAMOUS MEN	0.00	0.00
NUMBER OF FAMOUS WOMEN	0.66	0.57

FEMALES DRESSED ONLY IN SKIRTS	NA
DEMEANING OR STERO. STATEMENTS	NA
STERO. EMOTIONAL RESPONSES	NO
LANGUAGE EXCLUDING WOMEN	YES
SEPARATE FORMS	NO
SEPARATE NORMS	YES

JUNIOR AND SENIOR HIGH SCHOOL PERSONALITY QUESTIONNAIRE - FORM B

	MEAN	STANDARD DEVIATION
ILLUSTRATIONS-NUMBER OF MALE ADULTS	•	•
ILLUSTRATIONS-NUMBER OF FEMALE ADULTS	•	•
ILLUSTRATIONS-NUMBER OF MALE CHILDREN	•	•
ILLUSTRATIONS-NUMBER OF FEMALE CHILDREN	•	•
ILLUSTRATIONS-NUMBER OF MALE ANIMALS	•	•
ILLUSTRATIONS-NUMBER OF FEMALE ANIMALS	•	•
CONTENT-NUMBER OF MALE ADULTS	1.50	0.70
CONTENT-NUMBER OF FEMALE ADULTS	0.00	0.00
CONTENT-NUMBER OF MALE CHILDREN	3.00	0.00
CONTENT-NUMBER OF FEMALE CHILDREN	0.00	0.00
CONTENT-NUMBER OF MALE ANIMALS	0.00	0.00
CONTENT-NUMBER CF FEMALE ANIMALS	0.00	0.00
MALES IN STERO. NONOCC. ROLES	0.00	0.00
FEMALES IN STERO. NONOCC. ROLES	0.00	0.00
TOTAL MALES IN NONOCC. ROLES	0.00	0.00
TOTAL FEMALES IN NONOCC. ROLES	0.00	0.00
MALES IN STERO. OCCUPATIONAL ROLES	0.00	0.00
FEMALES IN STERO. OCCUPATIONAL ROLES	0.00	0.00
TOTAL MALES IN OCCUPATIONAL ROLES	0.00	0.00
TOTAL FEMALES IN OCCUPATIONAL ROLES	0.00	0.00
TOTAL OCCUPATIONS DEPICTED FOR MALES	0.00	0.00
TOTAL OCCUPATIONS DEPICTED FOR FEMALES	0.00	0.00
NUMBER OF FAMOUS MEN	0.00	0.00
NUMBER OF FAMOUS WOMEN	0.00	0.00

FEMALES DRESSED ONLY IN SKIRTS	NA
DEMEANING OR STERO. STATEMENTS	NA
STERO. EMOTIONAL RESPONSES	NO
LANGUAGE EXCLUDING WOMEN	YES
SEPARATE FORMS	NO
SEPARATE NORMS	YES

KUHLMAN-ANDERSON TESTS - BOOKLET D

	MEAN	STANDARD DEVIATION
ILLUSTRATIONS-NUMBER OF MALE ADULTS	.	.
ILLUSTRATIONS-NUMBER OF FEMALE ADULTS	.	.
ILLUSTRATIONS-NUMBER OF MALE CHILDREN	.	.
ILLUSTRATIONS-NUMBER OF FEMALE CHILDREN	.	.
ILLUSTRATIONS-NUMBER OF MALE ANIMALS	.	.
ILLUSTRATIONS-NUMBER OF FEMALE ANIMALS	.	.
CONTENT-NUMBER OF MALE ADULTS	1.00	0.00
CONTENT-NUMBER OF FEMALE ADULTS	0.00	0.00
CONTENT-NUMBER OF MALE CHILDREN	4.00	0.00
CONTENT-NUMBER CF FEMALE CHILDREN	4.50	0.70
CONTENT-NUMBER CF MALE ANIMALS	0.00	0.00
CONTENT-NUMBER OF FEMALE ANIMALS	0.00	0.00
MALES IN STERO. NONOCC. ROLES	.	.
FEMALES IN STERO. NONOCC. ROLES	0.00	0.00
TOTAL MALES IN NONOCC. ROLES	.	.
TOTAL FEMALES IN NONOCC. ROLES	0.00	0.00
MALES IN STERO. OCCUPATIONAL ROLES	.	.
FEMALES IN STERO. OCCUPATIONAL ROLES	0.00	0.00
TOTAL MALES IN OCCUPATIONAL ROLES	.	.
TOTAL FEMALES IN OCCUPATIONAL ROLES	0.00	0.00
TOTAL OCCUPATIONS DEPICTED FOR MALES	0.00	0.00
TOTAL OCCUPATIONS DEPICTED FOR FEMALES	0.00	0.00
NUMBER OF FAMOUS MEN	0.00	0.00
NUMBER OF FAMOUS WOMEN	0.00	0.00

FEMALES DRESSED ONLY IN SKIRTS   NA

DEMEANING OR STERO. STATEMENTS   NA

STERO. EMOTIONAL RESPONSES   NO

LANGUAGE EXCLUDING WOMEN   NO

SEPARATE FORMS   NO

SEPARATE NORMS   NO

KUHLMAN-ANDERSON TESTS - BOOKLET E & F

	MEAN	STANDARD DEVIATION
ILLUSTRATIONS-NUMBER OF MALE ADULTS	•	•
ILLUSTRATIONS-NUMBER OF FEMALE ADULTS	•	•
ILLUSTRATIONS-NUMBER OF MALE CHILDREN	•	•
ILLUSTRATIONS-NUMBER OF FEMALE CHILDREN	•	•
ILLUSTRATIONS-NUMBER OF MALE ANIMALS	•	•
ILLUSTRATIONS-NUMBER OF FEMALE ANIMALS	•	•
CONTENT-NUMBER OF MALE ADULTS	3.00	0.00
CONTENT-NUMBER OF FEMALE ADULTS	0.66	0.57
CONTENT-NUMBER OF MALE CHILDREN	5.66	0.57
CONTENT-NUMBER OF FEMALE CHILDREN	2.66	0.57
CONTENT-NUMBER OF MALE ANIMALS	0.00	0.00
CONTENT-NUMBER OF FEMALE ANIMALS	0.00	0.00
MALES IN STERO. NONOCC. ROLES	0.00	0.00
FEMALES IN STERO. NONOCC. ROLES	0.00	0.00
TOTAL MALES IN NONOCC. ROLES	0.00	0.00
TOTAL FEMALES IN NONOCC. ROLES	0.00	0.00
MALES IN STERO. OCCUPATIONAL ROLES	0.33	0.57
FEMALES IN STERO. OCCUPATIONAL ROLES	0.00	0.00
TOTAL MALES IN OCCUPATIONAL ROLES	0.33	0.57
TOTAL FEMALES IN OCCUPATIONAL ROLES	0.33	0.57
TOTAL OCCUPATIONS DEPICTED FOR MALES	0.33	0.57
TOTAL OCCUPATIONS DEPICTED FOR FEMALES	0.33	0.57
NUMBER OF FAMOUS MEN	0.00	0.00
NUMBER OF FAMOUS WOMEN	0.00	0.00

FEMALES DRESSED ONLY IN SKIRTS	NA
DEMEANING OR STERO. STATEMENTS	NA
STERO. EMOTIONAL RESPONSES	NO
LANGUAGE EXCLUDING WOMEN	NO
SEPARATE FORMS	NO
SEPARATE NORMS	NO

KUHLMAN-ANDERSON TESTS - BOOKLET G

	MEAN	STANDARD DEVIATION
ILLUSTRATIONS-NUMBER OF MALE ADULTS	•	•
ILLUSTRATIONS-NUMBER OF FEMALE ADULTS	•	•
ILLUSTRATIONS-NUMBER OF MALE CHILDREN	•	•
ILLUSTRATIONS-NUMBER OF FEMALE CHILDREN	•	•
ILLUSTRATIONS-NUMBER OF MALE ANIMALS	•	•
ILLUSTRATIONS-NUMBER OF FEMALE ANIMALS	•	•
CONTENT-NUMBER OF MALE ADULTS	2.00	1.73
CONTENT-NUMBER OF FEMALE ADULTS	1.33	1.52
CONTENT-NUMBER OF MALE CHILDREN	0.66	0.57
CONTENT-NUMBER OF FEMALE CHILDREN	2.00	1.00
CONTENT-NUMBER OF MALE ANIMALS	0.00	0.00
CONTENT-NUMBER OF FEMALE ANIMALS	0.00	0.00
MALES IN STERO. NONOCC. ROLES	0.00	0.00
FEMALES IN STERO. NONOCC. ROLES	0.00	0.00
TOTAL MALES IN NONOCC. ROLES	0.00	0.00
TOTAL FEMALES IN NONOCC. ROLES	0.00	0.00
MALES IN STERO. OCCUPATIONAL ROLES	0.00	0.00
FEMALES IN STERO. OCCUPATIONAL ROLES	0.00	0.00
TOTAL MALES IN OCCUPATIONAL ROLES	0.00	0.00
TOTAL FEMALES IN OCCUPATIONAL ROLES	0.00	0.00
TOTAL OCCUPATIONS DEPICTED FOR MALES	0.00	0.00
TOTAL OCCUPATIONS DEPICTED FOR FEMALES	0.00	0.00
NUMBER OF FAMOUS MEN	0.00	0.00
NUMBER OF FAMOUS WOMEN	0.00	0.00

FEMALES DRESSED ONLY IN SKIRTS	NA
DEMEANING OR STERO. STATEMENTS	NA
STERO. EMOTIONAL RESPONSES	NO
LANGUAGE EXCLUDING WOMEN	YES
SEPARATE FORMS	NA
SEPARATE NORMS	NA

KUHLMAN-ANDERSON TESTS - BOOKLET H

	MEAN	STANDARD DEVIATION
ILLUSTRATIONS-NUMBER OF MALE ADULTS	•	•
ILLUSTRATIONS-NUMBER OF FEMALE ADULTS	•	•
ILLUSTRATIONS-NUMBER OF MALE CHILDREN	•	•
ILLUSTRATIONS-NUMBER OF FEMALE CHILDREN	•	•
ILLUSTRATIONS-NUMBER OF MALE ANIMALS	•	•
ILLUSTRATIONS-NUMBER OF FEMALE ANIMALS	•	•
CONTENT-NUMBER OF MALE ADULTS	1.00	0.00
CONTENT-NUMBER OF FEMALE ADULTS	0.50	0.70
CONTENT-NUMBER OF MALE CHILDREN	1.66	0.57
CONTENT-NUMBER OF FEMALE CHILDREN	2.33	1.52
CONTENT-NUMBER OF MALE ANIMALS	0.00	0.00
CONTENT-NUMBER OF FEMALE ANIMALS	0.00	0.00
MALES IN STERO. NONOCC. ROLES	0.00	0.00
FEMALES IN STERO. NONOCC. ROLES	0.00	0.00
TOTAL MALES IN NONOCC. ROLES	0.00	0.00
TOTAL FEMALES IN NONOCC. ROLES	0.00	0.00
MALES IN STERO. OCCUPATIONAL ROLES	0.00	0.00
FEMALES IN STERO. OCCUPATIONAL ROLES	0.00	0.00
TOTAL MALES IN OCCUPATIONAL ROLES	0.00	0.00
TOTAL FEMALES IN OCCUPATIONAL ROLES	0.00	0.00
TOTAL OCCUPATIONS DEPICTED FOR MALES	0.00	0.00
TOTAL OCCUPATIONS DEPICTED FOR FEMALES	0.00	0.00
NUMBER OF FAMOUS MEN	0.00	0.00
NUMBER OF FAMOUS WOMEN	0.00	0.00

FEMALES DRESSED ONLY IN SKIRTS	NA
DEMEANING OR STERO. STATEMENTS	NA
STERO. EMOTIONAL RESPONSES	NO
LANGUAGE EXCLUDING WOMEN	NO
SEPARATE FORMS	NO
SEPARATE NORMS	NO

LEE-CLARK READING READINESS TEST

	MEAN	STANDARD DEVIATION
ILLUSTRATIONS-NUMBER OF MALE ADULTS	3.75	1.89
ILLUSTRATIONS-NUMBER OF FEMALE ADULTS	0.00	0.00
ILLUSTRATIONS-NUMBER OF MALE CHILDREN	7.00	1.63
ILLUSTRATIONS-NUMBER OF FEMALE CHILDREN	17.00	0.00
ILLUSTRATIONS-NUMBER OF MALE ANIMALS	0.00	0.00
ILLUSTRATIONS-NUMBER OF FEMALE ANIMALS	0.00	0.00
CONTENT-NUMBER OF MALE ADULTS	0.75	0.50
CONTENT-NUMBER OF FEMALE ADULTS	0.25	0.50
CONTENT-NUMBER OF MALE CHILDREN	2.00	0.81
CONTENT-NUMBER OF FEMALE CHILDREN	2.75	1.25
CONTENT-NUMBER OF MALE ANIMALS	0.00	0.00
CONTENT-NUMBER OF FEMALE ANIMALS	0.00	0.00
MALES IN STERO. NONOCC. ROLES	2.33	0.57
FEMALES IN STERO. NONOCC. ROLES	1.33	1.15
TOTAL MALES IN NONOCC. ROLES	3.00	1.00
TOTAL FEMALES IN NONOCC. ROLES	1.33	1.15
MALES IN STERO. OCCUPATIONAL ROLES	0.00	0.00
FEMALES IN STERO. OCCUPATIONAL ROLES	0.00	0.00
TOTAL MALES IN OCCUPATIONAL ROLES	0.00	0.00
TOTAL FEMALES IN OCCUPATIONAL ROLES	0.00	0.00
TOTAL OCCUPATIONS DEPICTED FOR MALES	0.00	0.00
TOTAL OCCUPATIONS DEPICTED FOR FEMALES	.	.
NUMBER OF FAMOUS MEN	0.00	0.00
NUMBER OF FAMOUS WOMEN	0.00	0.00

FEMALES DRESSED ONLY IN SKIRTS	YES
DEMEANING OR STERO. STATEMENTS	NO
STERO. EMOTIONAL RESPONSES	NO
LANGUAGE EXCLUDING WOMEN	NO
SEPARATE FORMS	NO
SEPARATE NORMS	NO

LORGE-THORNDIKE INTELLIGENCE TEST - FORM 1

	MEAN	STANDARD DEVIATION
ILLUSTRATIONS-NUMBER OF MALE ADULTS	3.33	2.30
ILLUSTRATIONS-NUMBER OF FEMALE ADULTS	1.66	1.15
ILLUSTRATIONS-NUMBER OF MALE CHILDREN	2.50	2.12
ILLUSTRATIONS-NUMBER OF FEMALE CHILDREN	1.50	0.70
ILLUSTRATIONS-NUMBER OF MALE ANIMALS	0.00	0.00
ILLUSTRATIONS-NUMBER OF FEMALE ANIMALS	0.00	0.00
CONTENT-NUMBER OF MALE ADULTS	9.66	2.08
CONTENT-NUMBER OF FEMALE ADULTS	5.33	4.93
CONTENT-NUMBER OF MALE CHILDREN	7.00	3.46
CONTENT-NUMBER OF FEMALE CHILDREN	3.00	2.00
CONTENT-NUMBER OF MALE ANIMALS	28.00	.
CONTENT-NUMBER OF FEMALE ANIMALS	11.00	.
MALES IN STERO. NONOCC. ROLES	.	.
FEMALES IN STERO. NONOCC. ROLES	.	.
TOTAL MALES IN NONOCC. ROLES	.	.
TOTAL FEMALES IN NONOCC. ROLES	.	.
MALES IN STERO. OCCUPATIONAL ROLES	0.66	0.57
FEMALES IN STERO. OCCUPATIONAL ROLES	.	.
TOTAL MALES IN OCCUPATIONAL ROLES	0.66	0.57
TOTAL FEMALES IN OCCUPATIONAL ROLES	.	.
TOTAL OCCUPATIONS DEPICTED FOR MALES	1.33	0.57
TOTAL OCCUPATIONS DEPICTED FOR FEMALES	0.00	0.00
NUMBER OF FAMOUS MEN	1.00	0.00
NUMBER OF FAMOUS WOMEN	0.00	0.00

FEMALES DRESSED ONLY IN SKIRTS	YES
DEMEANING OR STERO. STATEMENTS	NO
STERO. EMOTIONAL RESPONSES	NO
LANGUAGE EXCLUDING WOMEN	YES
SEPARATE FORMS	NO
SEPARATE NORMS	NO

LORGE-THORNDIKE INTELLIGENCE TEST - FORM 2

	MEAN	STANDARD DEVIATION
ILLUSTRATIONS-NUMBER OF MALE ADULTS	1.00	0.00
ILLUSTRATIONS-NUMBER OF FEMALE ADULTS	1.50	0.70
ILLUSTRATIONS-NUMBER OF MALE CHILDREN	7.50	0.70
ILLUSTRATIONS-NUMBER OF FEMALE CHILDREN	3.00	1.41
ILLUSTRATIONS-NUMBER OF MALE ANIMALS	0.00	0.00
ILLUSTRATIONS-NUMBER OF FEMALE ANIMALS	0.00	0.C0
CONTENT-NUMBER OF MALE ADULTS	18.00	7.07
CONTENT-NUMBER OF FEMALE ADULTS	8.00	7.07
CONTENT-NUMBER OF MALE CHILDREN	5.50	2.12
CONTENT-NUMBER OF FEMALE CHILDREN	4.50	0.70
CONTENT-NUMBER OF MALE ANIMALS	.	.
CONTENT-NUMBER OF FEMALE ANIMALS	.	.
MALES IN STERO. NONOCC. ROLES	.	.
FEMALES IN STERO. NONOCC. ROLES	1.00	.
TOTAL MALES IN NONOCC. ROLES	.	.
TOTAL FEMALES IN NONOCC. ROLES	0.00	.
MALES IN STERO. OCCUPATIONAL ROLES	1.00	0.00
FEMALES IN STERO. OCCUPATIONAL ROLES	.	.
TOTAL MALES IN OCCUPATIONAL ROLES	1.00	0.00
TOTAL FEMALES IN OCCUPATIONAL ROLES	.	.
TOTAL OCCUPATIONS DEPICTED FOR MALES	1.00	.
TOTAL OCCUPATIONS DEPICTED FOR FEMALES	0.00	.
NUMBER OF FAMOUS MEN	.	.
NUMBER OF FAMOUS WOMEN	.	.

FEMALES DRESSED ONLY IN SKIRTS	YES
DEMEANING OR STERO. STATEMENTS	NO
STERO. EMOTIONAL RESPONSES	NO
LANGUAGE EXCLUDING WOMEN	YES
SEPARATE FORMS	NO
SEPARATE NORMS	NO

MACMILLAN READING READINESS TEST

	MEAN	STANDARD DEVIATION
ILLUSTRATIONS-NUMBER OF MALE ADULTS	9.75	2.06
ILLUSTRATIONS-NUMBER OF FEMALE ADULTS	3.25	0.50
ILLUSTRATIONS-NUMBER OF MALE CHILDREN	10.00	2.00
ILLUSTRATIONS-NUMBER OF FEMALE CHILDREN	4.25	0.95
ILLUSTRATIONS-NUMBER OF MALE ANIMALS	0.00	0.00
ILLUSTRATIONS-NUMBER OF FEMALE ANIMALS	0.00	0.00
CONTENT-NUMBER OF MALE ADULTS	0.50	1.00
CONTENT-NUMBER OF FEMALE ADULTS	0.25	0.50
CONTENT-NUMBER OF MALE CHILDREN	3.25	2.21
CONTENT-NUMBER OF FEMALE CHILDREN	2.50	1.29
CONTENT-NUMBER OF MALE ANIMALS	0.00	0.00
CONTENT-NUMBER OF FEMALE ANIMALS	0.00	0.00
MALES IN STERO. NONOCC. ROLES	0.00	0.00
FEMALES IN STERO. NONOCC. ROLES	0.50	0.57
TOTAL MALES IN NONOCC. ROLES	0.00	0.00
TOTAL FEMALES IN NONOCC. ROLES	0.75	0.95
MALES IN STERO. OCCUPATIONAL ROLES	5.25	2.21
FEMALES IN STERO. OCCUPATIONAL ROLES	0.25	0.50
TOTAL MALES IN OCCUPATIONAL ROLES	5.50	2.38
TOTAL FEMALES IN OCCUPATIONAL ROLES	0.50	1.00
TOTAL OCCUPATIONS DEPICTED FOR MALES	5.66	1.52
TOTAL OCCUPATIONS DEPICTED FOR FEMALES	0.50	1.00
NUMBER OF FAMOUS MEN	0.00	0.00
NUMBER OF FAMOUS WOMEN	0.00	0.00

FEMALES DRESSED ONLY IN SKIRTS	YES
DEMEANING OR STERO. STATEMENTS	NO
STERO. EMOTIONAL RESPONSES	NO
LANGUAGE EXCLUDING WOMEN	NO
SEPARATE FORMS	NO
SEPARATE NORMS	NO

MCCARTHY SCALES

	MEAN	STANDARD DEVIATION
ILLUSTRATIONS-NUMBER OF MALE ADULTS	.	.
ILLUSTRATIONS-NUMBER OF FEMALE ADULTS	1.00	0.00
ILLUSTRATIONS-NUMBER OF MALE CHILDREN	1.00	.
ILLUSTRATIONS-NUMBER OF FEMALE CHILDREN	0.00	0.00
ILLUSTRATIONS-NUMBER OF MALE ANIMALS	.	.
ILLUSTRATIONS-NUMBER OF FEMALE ANIMALS	.	.
CONTENT-NUMBER CF MALE ADULTS	0.00	0.00
CONTENT-NUMBER OF FEMALE ADULTS	1.25	0.50
CONTENT-NUMBER OF MALE CHILDREN	2.50	0.57
CONTENT-NUMBER OF FEMALE CHILDREN	0.50	0.57
CONTENT-NUMBER CF MALE ANIMALS	.	.
CONTENT-NUMBER OF FEMALE ANIMALS	.	.
MALES IN STERO. NONOCC. ROLES	1.00	1.41
FEMALES IN STERO. NONOCC. ROLES	1.00	1.00
TOTAL MALES IN NONOCC. ROLES	1.50	0.70
TOTAL FEMALES IN NONOCC. ROLES	1.00	1.00
MALES IN STERO. OCCUPATIONAL ROLES	.	.
FEMALES IN STERO. OCCUPATIONAL ROLES	.	.
TOTAL MALES IN OCCUPATIONAL ROLES	.	.
TOTAL FEMALES IN OCCUPATIONAL ROLES	.	.
TOTAL OCCUPATIONS DEPICTED FOR MALES	.	.
TOTAL OCCUPATIONS DEPICTED FOR FEMALES	.	.
NUMBER OF FAMOUS MEN	.	.
NUMBER OF FAMOUS WOMEN	.	.

FEMALES DRESSED ONLY IN SKIRTS	YES
DEMEANING OR STERO. STATEMENTS	NO
STERO. EMOTIONAL RESPONSES	NO
LANGUAGE EXCLUDING WOMEN	YES
SEPARATE FORMS	NO
SEPARATE NORMS	NO

METROPOLITAN ACHIEVEMENT TESTS - MATH - FORM JI, PRIMER

	MEAN	STANDARD DEVIATION
ILLUSTRATIONS-NUMBER OF MALE ADULTS	6.00	2.64
ILLUSTRATIONS-NUMBER OF FEMALE ADULTS	0.33	0.57
ILLUSTRATIONS-NUMBER OF MALE CHILDREN	2.00	3.46
ILLUSTRATIONS-NUMBER OF FEMALE CHILDREN	8.66	1.52
ILLUSTRATIONS-NUMBER OF MALE ANIMALS	0.00	0.00
ILLUSTRATIONS-NUMBER OF FEMALE ANIMALS	0.00	0.00
CONTENT-NUMBER OF MALE ADULTS	.	.
CONTENT-NUMBER CF FEMALE ADULTS	.	.
CONTENT-NUMBER CF MALE CHILDREN	.	.
CONTENT-NUMBER OF FEMALE CHILDREN	.	.
CONTENT-NUMBER CF MALE ANIMALS	.	.
CONTENT-NUMBER OF FEMALE ANIMALS	.	.
MALES IN STERO. NONOCC. ROLES	0.00	0.00
FEMALES IN STERO. NONOCC. ROLES	0.00	0.00
TOTAL MALES IN NONOCC. ROLES	0.00	0.00
TOTAL FEMALES IN NONOCC. ROLES	0.00	0.00
MALES IN STERO. OCCUPATIONAL ROLES	0.00	0.00
FEMALES IN STERC. OCCUPATIONAL ROLES	0.00	0.00
TOTAL MALES IN OCCUPATIONAL ROLES	0.00	0.00
TOTAL FEMALES IN OCCUPATIONAL ROLES	0.00	0.00
TOTAL OCCUPATIONS DEPICTED FOR MALES	0.00	0.00
TOTAL OCCUPATIONS DEPICTED FOR FEMALES	0.00	0.00
NUMBER OF FAMOUS MEN	0.00	0.00
NUMBER OF FAMOUS WOMEN	0.00	0.00

FEMALES DRESSED ONLY IN SKIRTS	NO
DEMEANING OR STERO. STATEMENTS	NO
STERO. EMOTIONAL RESPONSES	NO
LANGUAGE EXCLUDING WOMEN	NO
SEPARATE FORMS	NO
SEPARATE NORMS	NO

METROPOLITAN ACHIEVEMENT TEST - MATH - FORM JI, PRIMARY 1

	MEAN	STANDARD DEVIATION
ILLUSTRATIONS-NUMBER OF MALE ADULTS	6.00	.
ILLUSTRATIONS-NUMBER OF FEMALE ADULTS	1.00	.
ILLUSTRATIONS-NUMBER OF MALE CHILDREN	0.00	0.00
ILLUSTRATIONS-NUMBER OF FEMALE CHILDREN	3.66	0.57
ILLUSTRATIONS-NUMBER OF MALE ANIMALS	0.00	0.00
ILLUSTRATIONS-NUMBER OF FEMALE ANIMALS	0.00	0.00
CONTENT-NUMBER OF MALE ADULTS	0.00	0.00
CONTENT-NUMBER CF FEMALE ADULTS	0.00	0.00
CONTENT-NUMBER OF MALE CHILDREN	0.25	0.50
CONTENT-NUMBER OF FEMALE CHILDREN	0.50	1.00
CONTENT-NUMBER OF MALE ANIMALS	0.00	0.00
CONTENT-NUMBER CF FEMALE ANIMALS	0.00	0.00
MALES IN STERO. NONOCC. ROLES	0.00	0.00
FEMALES IN STERO. NONOCC. ROLES	0.00	0.00
TOTAL MALES IN NONOCC. ROLES	0.00	0.00
TOTAL FEMALES IN NONOCC. ROLES	0.00	0.00
MALES IN STERO. OCCUPATIONAL ROLES	0.00	0.00
FEMALES IN STERO. OCCUPATIONAL ROLES	0.00	0.00
TOTAL MALES IN OCCUPATIONAL ROLES	0.00	0.00
TOTAL FEMALES IN OCCUPATIONAL ROLES	0.00	0.00
TOTAL OCCUPATIONS DEPICTED FOR MALES	0.00	0.00
TOTAL OCCUPATIONS DEPICTED FOR FEMALES	0.00	0.00
NUMBER OF FAMOUS MEN	1.25	2.50
NUMBER OF FAMOUS WOMEN	0.00	0.00

FEMALES DRESSED ONLY IN SKIRTS	YES
DEMEANING OR STERO. STATEMENTS	NO
STERO. EMOTIONAL RESPONSES	NO
LANGUAGE EXCLUDING WOMEN	NO
SEPARATE FORMS	NO
SEPARATE NORMS	NO

METROPOLITAN ACHIEVEMENT TESTS - MATH - FORM JI, PRIMARY 2

	MEAN	STANDARD DEVIATION
ILLUSTRATIONS-NUMBER OF MALE ADULTS	1.00	2.00
ILLUSTRATIONS-NUMBER OF FEMALE ADULTS	0.00	0.00
ILLUSTRATIONS-NUMBER OF MALE CHILDREN	0.00	0.00
ILLUSTRATIONS-NUMBER OF FEMALE CHILDREN	3.75	0.50
ILLUSTRATIONS-NUMBER OF MALE ANIMALS	0.00	0.00
ILLUSTRATIONS-NUMBER OF FEMALE ANIMALS	0.00	0.00
CONTENT-NUMBER OF MALE ADULTS	2.75	0.50
CONTENT-NUMBER CF FEMALE ADULTS	0.25	0.50
CONTENT-NUMBER OF MALE CHILDREN	3.75	0.50
CONTENT-NUMBER OF FEMALE CHILDREN	7.25	2.06
CONTENT-NUMBER OF MALE ANIMALS	0.00	0.00
CONTENT-NUMBER CF FEMALE ANIMALS	0.00	0.00
MALES IN STERO. NONOCC. ROLES	0.25	0.50
FEMALES IN STERO. NONOCC. ROLES	0.25	0.50
TOTAL MALES IN NONOCC. ROLES	0.25	0.50
TOTAL FEMALES IN NONOCC. ROLES	0.25	0.50
MALES IN STERO. OCCUPATIONAL ROLES	1.00	0.00
FEMALES IN STERO. OCCUPATIONAL ROLES	0.50	0.57
TOTAL MALES IN OCCUPATIONAL ROLES	1.00	0.00
TOTAL FEMALES IN OCCUPATIONAL ROLES	0.50	0.57
TOTAL OCCUPATIONS DEPICTED FOR MALES	1.00	1.15
TOTAL OCCUPATIONS DEPICTED FOR FEMALES	0.50	0.57
NUMBER OF FAMOUS MEN	1.50	3.00
NUMBER OF FAMOUS WOMEN	0.00	0.00

FEMALES DRESSED ONLY IN SKIRTS	YES
DEMEANING OR STERO. STATEMENTS	NO
STERO. EMOTIONAL RESPONSES	NO
LANGUAGE EXCLUDING WOMEN	NO
SEPARATE FORMS	NO
SEPARATE NORMS	NO

METROPOLITAN ACHIEVEMENT TESTS - MATH - FORM JI, ELEMENTARY

	MEAN	STANDARD DEVIATION
ILLUSTRATIONS-NUMBER OF MALE ADULTS	.	.
ILLUSTRATIONS-NUMBER OF FEMALE ADULTS	.	.
ILLUSTRATIONS-NUMBER OF MALE CHILDREN	.	.
ILLUSTRATIONS-NUMBER OF FEMALE CHILDREN	.	.
ILLUSTRATIONS-NUMBER OF MALE ANIMALS	.	.
ILLUSTRATIONS-NUMBER OF FEMALE ANIMALS	.	.
CONTENT-NUMBER OF MALE ADULTS	1.50	1.00
CONTENT-NUMBER OF FEMALE ADULTS	1.00	0.00
CONTENT-NUMBER CF MALE CHILDREN	2.50	0.57
CONTENT-NUMBER OF FEMALE CHILDREN	7.75	0.50
CONTENT-NUMBER CF MALE ANIMALS	0.00	0.00
CONTENT-NUMBER CF FEMALE ANIMALS	0.00	0.00
MALES IN STERO. NONOCC. ROLES	0.75	0.50
FEMALES IN STERC. NONOCC. ROLES	0.00	0.00
TOTAL MALES IN NONOCC. ROLES	0.75	0.50
TOTAL FEMALES IN NONOCC. ROLES	0.50	0.57
MALES IN STERO. OCCUPATIONAL ROLES	0.00	0.00
FEMALES IN STERC. OCCUPATIONAL ROLES	0.00	0.00
TOTAL MALES IN OCCUPATIONAL ROLES	0.00	0.00
TOTAL FEMALES IN OCCUPATIONAL ROLES	0.00	0.00
TOTAL OCCUPATIONS DEPICTED FOR MALES	0.00	0.00
TOTAL OCCUPATIONS DEPICTED FOR FEMALES	0.00	0.00
NUMBER OF FAMOUS MEN	0.00	0.00
NUMBER OF FAMOUS WOMEN	.	.

FEMALES DRESSED ONLY IN SKIRTS	NA
DEMEANING OR STERO. STATEMENTS	NO
STERO. EMOTIONAL RESPONSES	NO
LANGUAGE EXCLUDING WOMEN	NO
SEPARATE FORMS	NO
SEPARATE NORMS	NO

METROPOLITAN ACHIEVEMENT TESTS - MATH - FORM JI, INTERMEDIATE

	MEAN	STANDARD DEVIATION
ILLUSTRATIONS-NUMBER OF MALE ADULTS	•	•
ILLUSTRATIONS-NUMBER OF FEMALE ADULTS	•	•
ILLUSTRATIONS-NUMBER OF MALE CHILDREN	•	•
ILLUSTRATIONS-NUMBER OF FEMALE CHILDREN	•	•
ILLUSTRATIONS-NUMBER OF MALE ANIMALS	•	•
ILLUSTRATIONS-NUMBER OF FEMALE ANIMALS	•	•
CONTENT-NUMBER OF MALE ADULTS	0.00	0.00
CONTENT-NUMBER CF FEMALE ADULTS	0.66	0.57
CONTENT-NUMBER OF MALE CHILDREN	0.00	0.00
CONTENT-NUMBER CF FEMALE CHILDREN	4.33	1.52
CONTENT-NUMBER OF MALE ANIMALS	0.00	0.00
CONTENT-NUMBER CF FEMALE ANIMALS	0.00	0.00
MALES IN STERO. NONOCC. ROLES	0.00	0.00
FEMALES IN STERO. NONOCC. ROLES	0.00	0.00
TOTAL MALES IN NONOCC. ROLES	0.00	0.00
TOTAL FEMALES IN NONOCC. ROLES	0.00	0.00
MALES IN STERO. OCCUPATIONAL ROLES	0.00	0.00
FEMALES IN STERO. OCCUPATIONAL ROLES	0.00	0.00
TOTAL MALES IN OCCUPATIONAL ROLES	0.00	0.00
TOTAL FEMALES IN OCCUPATIONAL ROLES	0.00	0.00
TOTAL OCCUPATIONS DEPICTED FOR MALES	0.00	0.00
TOTAL OCCUPATIONS DEPICTED FOR FEMALES	0.00	0.00
NUMBER OF FAMOUS MEN	0.00	0.00
NUMBER OF FAMOUS WOMEN	0.00	0.00

FEMALES DRESSED ONLY IN SKIRTS	NA
DEMEANING OR STERO. STATEMENTS	NO
STERO. EMOTIONAL RESPONSES	NO
LANGUAGE EXCLUDING WOMEN	NO
SEPARATE FORMS	NO
SEPARATE NORMS	NO

METROPOLITAN ACHIEVEMENT TESTS - MATH - FORM JI, ADVANCED 1

	MEAN	STANDARD DEVIATION
ILLUSTRATIONS-NUMBER OF MALE ADULTS	•	•
ILLUSTRATIONS-NUMBER OF FEMALE ADULTS	•	•
ILLUSTRATIONS-NUMBER OF MALE CHILDREN	•	•
ILLUSTRATIONS-NUMBER OF FEMALE CHILDREN	•	•
ILLUSTRATIONS-NUMBER OF MALE ANIMALS	•	•
ILLUSTRATIONS-NUMBER OF FEMALE ANIMALS	•	•
CONTENT-NUMBER OF MALE ADULTS	1.33	0.57
CONTENT-NUMBER OF FEMALE ADULTS	2.00	0.00
CONTENT-NUMBER OF MALE CHILDREN	0.00	0.00
CONTENT-NUMBER OF FEMALE CHILDREN	2.00	0.00
CONTENT-NUMBER OF MALE ANIMALS	0.00	0.00
CONTENT-NUMBER OF FEMALE ANIMALS	0.00	0.00
MALES IN STERO. NONOCC. ROLES	0.00	0.00
FEMALES IN STERO. NONOCC. ROLES	0.00	0.00
TOTAL MALES IN NONOCC. ROLES	0.00	0.00
TOTAL FEMALES IN NONOCC. ROLES	0.00	0.00
MALES IN STERO. OCCUPATIONAL ROLES	0.00	0.00
FEMALES IN STERO. OCCUPATIONAL ROLES	0.00	0.00
TOTAL MALES IN OCCUPATIONAL ROLES	0.00	0.00
TOTAL FEMALES IN OCCUPATIONAL ROLES	0.00	0.00
TOTAL OCCUPATIONS DEPICTED FOR MALES	0.00	0.00
TOTAL OCCUPATIONS DEPICTED FOR FEMALES	0.00	0.00
NUMBER OF FAMOUS MEN	0.00	0.00
NUMBER OF FAMOUS WOMEN	0.00	0.00

FEMALES DRESSED ONLY IN SKIRTS	NA
DEMEANING OR STERO. STATEMENTS	NO
STERO. EMOTIONAL RESPONSES	NO
LANGUAGE EXCLUDING WOMEN	NO
SEPARATE FORMS	NO
SEPARATE NORMS	NO

METROPOLITAN READINESS TEST - FORM P, LEVEL I

	MEAN	STANDARD DEVIATION
ILLUSTRATIONS-NUMBER OF MALE ADULTS	4.25	1.50
ILLUSTRATIONS-NUMBER OF FEMALE ADULTS	2.00	0.00
ILLUSTRATIONS-NUMBER OF MALE CHILDREN	17.00	11.34
ILLUSTRATIONS-NUMBER OF FEMALE CHILDREN	15.75	9.53
ILLUSTRATIONS-NUMBER OF MALE ANIMALS	0.00	0.00
ILLUSTRATIONS-NUMBER OF FEMALE ANIMALS	0.00	0.00
CONTENT-NUMBER OF MALE ADULTS	0.25	0.50
CONTENT-NUMBER CF FEMALE ADULTS	0.25	0.50
CONTENT-NUMBER OF MALE CHILDREN	8.00	.
CONTENT-NUMBER OF FEMALE CHILDREN	8.00	.
CONTENT-NUMBER CF MALE ANIMALS	0.00	0.00
CONTENT-NUMBER CF FEMALE ANIMALS	0.00	0.00
MALES IN STERO. NONOCC. ROLES	0.00	0.00
FEMALES IN STERO. NONOCC. ROLES	0.00	0.00
TOTAL MALES IN NONOCC. ROLES	0.00	0.00
TOTAL FEMALES IN NONOCC. ROLES	0.00	0.00
MALES IN STERO. OCCUPATIONAL ROLES	0.00	0.00
FEMALES IN STERO. OCCUPATIONAL ROLES	0.00	0.00
TOTAL MALES IN OCCUPATIONAL ROLES	0.00	0.00
TOTAL FEMALES IN OCCUPATIONAL ROLES	0.00	0.00
TOTAL OCCUPATIONS DEPICTED FOR MALES	0.00	0.00
TOTAL OCCUPATIONS DEPICTED FOR FEMALES	0.00	0.00
NUMBER OF FAMOUS MEN	0.00	0.00
NUMBER OF FAMOUS WOMEN	0.00	0.00

FEMALES DRESSED ONLY IN SKIRTS	YES
DEMEANING OR STERO. STATEMENTS	NO
STERO. EMOTIONAL RESPONSES	NO
LANGUAGE EXCLUDING WOMEN	NO
SEPARATE FORMS	NO
SEPARATE NORMS	NO

METROPOLITAN READINESS TEST - FORM P, LEVEL II

	MEAN	STANDARD DEVIATION
ILLUSTRATIONS-NUMBER OF MALE ADULTS	2.00	0.00
ILLUSTRATIONS-NUMBER OF FEMALE ADULTS	2.00	0.00
ILLUSTRATIONS-NUMBER OF MALE CHILDREN	13.75	9.50
ILLUSTRATIONS-NUMBER OF FEMALE CHILDREN	15.25	8.61
ILLUSTRATIONS-NUMBER OF MALE ANIMALS	1.00	0.00
ILLUSTRATIONS-NUMBER OF FEMALE ANIMALS	1.00	0.00
CONTENT-NUMBER OF MALE ADULTS	1.00	.
CONTENT-NUMBER OF FEMALE ADULTS	3.00	.
CONTENT-NUMBER OF MALE CHILDREN	13.00	.
CONTENT-NUMBER OF FEMALE CHILDREN	11.00	.
CONTENT-NUMBER OF MALE ANIMALS	.	.
CONTENT-NUMBER OF FEMALE ANIMALS	.	.
MALES IN STERO. NONOCC. ROLES	.	.
FEMALES IN STERO. NONOCC. ROLES	.	.
TOTAL MALES IN NONOCC. ROLES	.	.
TOTAL FEMALES IN NONOCC. ROLES	.	.
MALES IN STERO. OCCUPATIONAL ROLES	.	.
FEMALES IN STERO. OCCUPATIONAL ROLES	.	.
TOTAL MALES IN OCCUPATIONAL ROLES	.	.
TOTAL FEMALES IN OCCUPATIONAL ROLES	.	.
TOTAL OCCUPATIONS DEPICTED FOR MALES	.	.
TOTAL OCCUPATIONS DEPICTED FOR FEMALES	.	.
NUMBER OF FAMOUS MEN	.	.
NUMBER OF FAMOUS WOMEN	.	.

FEMALES DRESSED ONLY IN SKIRTS	YES
DEMEANING OR STERO. STATEMENTS	NA
STERO. EMOTIONAL RESPONSES	NO
LANGUAGE EXCLUDING WOMEN	NA
SEPARATE FORMS	NO
SEPARATE NORMS	NO

MINNESOTA MULTIPHASIC PERSONALITY INVENTORY

	MEAN	STANDARD DEVIATION
ILLUSTRATIONS-NUMBER OF MALE ADULTS	•	•
ILLUSTRATIONS-NUMBER OF FEMALE ADULTS	•	•
ILLUSTRATIONS-NUMBER OF MALE CHILDREN	•	•
ILLUSTRATIONS-NUMBER OF FEMALE CHILDREN	•	•
ILLUSTRATIONS-NUMBER OF MALE ANIMALS	•	•
ILLUSTRATIONS-NUMBER OF FEMALE ANIMALS	•	•
CONTENT-NUMBER OF MALE ADULTS	3.5	3.53
CONTENT-NUMBER OF FEMALE ADULTS	3.0	•
CONTENT-NUMBER OF MALE CHILDREN	0.00	0.00
CONTENT-NUMBER OF FEMALE CHILDREN	0.00	0.00
CONTENT-NUMBER OF MALE ANIMALS	0.00	0.00
CONTENT-NUMBER OF FEMALE ANIMALS	0.00	0.00
MALES IN STERO. NONOCC. ROLES	0.00	0.00
FEMALES IN STERO. NONOCC. ROLES	0.00	0.00
TOTAL MALES IN NONOCC. ROLES	0.00	0.00
TOTAL FEMALES IN NONOCC. ROLES	0.00	0.00
MALES IN STERO. OCCUPATIONAL ROLES	0.00	0.00
FEMALES IN STERO. OCCUPATIONAL ROLES	0.00	0.00
TOTAL MALES IN OCCUPATIONAL ROLES	0.00	0.00
TOTAL FEMALES IN OCCUPATIONAL ROLES	0.00	0.00
TOTAL OCCUPATIONS DEPICTED FOR MALES	0.00	•
TOTAL OCCUPATIONS DEPICTED FOR FEMALES	2.00	•
NUMBER OF FAMOUS MEN	3.00	0.00
NUMBER OF FAMOUS WOMEN	0.00	0.00

FEMALES DRESSED ONLY IN SKIRTS	NA
DEMEANING OR STERO. STATEMENTS	NA
STERO. EMOTIONAL RESPONSES	NO
LANGUAGE EXCLUDING WOMEN	YES
SEPARATE FORMS	NO
SEPARATE NORMS	YES

MINNESOTA SCHOLASTIC APTITUDE TEST - FORM A

	MEAN	STANDARD DEVIATION
ILLUSTRATIONS-NUMBER OF MALE ADULTS	.	.
ILLUSTRATIONS-NUMBER OF FEMALE ADULTS	.	.
ILLUSTRATIONS-NUMBER OF MALE CHILDREN	.	.
ILLUSTRATIONS-NUMBER OF FEMALE CHILDREN	.	.
ILLUSTRATIONS-NUMBER OF MALE ANIMALS	.	.
ILLUSTRATIONS-NUMBER OF FEMALE ANIMALS	.	.
CONTENT-NUMBER CF MALE ADULTS	3.50	3.53
CONTENT-NUMBER CF FEMALE ADULTS	3.00	.
CONTENT-NUMBER OF MALE CHILDREN	.	.
CONTENT-NUMBER OF FEMALE CHILDREN	.	.
CONTENT-NUMBER OF MALE ANIMALS	.	.
CONTENT-NUMBER CF FEMALE ANIMALS	.	.
MALES IN STERO. NONOCC. ROLES	.	.
FEMALES IN STERO. NONOCC. ROLES	.	.
TOTAL MALES IN NONOCC. ROLES	.	.
TOTAL FEMALES IN NONOCC. ROLES	.	.
MALES IN STERO. OCCUPATIONAL ROLES	3.00	.
FEMALES IN STERO. OCCUPATIONAL ROLES	.	.
TOTAL MALES IN OCCUPATIONAL ROLES	3.00	.
TOTAL FEMALES IN OCCUPATIONAL ROLES	.	.
TOTAL OCCUPATIONS DEPICTED FOR MALES	4.00	.
TOTAL OCCUPATIONS DEPICTED FOR FEMALES	0.00	.
NUMBER OF FAMOUS MEN	0.00	0.00
NUMBER OF FAMOUS WOMEN	.	.

FEMALES DRESSED ONLY IN SKIRTS   NA

DEMEANING OR STERO. STATEMENTS   NO

STERO. EMOTIONAL RESPONSES   NO

LANGUAGE EXCLUDING WOMEN   NO

SEPARATE FORMS   NO

SEPARATE NORMS   . NO

OHIO STATE UNIVERSITY PSYCHOLOGICAL TEST

	MEAN	STANDARD DEVIATION
ILLUSTRATIONS-NUMBER OF MALE ADULTS	.	.
ILLUSTRATIONS-NUMBER OF FEMALE ADULTS	.	.
ILLUSTRATIONS-NUMBER OF MALE CHILDREN	.	.
ILLUSTRATIONS-NUMBER OF FEMALE CHILDREN	.	.
ILLUSTRATIONS-NUMBER OF MALE ANIMALS	.	.
ILLUSTRATIONS-NUMBER OF FEMALE ANIMALS	.	.
CONTENT-NUMBER OF MALE ADULTS	0.25	0.50
CONTENT-NUMBER CF FEMALE ADULTS	0.00	0.00
CONTENT-NUMBER OF MALE CHILDREN	0.00	0.00
CONTENT-NUMBER OF FEMALE CHILDREN	0.00	0.00
CONTENT-NUMBER OF MALE ANIMALS	0.00	0.00
CONTENT-NUMBER OF FEMALE ANIMALS	0.00	0.00
MALES IN STERO. NONOCC. ROLES	.	.
FEMALES IN STERO. NONOCC. ROLES	.	.
TOTAL MALES IN NONOCC. ROLES	.	.
TOTAL FEMALES IN NONOCC. ROLES	.	.
MALES IN STERO. OCCUPATIONAL ROLES	.	.
FEMALES IN STERO. OCCUPATIONAL ROLES	.	.
TOTAL MALES IN OCCUPATIONAL ROLES	.	.
TOTAL FEMALES IN OCCUPATIONAL ROLES	.	.
TOTAL OCCUPATIONS DEPICTED FOR MALES	0.00	.
TOTAL OCCUPATIONS DEPICTED FOR FEMALES	1.00	.
NUMBER OF FAMOUS MEN	2.00	1.41
NUMBER OF FAMOUS WOMEN	0.00	0.00

FEMALES DRESSED ONLY IN SKIRTS	NA
DEMEANING OR STERO. STATEMENTS	NA
STERO. EMOTIONAL RESPONSES	NA
LANGUAGE EXCLUDING WOMEN	NA
SEPARATE FORMS	NO
SEPARATE NORMS	NO

ORAL READING CRITERION TEST

	MEAN	STANDARD DEVIATION
ILLUSTRATIONS-NUMBER OF MALE ADULTS	.	.
ILLUSTRATIONS-NUMBER OF FEMALE ADULTS	.	.
ILLUSTRATIONS-NUMBER OF MALE CHILDREN	.	.
ILLUSTRATIONS-NUMBER OF FEMALE CHILDREN	.	.
ILLUSTRATIONS-NUMBER OF MALE ANIMALS	.	.
ILLUSTRATIONS-NUMBER OF FEMALE ANIMALS	.	.
CONTENT-NUMBER OF MALE ADULTS	18.50	2.12
CONTENT-NUMBER OF FEMALE ADULTS	10.00	1.41
CONTENT-NUMBER OF MALE CHILDREN	31.00	1.41
CONTENT-NUMBER OF FEMALE CHILDREN	15.00	2.82
CONTENT-NUMBER OF MALE ANIMALS	7.50	0.70
CONTENT-NUMBER OF FEMALE ANIMALS	0.00	0.00
MALES IN STERO. NONOCC. ROLES	4.00	1.41
FEMALES IN STERO. NONOCC. ROLES	1.00	0.00
TOTAL MALES IN NONOCC. ROLES	4.50	0.70
TOTAL FEMALES IN NONOCC. ROLES	1.00	0.00
MALES IN STERO. OCCUPATIONAL ROLES	1.00	0.00
FEMALES IN STERO. OCCUPATIONAL ROLES	0.50	0.70
TOTAL MALES IN OCCUPATIONAL ROLES	0.00	0.00
TOTAL FEMALES IN OCCUPATIONAL ROLES	0.50	0.70
TOTAL OCCUPATIONS DEPICTED FOR MALES	2.00	2.00
TOTAL OCCUPATIONS DEPICTED FOR FEMALES	0.50	0.70
NUMBER OF FAMOUS MEN	2.00	0.00
NUMBER OF FAMOUS WOMEN	0.00	0.00

FEMALES DRESSED ONLY IN SKIRTS	NA
DEMEANING OR STERO. STATEMENTS	YES
STERO. EMOTIONAL RESPONSES	NO
LANGUAGE EXCLUDING WOMEN	YES
SEPARATE FORMS	NO
SEPARATE NORMS	NO

OTIS-LENNON MENTAL ABILITY TEST - FORM J, PRIMARY II LEVEL

	MEAN	STANDARD DEVIATION
ILLUSTRATIONS-NUMBER OF MALE ADULTS	13.75	2.21
ILLUSTRATIONS-NUMBER OF FEMALE ADULTS	1.75	1.50
ILLUSTRATIONS-NUMBER OF MALE CHILDREN	7.25	0.95
ILLUSTRATIONS-NUMBER OF FEMALE CHILDREN	11.25	2.50
ILLUSTRATIONS-NUMBER OF MALE ANIMALS	3.66	0.57
ILLUSTRATIONS-NUMBER OF FEMALE ANIMALS	3.33	0.57
CONTENT-NUMBER OF MALE ADULTS	0.00	0.00
CONTENT-NUMBER OF FEMALE ADULTS	0.00	0.00
CONTENT-NUMBER OF MALE CHILDREN	0.00	0.00
CONTENT-NUMBER OF FEMALE CHILDREN	0.00	0.00
CONTENT-NUMBER OF MALE ANIMALS	0.75	1.50
CONTENT-NUMBER OF FEMALE ANIMALS	0.75	1.50
MALES IN STERO. NONOCC. ROLES	2.66	0.57
FEMALES IN STERO. NONOCC. ROLES	1.66	1.15
TOTAL MALES IN NONOCC. ROLES	2.66	0.57
TOTAL FEMALES IN NONOCC. ROLES	2.66	1.52
MALES IN STERO. OCCUPATIONAL ROLES	10.66	2.08
FEMALES IN STERO. OCCUPATIONAL ROLES	1.00	0.00
TOTAL MALES IN OCCUPATIONAL ROLES	10.66	2.08
TOTAL FEMALES IN OCCUPATIONAL ROLES	1.33	0.57
TOTAL OCCUPATIONS DEPICTED FOR MALES	10.66	2.08
TOTAL OCCUPATIONS DEPICTED FOR FEMALES	1.00	0.00
NUMBER OF FAMOUS MEN	0.00	0.00
NUMBER OF FAMOUS WOMEN	0.00	0.00

FEMALES DRESSED ONLY IN SKIRTS	YES
DEMEANING OR STERO. STATEMENTS	NO
STERO. EMOTIONAL RESPONSES	NO
LANGUAGE EXCLUDING WOMEN	NO
SEPARATE FORMS	NO
SEPARATE NORMS	NO

PEABODY INDIVIDUAL ACHIEVEMENT TEST - VOL I

	MEAN	STANDARD DEVIATION
ILLUSTRATIONS-NUMBER OF MALE ADULTS	0.00	0.00
ILLUSTRATIONS-NUMBER OF FEMALE ADULTS	0.00	0.00
ILLUSTRATIONS-NUMBER OF MALE CHILDREN	0.00	.
ILLUSTRATIONS-NUMBER OF FEMALE CHILDREN	2.00	.
ILLUSTRATIONS-NUMBER OF MALE ANIMALS	0.00	0.00
ILLUSTRATIONS-NUMBER OF FEMALE ANIMALS	0.00	0.00
CONTENT-NUMBER OF MALE ADULTS	4.00	0.00
CONTENT-NUMBER OF FEMALE ADULTS	5.00	0.00
CONTENT-NUMBER OF MALE CHILDREN	8.33	1.15
CONTENT-NUMBER OF FEMALE CHILDREN	5.00	1.73
CONTENT-NUMBER OF MALE ANIMALS	0.00	0.00
CONTENT-NUMBER OF FEMALE ANIMALS	0.00	0.00
MALES IN STERO. NONOCC. ROLES	.	.
FEMALES IN STERO. NONOCC. ROLES	.	.
TOTAL MALES IN NONOCC. ROLES	.	.
TOTAL FEMALES IN NONOCC. ROLES	.	.
MALES IN STERO. OCCUPATIONAL ROLES	1.00	.
FEMALES IN STERO. OCCUPATIONAL ROLES	2.00	.
TOTAL MALES IN OCCUPATIONAL ROLES	1.00	.
TOTAL FEMALES IN OCCUPATIONAL ROLES	2.00	.
TOTAL OCCUPATIONS DEPICTED FOR MALES	1.00	0.00
TOTAL OCCUPATIONS DEPICTED FOR FEMALES	0.33	0.57
NUMBER OF FAMOUS MEN	0.00	0.00
NUMBER OF FAMOUS WOMEN	0.00	0.00

FEMALES DRESSED ONLY IN SKIRTS	NA
DEMEANING OR STERO. STATEMENTS	NO
STERO. EMOTIONAL RESPONSES	NO
LANGUAGE EXCLUDING WOMEN	NA
SEPARATE FORMS	YES
SEPARATE NORMS	YES

PEABODY INDIVIDUAL ACHIEVEMENT TEST - VOL. II

	MEAN	STANDARD DEVIATION
ILLUSTRATIONS-NUMBER OF MALE ADULTS	89.00	32.28
ILLUSTRATIONS-NUMBER OF FEMALE ADULTS	31.75	12.14
ILLUSTRATIONS-NUMBER OF MALE CHILDREN	13.33	0.57
ILLUSTRATIONS-NUMBER OF FEMALE CHILDREN	12.66	1.15
ILLUSTRATIONS-NUMBER OF MALE ANIMALS	0.00	0.00
ILLUSTRATIONS-NUMBER OF FEMALE ANIMALS	0.00	0.00
CONTENT-NUMBER OF MALE ADULTS	18.25	6.39
CONTENT-NUMBER OF FEMALE ADULTS	6.25	0.50
CONTENT-NUMBER OF MALE CHILDREN	1.50	0.57
CONTENT-NUMBER OF FEMALE CHILDREN	2.25	0.50
CONTENT-NUMBER OF MALE ANIMALS	0.00	0.00
CONTENT-NUMBER OF FEMALE ANIMALS	0.00	0.00
MALES IN STERO. NONOCC. ROLES	6.00	1.41
FEMALES IN STERO. NONOCC. ROLES	3.00	1.41
TOTAL MALES IN NONOCC. ROLES	6.00	1.41
TOTAL FEMALES IN NONOCC. ROLES	4.00	1.41
MALES IN STERO. OCCUPATIONAL ROLES	10.00	9.53
FEMALES IN STERO. OCCUPATIONAL ROLES	1.00	1.41
TOTAL MALES IN OCCUPATIONAL ROLES	11.00	9.53
TOTAL FEMALES IN OCCUPATIONAL ROLES	2.00	1.41
TOTAL OCCUPATIONS DEPICTED FOR MALES	16.66	4.93
TOTAL OCCUPATIONS DEPICTED FOR FEMALES	2.00	1.00
NUMBER OF FAMOUS MEN	4.50	2.64
NUMBER OF FAMOUS WOMEN	0.25	0.50

FEMALES DRESSED ONLY IN SKIRTS	NO
DEMEANING OR STERO. STATEMENTS	NO
STERO. EMOTIONAL RESPONSES	NO
LANGUAGE EXCLUDING WOMEN	YES
SEPARATE FORMS	NO
SEPARATE NORMS	NO

PEABODY PICTURE VOCABULARY TEST

	MEAN	STANDARD DEVIATION
ILLUSTRATIONS-NUMBER OF MALE ADULTS	123.75	9.17
ILLUSTRATIONS-NUMBER OF FEMALE ADULTS	41.50	4.79
ILLUSTRATIONS-NUMBER OF MALE CHILDREN	44.00	2.16
ILLUSTRATIONS-NUMBER OF FEMALE CHILDREN	42.75	3.59
ILLUSTRATIONS-NUMBER OF MALE ANIMALS	0.50	1.00
ILLUSTRATIONS-NUMBER OF FEMALE ANIMALS	2.00	4.00
CONTENT-NUMBER OF MALE ADULTS	2.00	.
CONTENT-NUMBER OF FEMALE ADULTS	.	.
CONTENT-NUMBER OF MALE CHILDREN	.	.
CONTENT-NUMBER OF FEMALE CHILDREN	.	.
CONTENT-NUMBER OF MALE ANIMALS	.	.
CONTENT-NUMBER OF FEMALE ANIMALS	.	.
MALES IN STERO. NONOCC. ROLES	13.50	18.44
FEMALES IN STERO. NONOCC. ROLES	9.50	3.69
TOTAL MALES IN NONOCC. ROLES	15.25	17.91
TOTAL FEMALES IN NONOCC. ROLES	11.25	2.75
MALES IN STERO. OCCUPATIONAL ROLES	31.00	23.38
FEMALES IN STERO. OCCUPATIONAL ROLES	6.66	4.93
TOTAL MALES IN OCCUPATIONAL ROLES	31.33	23.09
TOTAL FEMALES IN OCCUPATIONAL ROLES	7.33	5.50
TOTAL OCCUPATIONS DEPICTED FOR MALES	22.50	6.36
TOTAL OCCUPATIONS DEPICTED FOR FEMALES	6.50	3.53
NUMBER OF FAMOUS MEN	0.00	0.00
NUMBER OF FAMOUS WOMEN	0.25	0.50

FEMALES DRESSED ONLY IN SKIRTS	YES
DEMEANING OR STERO. STATEMENTS	NO
STERO. EMOTIONAL RESPONSES	NO
LANGUAGE EXCLUDING WOMEN	NA
SEPARATE FORMS	NO
SEPARATE NORMS	NO

PERSONAL ORIENTATION INVENTORY

	MEAN	STANDARD DEVIATION
ILLUSTRATIONS-NUMBER OF MALE ADULTS	.	.
ILLUSTRATIONS-NUMBER OF FEMALE ADULTS	.	.
ILLUSTRATIONS-NUMBER OF MALE CHILDREN	.	.
ILLUSTRATIONS-NUMBER OF FEMALE CHILDREN	.	.
ILLUSTRATIONS-NUMBER OF MALE ANIMALS	.	.
ILLUSTRATIONS-NUMBER OF FEMALE ANIMALS	.	.
CONTENT-NUMBER OF MALE ADULTS	6.00	0.00
CONTENT-NUMBER OF FEMALE ADULTS	3.00	0.00
CONTENT-NUMBER OF MALE CHILDREN	0.00	0.00
CONTENT-NUMBER OF FEMALE CHILDREN	0.00	0.00
CONTENT-NUMBER OF MALE ANIMALS	0.00	0.00
CONTENT-NUMBER OF FEMALE ANIMALS	0.00	0.00
MALES IN STERO. NONOCC. ROLES	0.00	0.00
FEMALES IN STERO. NONOCC. ROLES	0.00	0.00
TOTAL MALES IN NONOCC. ROLES	0.00	0.00
TOTAL FEMALES IN NONOCC. ROLES	0.00	0.00
MALES IN STERO. OCCUPATIONAL ROLES	0.00	0.00
FEMALES IN STERO. OCCUPATIONAL ROLES	0.00	0.00
TOTAL MALES IN OCCUPATIONAL ROLES	0.00	0.00
TOTAL FEMALES IN OCCUPATIONAL ROLES	0.00	0.00
TOTAL OCCUPATIONS DEPICTED FOR MALES	0.00	0.00
TOTAL OCCUPATIONS DEPICTED FOR FEMALES	0.00	0.00
NUMBER OF FAMOUS MEN	0.00	0.00
NUMBER OF FAMOUS WOMEN	0.00	0.00

FEMALES DRESSED ONLY IN SKIRTS	NA
DEMEANING OR STERO. STATEMENTS	NO
STERO. EMOTIONAL RESPONSES	NO
LANGUAGE EXCLUDING WOMEN	NO
SEPARATE FORMS	NO
SEPARATE NORMS	NO

PERSONAL VALUES ABSTRACT

	MEAN	STANDARD DEVIATION
ILLUSTRATIONS-NUMBER OF MALE ADULTS	.	.
ILLUSTRATIONS-NUMBER OF FEMALE ADULTS	.	.
ILLUSTRATIONS-NUMBER OF MALE CHILDREN	.	.
ILLUSTRATIONS-NUMBER OF FEMALE CHILDREN	.	.
ILLUSTRATIONS-NUMBER OF MALE ANIMALS	.	.
ILLUSTRATIONS-NUMBER OF FEMALE ANIMALS	.	.
CONTENT-NUMBER OF MALE ADULTS	.	.
CONTENT-NUMBER OF FEMALE ADULTS	.	.
CONTENT-NUMBER OF MALE CHILDREN	.	.
CONTENT-NUMBER OF FEMALE CHILDREN	.	.
CONTENT-NUMBER OF MALE ANIMALS	.	.
CONTENT-NUMBER OF FEMALE ANIMALS	.	.
MALES IN STERO. NONOCC. ROLES	.	.
FEMALES IN STERO. NONOCC. ROLES	.	.
TOTAL MALES IN NONOCC. ROLES	.	.
TOTAL FEMALES IN NONOCC. ROLES	.	.
MALES IN STERO. OCCUPATIONAL ROLES	.	.
FEMALES IN STERO. OCCUPATIONAL ROLES	.	.
TOTAL MALES IN OCCUPATIONAL ROLES	.	.
TOTAL FEMALES IN OCCUPATIONAL ROLES	.	.
TOTAL OCCUPATIONS DEPICTED FOR MALES	.	.
TOTAL OCCUPATIONS DEPICTED FOR FEMALES	.	.
NUMBER OF FAMOUS MEN	.	.
NUMBER OF FAMOUS WOMEN	.	.

FEMALES DRESSED ONLY IN SKIRTS   NA

DEMEANING OR STERO. STATEMENTS   YES

STERO. EMOTIONAL RESPONSES   NO

LANGUAGE EXCLUDING WOMEN   YES

SEPARATE FORMS   NO

SEPARATE NORMS   YES

PICTURE STORY LANGUAGE TEST

	MEAN	STANDARD DEVIATION
ILLUSTRATIONS-NUMBER OF MALE ADULTS	0.66	0.57
ILLUSTRATIONS-NUMBER OF FEMALE ADULTS	0.66	0.57
ILLUSTRATIONS-NUMBER OF MALE CHILDREN	2.00	0.00
ILLUSTRATIONS-NUMBER OF FEMALE CHILDREN	1.00	0.00
ILLUSTRATIONS-NUMBER OF MALE ANIMALS	0.00	0.00
ILLUSTRATIONS-NUMBER OF FEMALE ANIMALS	0.00	0.00
CONTENT-NUMBER OF MALE ADULTS	.	.
CONTENT-NUMBER OF FEMALE ADULTS	.	.
CONTENT-NUMBER OF MALE CHILDREN	.	.
CONTENT-NUMBER OF FEMALE CHILDREN	.	.
CONTENT-NUMBER OF MALE ANIMALS	.	.
CONTENT-NUMBER OF FEMALE ANIMALS	.	.
MALES IN STERO. NONOCC. ROLES	0.00	0.00
FEMALES IN STERO. NONOCC. ROLES	1.00	1.00
TOTAL MALES IN NONOCC. ROLES	1.33	1.15
TOTAL FEMALES IN NONOCC. ROLES	1.00	1.00
MALES IN STERO. OCCUPATIONAL ROLES	0.00	0.00
FEMALES IN STERO. OCCUPATIONAL ROLES	0.00	0.00
TOTAL MALES IN OCCUPATIONAL ROLES	0.00	0.00
TOTAL FEMALES IN OCCUPATIONAL ROLES	0.00	0.00
TOTAL OCCUPATIONS DEPICTED FOR MALES	0.00	0.00
TOTAL OCCUPATIONS DEPICTED FOR FEMALES	0.00	0.00
NUMBER OF FAMOUS MEN	0.00	0.00
NUMBER OF FAMOUS WOMEN	0.00	0.00

FEMALES DRESSED ONLY IN SKIRTS	YES
DEMEANING OR STERO. STATEMENTS	NO
STERO. EMOTIONAL RESPONSES	NO
LANGUAGE EXCLUDING WOMEN	NO
SEPARATE FORMS	NO
SEPARATE NORMS	NO

PINTNER-CUNNINGHAM PRIMARY TEST - FORM A

	MEAN	STANDARD DEVIATION
ILLUSTRATIONS-NUMBER OF MALE ADULTS	2.50	1.73
ILLUSTRATIONS-NUMBER OF FEMALE ADULTS	0.00	0.00
ILLUSTRATIONS-NUMBER OF MALE CHILDREN	7.75	2.50
ILLUSTRATIONS-NUMBER OF FEMALE CHILDREN	14.00	6.68
ILLUSTRATIONS-NUMBER OF MALE ANIMALS	0.00	0.00
ILLUSTRATIONS-NUMBER OF FEMALE ANIMALS	0.00	0.00
CONTENT-NUMBER OF MALE ADULTS	1.25	0.50
CONTENT-NUMBER OF FEMALE ADULTS	1.00	0.00
CONTENT-NUMBER OF MALE CHILDREN	2.75	1.70
CONTENT-NUMBER OF FEMALE CHILDREN	3.00	1.41
CONTENT-NUMBER OF MALE ANIMALS	0.00	0.00
CONTENT-NUMBER OF FEMALE ANIMALS	0.00	0.00
MALES IN STERO. NONOCC. ROLES	2.00	1.82
FEMALES IN STERO. NONOCC. ROLES	3.33	1.15
TOTAL MALES IN NONOCC. ROLES	3.00	0.81
TOTAL FEMALES IN NONOCC. ROLES	3.00	1.41
MALES IN STERO. OCCUPATIONAL ROLES	1.00	0.00
FEMALES IN STERO. OCCUPATIONAL ROLES	0.00	0.00
TOTAL MALES IN OCCUPATIONAL ROLES	1.00	0.00
TOTAL FEMALES IN OCCUPATIONAL ROLES	0.00	0.00
TOTAL OCCUPATIONS DEPICTED FOR MALES	1.00	0.00
TOTAL OCCUPATIONS DEPICTED FOR FEMALES	0.00	0.00
NUMBER OF FAMOUS MEN	0.00	0.00
NUMBER OF FAMOUS WOMEN	0.00	0.00

FEMALES DRESSED ONLY IN SKIRTS	YES
DEMEANING OR STERO. STATEMENTS	NO
STERO. EMOTIONAL RESPONSES	NO
LANGUAGE EXCLUDING WOMEN	NA
SEPARATE FORMS	NO
SEPARATE NORMS	NO

PRE-ASSESSMENT TESTS   POST-ASSESSMENT TESTS - LEVEL 1

	MEAN	STANDARD DEVIATION
ILLUSTRATIONS-NUMBER OF MALE ADULTS	2.00	1.00
ILLUSTRATIONS-NUMBER OF FEMALE ADULTS	2.66	0.57
ILLUSTRATIONS-NUMBER OF MALE CHILDREN	22.00	10.44
ILLUSTRATIONS-NUMBER OF FEMALE CHILDREN	21.33	15.37
ILLUSTRATIONS-NUMBER OF MALE ANIMALS	0.00	0.00
ILLUSTRATIONS-NUMBER OF FEMALE ANIMALS	0.00	0.00
CONTENT-NUMBER OF MALE ADULTS	3.66	2.88
CONTENT-NUMBER OF FEMALE ADULTS	1.66	1.15
CONTENT-NUMBER OF MALE CHILDREN	5.33	1.52
CONTENT-NUMBER OF FEMALE CHILDREN	1.66	1.15
CONTENT-NUMBER OF MALE ANIMALS	0.00	0.00
CONTENT-NUMBER OF FEMALE ANIMALS	0.00	0.00
MALES IN STERO. NONOCC. ROLES	3.00	3.00
FEMALES IN STERO. NONOCC. ROLES	0.00	0.00
TOTAL MALES IN NONOCC. ROLES	7.00	4.35
TOTAL FEMALES IN NONOCC. ROLES	7.33	4.93
MALES IN STERO. OCCUPATIONAL ROLES	0.00	0.00
FEMALES IN STERO. OCCUPATIONAL ROLES	0.00	0.00
TOTAL MALES IN OCCUPATIONAL ROLES	0.00	0.00
TOTAL FEMALES IN OCCUPATIONAL ROLES	0.00	0.00
TOTAL OCCUPATIONS DEPICTED FOR MALES	0.00	0.00
TOTAL OCCUPATIONS DEPICTED FOR FEMALES	0.00	0.00
NUMBER OF FAMOUS MEN	0.00	0.00
NUMBER OF FAMOUS WOMEN	0.00	0.00

FEMALES DRESSED ONLY IN SKIRTS	NO
DEMEANING OR STERO. STATEMENTS	NO
STERO. EMOTIONAL RESPONSES	NO
LANGUAGE EXCLUDING WOMEN	NO
SEPARATE FORMS	NO
SEPARATE NORMS	NO

PRE-ASSESSMENT TESTS   POST ASSESSMENT TESTS - LEVEL 2

	MEAN	STANDARD DEVIATION
ILLUSTRATIONS-NUMBER OF MALE ADULTS	11.00	3.60
ILLUSTRATIONS-NUMBER OF FEMALE ADULTS	5.66	2.51
ILLUSTRATIONS-NUMBER OF MALE CHILDREN	16.00	6.00
ILLUSTRATIONS-NUMBER OF FEMALE CHILDREN	18.33	5.50
ILLUSTRATIONS-NUMBER OF MALE ANIMALS	0.00	0.00
ILLUSTRATIONS-NUMBER OF FEMALE ANIMALS	0.00	0.00
CONTENT-NUMBER OF MALE ADULTS	3.33	1.15
CONTENT-NUMBER OF FEMALE ADULTS	1.00	.
CONTENT-NUMBER OF MALE CHILDREN	1.33	0.57
CONTENT-NUMBER OF FEMALE CHILDREN	4.33	0.57
CONTENT-NUMBER OF MALE ANIMALS	0.00	0.00
CONTENT-NUMBER OF FEMALE ANIMALS	0.00	0.00
MALES IN STERO. NONOCC. ROLES	0.66	0.57
FEMALES IN STERO. NONOCC. ROLES	0.00	0.00
TOTAL MALES IN NONOCC. ROLES	4.33	2.30
TOTAL FEMALES IN NONOCC. ROLES	1.66	2.08
MALES IN STERO. OCCUPATIONAL ROLES	0.66	0.57
FEMALES IN STERO. OCCUPATIONAL ROLES	0.00	0.00
TOTAL MALES IN OCCUPATIONAL ROLES	0.66	0.57
TOTAL FEMALES IN OCCUPATIONAL ROLES	0.00	0.00
TOTAL OCCUPATIONS DEPICTED FOR MALES	0.33	0.57
TOTAL OCCUPATIONS DEPICTED FOR FEMALES	0.00	0.00
NUMBER OF FAMOUS MEN	0.00	0.00
NUMBER OF FAMOUS WOMEN	0.00	0.00

FEMALES DRESSED ONLY IN SKIRTS	NO
DEMEANING OR STERO. STATEMENTS	NO
STERO. EMOTIONAL RESPONSES	NO
LANGUAGE EXCLUDING WOMEN	NO
SEPARATE FORMS	NO
SEPARATE NORMS	NO

PRE-ASSESSMENT TESTS - POST ASSESSMENT TESTS - LEVEL 3

	MEAN	STANDARD DEVIATION
ILLUSTRATIONS-NUMBER OF MALE ADULTS	11.00	3.60
ILLUSTRATIONS-NUMBER OF FEMALE ADULTS	3.33	1.15
ILLUSTRATIONS-NUMBER OF MALE CHILDREN	25.33	11.23
ILLUSTRATIONS-NUMBER OF FEMALE CHILDREN	16.00	4.00
ILLUSTRATIONS-NUMBER OF MALE ANIMALS	0.00	0.00
ILLUSTRATIONS-NUMBER OF FEMALE ANIMALS	0.00	0.00
CONTENT-NUMBER OF MALE ADULTS	1.66	0.57
CONTENT-NUMBER OF FEMALE ADULTS	0.00	0.00
CONTENT-NUMBER OF MALE CHILDREN	6.00	6.08
CONTENT-NUMBER OF FEMALE CHILDREN	4.00	2.64
CONTENT-NUMBER OF MALE ANIMALS	0.00	0.00
CONTENT-NUMBER OF FEMALE ANIMALS	0.00	0.00
MALES IN STERO. NONOCC. ROLES	3.33	1.52
FEMALES IN STERO. NONOCC. ROLES	0.33	0.57
TOTAL MALES IN NONOCC. ROLES	6.66	1.15
TOTAL FEMALES IN NONOCC. ROLES	4.66	2.51
MALES IN STERO. OCCUPATIONAL ROLES	0.50	0.70
FEMALES IN STERO. OCCUPATIONAL ROLES	0.66	1.15
TOTAL MALES IN OCCUPATIONAL ROLES	0.50	0.70
TOTAL FEMALES IN OCCUPATIONAL ROLES	1.00	1.00
TOTAL OCCUPATIONS DEPICTED FOR MALES	0.00	0.00
TOTAL OCCUPATIONS DEPICTED FOR FEMALES	0.00	0.00
NUMBER OF FAMOUS MEN	0.00	0.00
NUMBER OF FAMOUS WOMEN	0.00	0.00

FEMALES DRESSED ONLY IN SKIRTS	NO
DEMEANING OR STERO. STATEMENTS	NO
STERO. EMOTIONAL RESPONSES	NO
LANGUAGE EXCLUDING WOMEN	NO
SEPARATE FORMS	NO
SEPARATE NORMS	NO

PRE-READING SCREENING PROCEDURES

	MEAN	STANDARD DEVIATION
ILLUSTRATIONS-NUMBER OF MALE ADULTS	0.25	0.50
ILLUSTRATIONS-NUMBER OF FEMALE ADULTS	1.25	0.95
ILLUSTRATIONS-NUMBER OF MALE CHILDREN	7.33	2.51
ILLUSTRATIONS-NUMBER OF FEMALE CHILDREN	3.75	0.95
ILLUSTRATIONS-NUMBER OF MALE ANIMALS	0.00	0.00
ILLUSTRATIONS-NUMBER OF FEMALE ANIMALS	0.00	0.00
CONTENT-NUMBER OF MALE ADULTS	0.75	0.50
CONTENT-NUMBER OF FEMALE ADULTS	1.50	1.29
CONTENT-NUMBER OF MALE CHILDREN	1.75	2.87
CONTENT-NUMBER OF FEMALE CHILDREN	2.00	2.64
CONTENT-NUMBER CF MALE ANIMALS	0.00	0.00
CONTENT-NUMBER CF FEMALE ANIMALS	0.50	0.57
MALES IN STERO. NONOCC. ROLES	0.75	0.95
FEMALES IN STERO. NONOCC. ROLES	0.50	0.57
TOTAL MALES IN NONOCC. ROLES	0.75	0.95
TOTAL FEMALES IN NONOCC. ROLES	1.00	1.41
MALES IN STERO. OCCUPATIONAL ROLES	0.00	0.00
FEMALES IN STERO. OCCUPATIONAL ROLES	0.00	0.00
TOTAL MALES IN OCCUPATIONAL ROLES	0.00	0.00
TOTAL FEMALES IN OCCUPATIONAL ROLES	0.00	0.00
TOTAL OCCUPATIONS DEPICTED FOR MALES	0.00	0.00
TOTAL OCCUPATIONS DEPICTED FOR FEMALES	0.00	0.00
NUMBER OF FAMOUS MEN	0.00	0.00
NUMBER OF FAMOUS WOMEN	0.00	0.00

FEMALES DRESSED ONLY IN SKIRTS	YES
DEMEANING OR STERO. STATEMENTS	NO
STERO. EMOTIONAL RESPONSES	NO
LANGUAGE EXCLUDING WOMEN	NO
SEPARATE FORMS	NO
SEPARATE NORMS	NO

PRESCRIPTIVE READING INVENTORY - LEVEL A

	MEAN	STANDARD DEVIATION
ILLUSTRATIONS-NUMBER OF MALE ADULTS	0.00	0.00
ILLUSTRATIONS-NUMBER OF FEMALE ADULTS	0.00	0.00
ILLUSTRATIONS-NUMBER OF MALE CHILDREN	0.75	0.50
ILLUSTRATIONS-NUMBER OF FEMALE CHILDREN	0.00	0.00
ILLUSTRATIONS-NUMBER OF MALE ANIMALS	0.00	0.00
ILLUSTRATIONS-NUMBER OF FEMALE ANIMALS	0.75	0.50
CONTENT-NUMBER OF MALE ADULTS	3.50	0.57
CONTENT-NUMBER OF FEMALE ADULTS	2.50	1.29
CONTENT-NUMBER OF MALE CHILDREN	12.75	4.71
CONTENT-NUMBER OF FEMALE CHILDREN	3.50	1.91
CONTENT-NUMBER OF MALE ANIMALS	1.75	0.95
CONTENT-NUMBER OF FEMALE ANIMALS	2.00	1.15
MALES IN STERO. NONOCC. ROLES	0.50	0.57
FEMALES IN STERO. NONOCC. ROLES	0.00	0.00
TOTAL MALES IN NONOCC. ROLES	0.75	0.95
TOTAL FEMALES IN NONOCC. ROLES	0.25	0.50
MALES IN STERO. OCCUPATIONAL ROLES	0.00	0.00
FEMALES IN STERO. OCCUPATIONAL ROLES	0.00	0.00
TOTAL MALES IN OCCUPATIONAL ROLES	0.00	0.00
TOTAL FEMALES IN OCCUPATIONAL ROLES	0.00	0.00
TOTAL OCCUPATIONS DEPICTED FOR MALES	0.00	0.00
TOTAL OCCUPATIONS DEPICTED FOR FEMALES	0.00	0.00
NUMBER OF FAMOUS MEN	0.00	0.00
NUMBER OF FAMOUS WOMEN	0.00	0.00

FEMALES DRESSED ONLY IN SKIRTS	NO
DEMEANING OR STERO. STATEMENTS	NA
STERO. EMOTIONAL RESPONSES	NO
LANGUAGE EXCLUDING WOMEN	YES
SEPARATE FORMS	NO
SEPARATE NORMS	NO

PRESCRIPTIVE READING INVENTORY - LEVEL B

	MEAN	STANDARD DEVIATION
ILLUSTRATIONS-NUMBER OF MALE ADULTS	0.00	0.00
ILLUSTRATIONS-NUMBER OF FEMALE ADULTS	0.00	0.00
ILLUSTRATIONS-NUMBER OF MALE CHILDREN	2.75	0.50
ILLUSTRATIONS-NUMBER OF FEMALE CHILDREN	6.00	5.77
ILLUSTRATIONS-NUMBER OF MALE ANIMALS	0.00	0.00
ILLUSTRATIONS-NUMBER OF FEMALE ANIMALS	0.00	0.00
CONTENT-NUMBER OF MALE ADULTS	5.50	0.57
CONTENT-NUMBER OF FEMALE ADULTS	5.00	0.00
CONTENT-NUMBER OF MALE CHILDREN	10.50	3.51
CONTENT-NUMBER OF FEMALE CHILDREN	4.25	1.50
CONTENT-NUMBER OF MALE ANIMALS	4.25	2.62
CONTENT-NUMBER OF FEMALE ANIMALS	1.00	0.00
MALES IN STERO. NONOCC. ROLES	1.50	3.00
FEMALES IN STERO. NONOCC. ROLES	0.25	0.50
TOTAL MALES IN NONOCC. ROLES	2.00	4.00
TOTAL FEMALES IN NONOCC. ROLES	0.25	0.50
MALES IN STERO. OCCUPATIONAL ROLES	0.25	0.50
FEMALES IN STERO. OCCUPATIONAL ROLES	0.00	0.00
TOTAL MALES IN OCCUPATIONAL ROLES	0.25	0.50
TOTAL FEMALES IN OCCUPATIONAL ROLES	0.00	0.00
TOTAL OCCUPATIONS DEPICTED FOR MALES	0.25	0.50
TOTAL OCCUPATIONS DEPICTED FOR FEMALES	0.00	0.00
NUMBER OF FAMOUS MEN	0.00	0.00
NUMBER OF FAMOUS WOMEN	0.00	0.00

FEMALES DRESSED ONLY IN SKIRTS	YES
DEMEANING OR STERO. STATEMENTS	NO
STERO. EMOTIONAL RESPONSES	NO
LANGUAGE EXCLUDING WOMEN	NO
SEPARATE FORMS	NO
SEPARATE NORMS	NO

PRESCRIPTIVE READING INVENTORY - LEVEL C

	MEAN	STANDARD DEVIATION
ILLUSTRATIONS-NUMBER OF MALE ADULTS	0.75	0.95
ILLUSTRATIONS-NUMBER OF FEMALE ADULTS	0.00	0.00
ILLUSTRATIONS-NUMBER OF MALE CHILDREN	0.50	0.57
ILLUSTRATIONS-NUMBER OF FEMALE CHILDREN	0.00	0.00
ILLUSTRATIONS-NUMBER OF MALE ANIMALS	0.00	0.00
ILLUSTRATIONS-NUMBER OF FEMALE ANIMALS	0.00	0.00
CONTENT-NUMBER OF MALE ADULTS	6.25	0.50
CONTENT-NUMBER OF FEMALE ADULTS	2.75	0.50
CONTENT-NUMBER OF MALE CHILDREN	7.00	2.30
CONTENT-NUMBER OF FEMALE CHILDREN	2.25	0.50
CONTENT-NUMBER OF MALE ANIMALS	2.66	1.52
CONTENT-NUMBER OF FEMALE ANIMALS	0.00	0.00
MALES IN STERO. NONOCC. ROLES	1.00	2.00
FEMALES IN STERC. NONOCC. ROLES	0.25	0.50
TOTAL MALES IN NONOCC. ROLES	1.25	2.50
TOTAL FEMALES IN NONOCC. ROLES	0.25	0.50
MALES IN STERC. OCCUPATIONAL ROLES	1.00	.
FEMALES IN STERC. OCCUPATIONAL ROLES	0.25	0.50
TOTAL MALES IN OCCUPATIONAL ROLES	1.00	.
TOTAL FEMALES IN OCCUPATIONAL ROLES	0.50	0.57
TOTAL OCCUPATIONS DEPICTED FOR MALES	0.25	0.50
TOTAL OCCUPATIONS DEPICTED FOR FEMALES	0.75	0.50
NUMBER OF FAMCUS MEN	0.00	0.00
NUMBER OF FAMOUS WOMEN	0.00	0.00

FEMALES DRESSED ONLY IN SKIRTS	NO
DEMEANING OR STERO. STATEMENTS	NO
STERO. EMOTIONAL RESPONSES	NO
LANGUAGE EXCLUDING WOMEN	YES
SEPARATE FORMS	NO
SEPARATE NORMS	NO

PRESCRIPTIVE READING INVENTORY - LEVEL D

	MEAN	STANDARD DEVIATION
ILLUSTRATIONS-NUMBER OF MALE ADULTS	4.00	0.00
ILLUSTRATIONS-NUMBER OF FEMALE ADULTS	3.00	0.00
ILLUSTRATIONS-NUMBER OF MALE CHILDREN	3.00	0.00
ILLUSTRATIONS-NUMBER OF FEMALE CHILDREN	0.00	0.00
ILLUSTRATIONS-NUMBER OF MALE ANIMALS	0.00	0.00
ILLUSTRATIONS-NUMBER OF FEMALE ANIMALS	0.00	0.00
CONTENT-NUMBER OF MALE ADULTS	6.50	3.78
CONTENT-NUMBER OF FEMALE ADULTS	4.50	1.00
CONTENT-NUMBER OF MALE CHILDREN	6.00	1.63
CONTENT-NUMBER OF FEMALE CHILDREN	6.00	1.41
CONTENT-NUMBER OF MALE ANIMALS	0.50	0.57
CONTENT-NUMBER OF FEMALE ANIMALS	0.00	0.00
MALES IN STERO. NONOCC. ROLES	0.50	1.00
FEMALES IN STERO. NONOCC. ROLES	0.00	0.00
TOTAL MALES IN NONOCC. ROLES	0.75	1.50
TOTAL FEMALES IN NONOCC. ROLES	0.25	0.50
MALES IN STERO. OCCUPATIONAL ROLES	0.75	1.50
FEMALES IN STERO. OCCUPATIONAL ROLES	0.00	0.00
TOTAL MALES IN OCCUPATIONAL ROLES	0.75	1.50
TOTAL FEMALES IN OCCUPATIONAL ROLES	0.00	0.00
TOTAL OCCUPATIONS DEPICTED FOR MALES	0.75	1.50
TOTAL OCCUPATIONS DEPICTED FOR FEMALES	0.00	0.00
NUMBER OF FAMOUS MEN	0.00	0.00
NUMBER OF FAMOUS WOMEN	0.00	0.00

FEMALES DRESSED ONLY IN SKIRTS	YES
DEMEANING OR STERO. STATEMENTS	NO
STERO. EMOTIONAL RESPONSES	NO
LANGUAGE EXCLUDING WOMEN	NO
SEPARATE FORMS	NO
SEPARATE NORMS	NO

PRESCRIPTIVE READING INVENTORY - LEVEL I

	MEAN	STANDARD DEVIATION
ILLUSTRATIONS-NUMBER OF MALE ADULTS	1.00	0.00
ILLUSTRATIONS-NUMBER OF FEMALE ADULTS	5.00	2.82
ILLUSTRATIONS-NUMBER OF MALE CHILDREN	24.25	18.75
ILLUSTRATIONS-NUMBER OF FEMALE CHILDREN	19.25	12.65
ILLUSTRATIONS-NUMBER OF MALE ANIMALS	0.00	0.00
ILLUSTRATIONS-NUMBER OF FEMALE ANIMALS	0.00	0.00
CONTENT-NUMBER OF MALE ADULTS	0.75	0.50
CONTENT-NUMBER OF FEMALE ADULTS	1.25	0.95
CONTENT-NUMBER OF MALE CHILDREN	3.50	0.70
CONTENT-NUMBER OF FEMALE CHILDREN	2.50	1.91
CONTENT-NUMBER OF MALE ANIMALS	0.25	0.50
CONTENT-NUMBER OF FEMALE ANIMALS	0.00	0.00
MALES IN STERO. NONOCC. ROLES	1.50	1.73
FEMALES IN STERO. NONOCC. ROLES	0.00	0.00
TOTAL MALES IN NONOCC. ROLES	1.75	1.50
TOTAL FEMALES IN NONOCC. ROLES	2.25	2.06
MALES IN STERO. OCCUPATIONAL ROLES	0.00	0.00
FEMALES IN STERO. OCCUPATIONAL ROLES	0.00	0.00
TOTAL MALES IN OCCUPATIONAL ROLES	0.25	0.50
TOTAL FEMALES IN OCCUPATIONAL ROLES	0.00	0.00
TOTAL OCCUPATIONS DEPICTED FOR MALES	0.25	0.50
TOTAL OCCUPATIONS DEPICTED FOR FEMALES	0.00	0.00
NUMBER OF FAMOUS MEN	0.00	0.00
NUMBER OF FAMOUS WOMEN	0.00	0.00

FEMALES DRESSED ONLY IN SKIRTS	NO
DEMEANING OR STERO. STATEMENTS	NO
STERO. EMOTIONAL RESPONSES	NO
LANGUAGE EXCLUDING WOMEN	NO
SEPARATE FORMS	NO
SEPARATE NORMS	NO

PRESCRIPTIVE READING INVENTORY - LEVEL II

	MEAN	STANDARD DEVIATION
ILLUSTRATIONS-NUMBER OF MALE ADULTS	1.75	0.50
ILLUSTRATIONS-NUMBER OF FEMALE ADULTS	9.25	1.50
ILLUSTRATIONS-NUMBER OF MALE CHILDREN	10.25	5.31
ILLUSTRATIONS-NUMBER OF FEMALE CHILDREN	16.50	10.63
ILLUSTRATIONS-NUMBER OF MALE ANIMALS	0.00	0.00
ILLUSTRATIONS-NUMBER OF FEMALE ANIMALS	0.00	0.00
CONTENT-NUMBER OF MALE ADULTS	2.00	0.00
CONTENT-NUMBER OF FEMALE ADULTS	1.25	1.50
CONTENT-NUMBER OF MALE CHILDREN	3.50	1.00
CONTENT-NUMBER OF FEMALE CHILDREN	0.25	0.50
CONTENT-NUMBER OF MALE ANIMALS	0.50	0.57
CONTENT-NUMBER OF FEMALE ANIMALS	0.50	0.57
MALES IN STERO. NONOCC. ROLES	1.33	1.15
FEMALES IN STERO. NONOCC. ROLES	0.50	0.57
TOTAL MALES IN NONOCC. ROLES	1.66	0.57
TOTAL FEMALES IN NONOCC. ROLES	0.50	0.57
MALES IN STERO. OCCUPATIONAL ROLES	0.00	0.00
FEMALES IN STERO. OCCUPATIONAL ROLES	0.00	0.00
TOTAL MALES IN OCCUPATIONAL ROLES	0.00	0.00
TOTAL FEMALES IN OCCUPATIONAL ROLES	0.00	0.00
TOTAL OCCUPATIONS DEPICTED FOR MALES	0.00	0.00
TOTAL OCCUPATIONS DEPICTED FOR FEMALES	0.00	0.00
NUMBER OF FAMOUS MEN	0.00	0.00
NUMBER OF FAMOUS WOMEN	0.00	0.00

FEMALES DRESSED ONLY IN SKIRTS	YES
DEMEANING OR STERO. STATEMENTS	NO
STERO. EMOTIONAL RESPONSES	NO
LANGUAGE EXCLUDING WOMEN	NO
SEPARATE FORMS	NO
SEPARATE NORMS	NO

PRIMARY MENTAL ABILITIES - GRADE K-1

	MEAN	STANDARD DEVIATION
ILLUSTRATIONS-NUMBER OF MALE ADULTS	16.00	0.00
ILLUSTRATIONS-NUMBER OF FEMALE ADULTS	4.00	1.41
ILLUSTRATIONS-NUMBER OF MALE CHILDREN	12.00	11.31
ILLUSTRATIONS-NUMBER OF FEMALE CHILDREN	15.00	9.89
ILLUSTRATIONS-NUMBER OF MALE ANIMALS	0.00	0.00
ILLUSTRATIONS-NUMBER OF FEMALE ANIMALS	0.00	0.00
CONTENT-NUMBER OF MALE ADULTS	3.50	4.94
CONTENT-NUMBER OF FEMALE ADULTS	1.50	2.12
CONTENT-NUMBER OF MALE CHILDREN	6.00	8.48
CONTENT-NUMBER OF FEMALE CHILDREN	4.00	5.65
CONTENT-NUMBER OF MALE ANIMALS	0.00	0.00
CONTENT-NUMBER OF FEMALE ANIMALS	0.00	0.00
MALES IN STERO. NONOCC. ROLES	4.00	1.41
FEMALES IN STERO. NONOCC. ROLES	3.00	2.82
TOTAL MALES IN NONOCC. ROLES	7.00	4.24
TOTAL FEMALES IN NONOCC. ROLES	3.00	2.82
MALES IN STERO. OCCUPATIONAL ROLES	6.50	0.70
FEMALES IN STERO. OCCUPATIONAL ROLES	1.50	0.70
TOTAL MALES IN OCCUPATIONAL ROLES	6.50	0.70
TOTAL FEMALES IN OCCUPATIONAL ROLES	1.50	0.70
TOTAL OCCUPATIONS DEPICTED FOR MALES	6.50	0.70
TOTAL OCCUPATIONS DEPICTED FOR FEMALES	0.50	0.70
NUMBER OF FAMOUS MEN	0.00	0.00
NUMBER OF FAMOUS WOMEN	0.00	0.00

FEMALES DRESSED ONLY IN SKIRTS	YES
DEMEANING OR STERO. STATEMENTS	NA
STERO. EMOTIONAL RESPONSES	YES
LANGUAGE EXCLUDING WOMEN	NO
SEPARATE FORMS	NO
SEPARATE NORMS	NO

PRIMARY MENTAL ABILITIES - GRADES 2-4

	MEAN	STANDARD DEVIATION
ILLUSTRATIONS-NUMBER OF MALE ADULTS	25.00	1.41
ILLUSTRATIONS-NUMBER OF FEMALE ADULTS	6.50	3.53
ILLUSTRATIONS-NUMBER OF MALE CHILDREN	6.00	5.65
ILLUSTRATIONS-NUMBER OF FEMALE CHILDREN	7.50	6.36
ILLUSTRATIONS-NUMBER OF MALE ANIMALS	0.00	0.00
ILLUSTRATIONS-NUMBER OF FEMALE ANIMALS	0.00	0.00
CONTENT-NUMBER OF MALE ADULTS	6.00	.
CONTENT-NUMBER OF FEMALE ADULTS	6.00	.
CONTENT-NUMBER OF MALE CHILDREN	16.00	.
CONTENT-NUMBER OF FEMALE CHILDREN	3.00	.
CONTENT-NUMBER OF MALE ANIMALS	0.00	.
CONTENT-NUMBER OF FEMALE ANIMALS	0.00	.
MALES IN STERO. NONOCC. ROLES	5.00	0.00
FEMALES IN STERO. NONOCC. ROLES	2.00	0.00
TOTAL MALES IN NONOCC. ROLES	5.50	0.70
TOTAL FEMALES IN NONOCC. ROLES	2.00	0.00
MALES IN STERO. OCCUPATIONAL ROLES	4.50	0.70
FEMALES IN STERO. OCCUPATIONAL ROLES	3.00	4.24
TOTAL MALES IN OCCUPATIONAL ROLES	4.50	0.70
TOTAL FEMALES IN OCCUPATIONAL ROLES	3.00	4.24
TOTAL OCCUPATIONS DEPICTED FOR MALES	4.50	0.70
TOTAL OCCUPATIONS DEPICTED FOR FEMALES	0.50	0.70
NUMBER OF FAMOUS MEN	0.00	0.00
NUMBER OF FAMOUS WOMEN	0.00	0.00

FEMALES DRESSED ONLY IN SKIRTS   YES

DEMEANING OR STERO. STATEMENTS   NA

STERO. EMOTIONAL RESPONSES   NO

LANGUAGE EXCLUDING WOMEN   NA

SEPARATE FORMS   NO

SEPARATE NORMS   NO

PRIMARY MENTAL ABILITIES - GRADES 4-6

	MEAN	STANDARD DEVIATION
ILLUSTRATIONS-NUMBER OF MALE ADULTS	13.00	3.60
ILLUSTRATIONS-NUMBER OF FEMALE ADULTS	1.33	0.57
ILLUSTRATIONS-NUMBER OF MALE CHILDREN	3.00	1.00
ILLUSTRATIONS-NUMBER OF FEMALE CHILDREN	2.66	1.52
ILLUSTRATIONS-NUMBER OF MALE ANIMALS	0.00	0.00
ILLUSTRATIONS-NUMBER OF FEMALE ANIMALS	0.00	0.00
CONTENT-NUMBER OF MALE ADULTS	1.33	0.57
CONTENT-NUMBER OF FEMALE ADULTS	0.33	0.57
CONTENT-NUMBER OF MALE CHILDREN	3.50	0.70
CONTENT-NUMBER OF FEMALE CHILDREN	3.50	0.70
CONTENT-NUMBER OF MALE ANIMALS	0.00	0.00
CONTENT-NUMBER OF FEMALE ANIMALS	0.00	0.00
MALES IN STERO. NONOCC. ROLES	3.00	1.41
FEMALES IN STERO. NONOCC. ROLES	2.00	1.41
TOTAL MALES IN NONOCC. ROLES	3.00	1.41
TOTAL FEMALES IN NONOCC. ROLES	2.00	1.41
MALES IN STERO. OCCUPATIONAL ROLES	5.50	0.70
FEMALES IN STERO. OCCUPATIONAL ROLES	0.00	0.00
TOTAL MALES IN OCCUPATIONAL ROLES	5.50	0.70
TOTAL FEMALES IN OCCUPATIONAL ROLES	0.00	0.00
TOTAL OCCUPATIONS DEPICTED FOR MALES	6.00	0.00
TOTAL OCCUPATIONS DEPICTED FOR FEMALES	0.00	0.00
NUMBER OF FAMOUS MEN	.	.
NUMBER OF FAMOUS WOMEN	.	.

FEMALES DRESSED ONLY IN SKIRTS	YES
DEMEANING OR STERO. STATEMENTS	NA
STERO. EMOTIONAL RESPONSES	NA
LANGUAGE EXCLUDING WOMEN	NA
SEPARATE FORMS	YES
SEPARATE NORMS	YES

PRIMARY READING PROFILES - LEVEL 1

	MEAN	STANDARD DEVIATION
ILLUSTRATIONS-NUMBER OF MALE ADULTS	10.00	1.15
ILLUSTRATIONS-NUMBER OF FEMALE ADULTS	2.50	1.73
ILLUSTRATIONS-NUMBER OF MALE CHILDREN	12.00	2.30
ILLUSTRATIONS-NUMBER OF FEMALE CHILDREN	11.50	2.88
ILLUSTRATIONS-NUMBER OF MALE ANIMALS	0.00	0.00
ILLUSTRATIONS-NUMBER OF FEMALE ANIMALS	0.00	0.00
CONTENT-NUMBER OF MALE ADULTS	13.50	4.43
CONTENT-NUMBER OF FEMALE ADULTS	6.25	3.40
CONTENT-NUMBER OF MALE CHILDREN	20.25	8.22
CONTENT-NUMBER OF FEMALE CHILDREN	16.75	5.25
CONTENT-NUMBER OF MALE ANIMALS	2.33	1.15
CONTENT-NUMBER OF FEMALE ANIMALS	0.00	0.00
MALES IN STERO. NONOCC. ROLES	3.75	0.50
FEMALES IN STERO. NONOCC. ROLES	1.00	0.00
TOTAL MALES IN NONOCC. ROLES	3.75	0.50
TOTAL FEMALES IN NONOCC. ROLES	1.00	0.00
MALES IN STERO. OCCUPATIONAL ROLES	1.50	0.57
FEMALES IN STERO. OCCUPATIONAL ROLES	0.50	0.57
TOTAL MALES IN OCCUPATIONAL ROLES	1.50	0.57
TOTAL FEMALES IN OCCUPATIONAL ROLES	0.50	0.57
TOTAL OCCUPATIONS DEPICTED FOR MALES	0.75	0.95
TOTAL OCCUPATIONS DEPICTED FOR FEMALES	0.25	0.50
NUMBER OF FAMOUS MEN	0.00	0.00
NUMBER OF FAMOUS WOMEN	0.00	0.00

FEMALES DRESSED ONLY IN SKIRTS	YES
DEMEANING OR STERO. STATEMENTS	NO
STERO. EMOTIONAL RESPONSES	NO
LANGUAGE EXCLUDING WOMEN	NO
SEPARATE FORMS	NO
SEPARATE NORMS	NO

PRIMARY READING PROFILES - LEVEL 2

	MEAN	STANDARD DEVIATION
ILLUSTRATIONS-NUMBER OF MALE ADULTS	19.00	0.00
ILLUSTRATIONS-NUMBER OF FEMALE ADULTS	7.00	0.00
ILLUSTRATIONS-NUMBER OF MALE CHILDREN	6.00	0.00
ILLUSTRATIONS-NUMBER OF FEMALE CHILDREN	6.00	0.00
ILLUSTRATIONS-NUMBER OF MALE ANIMALS	0.00	0.00
ILLUSTRATIONS-NUMBER OF FEMALE ANIMALS	0.00	0.00
CONTENT-NUMBER OF MALE ADULTS	8.00	1.41
CONTENT-NUMBER OF FEMALE ADULTS	7.00	0.00
CONTENT-NUMBER OF MALE CHILDREN	12.50	3.53
CONTENT-NUMBER OF FEMALE CHILDREN	7.00	1.41
CONTENT-NUMBER OF MALE ANIMALS	0.00	0.00
CONTENT-NUMBER OF FEMALE ANIMALS	0.00	0.00
MALES IN STERO. NONOCC. ROLES	1.50	0.70
FEMALES IN STERO. NONOCC. ROLES	0.00	0.00
TOTAL MALES IN NONOCC. ROLES	1.50	0.70
TOTAL FEMALES IN NONOCC. ROLES	0.00	0.00
MALES IN STERO. OCCUPATIONAL ROLES	1.00	0.00
FEMALES IN STERO. OCCUPATIONAL ROLES	0.00	0.00
TOTAL MALES IN OCCUPATIONAL ROLES	1.00	0.00
TOTAL FEMALES IN OCCUPATIONAL ROLES	0.00	0.00
TOTAL OCCUPATIONS DEPICTED FOR MALES	0.00	0.00
TOTAL OCCUPATIONS DEPICTED FOR FEMALES	0.00	0.00
NUMBER OF FAMOUS MEN	0.00	0.00
NUMBER OF FAMOUS WOMEN	0.00	0.00

FEMALES DRESSED ONLY IN SKIRTS	YES
DEMEANING OR STERO. STATEMENTS	NO
STERO. EMOTIONAL RESPONSES	NO
LANGUAGE EXCLUDING WOMEN	NO
SEPARATE FORMS	NO
SEPARATE NORMS	NO

PRIMARY SURVEY TEST BATTERY - INITIAL SURVEY TEST

	MEAN	STANDARD DEVIATION
ILLUSTRATIONS-NUMBER OF MALE ADULTS	1.33	0.57
ILLUSTRATIONS-NUMBER OF FEMALE ADULTS	2.33	0.57
ILLUSTRATIONS-NUMBER OF MALE CHILDREN	21.66	12.85
ILLUSTRATIONS-NUMBER OF FEMALE CHILDREN	4.66	1.52
ILLUSTRATIONS-NUMBER OF MALE ANIMALS	0.00	0.00
ILLUSTRATIONS-NUMBER OF FEMALE ANIMALS	0.00	0.00
CONTENT-NUMBER OF MALE ADULTS	0.33	0.57
CONTENT-NUMBER OF FEMALE ADULTS	0.66	0.57
CONTENT-NUMBER CF MALE CHILDREN	3.33	2.88
CONTENT-NUMBER OF FEMALE CHILDREN	0.66	0.57
CONTENT-NUMBER CF MALE ANIMALS	0.00	0.00
CONTENT-NUMBER CF FEMALE ANIMALS	0.00	0.00
MALES IN STERO. NONOCC. ROLES	0.66	1.15
FEMALES IN STERO. NONOCC. ROLES	0.00	0.00
TOTAL MALES IN NONOCC. ROLES	1.33	1.52
TOTAL FEMALES IN NONOCC. ROLES	0.33	0.57
MALES IN STERO. OCCUPATIONAL ROLES	0.00	0.00
FEMALES IN STERO. OCCUPATIONAL ROLES	0.00	0.00
TOTAL MALES IN OCCUPATIONAL ROLES	0.00	0.00
TOTAL FEMALES IN OCCUPATIONAL ROLES	0.00	0.00
TOTAL OCCUPATIONS DEPICTED FOR MALES	0.00	0.00
TOTAL OCCUPATIONS DEPICTED FOR FEMALES	0.00	0.00
NUMBER OF FAMOUS MEN	0.00	0.00
NUMBER OF FAMOUS WOMEN	0.00	0.00

FEMALES DRESSED ONLY IN SKIRTS	YES
DEMEANING OR STERO. STATEMENTS	NO
STERO. EMOTIONAL RESPONSES	NO
LANGUAGE EXCLUDING WOMEN	NO
SEPARATE FORMS	NO
SEPARATE NORMS	NO

PRIMARY SURVEY TEST BATTERY - EARLY PRIMARY SURVEY TEST

	MEAN	STANDARD DEVIATION
ILLUSTRATIONS-NUMBER OF MALE ADULTS	7.25	2.87
ILLUSTRATIONS-NUMBER OF FEMALE ADULTS	5.00	2.70
ILLUSTRATIONS-NUMBER OF MALE CHILDREN	9.75	1.25
ILLUSTRATIONS-NUMBER OF FEMALE CHILDREN	7.00	1.41
ILLUSTRATIONS-NUMBER OF MALE ANIMALS	0.00	0.00
ILLUSTRATIONS-NUMBER OF FEMALE ANIMALS	0.00	0.00
CONTENT-NUMBER OF MALE ADULTS	6.00	2.16
CONTENT-NUMBER OF FEMALE ADULTS	5.00	1.41
CONTENT-NUMBER OF MALE CHILDREN	26.00	2.16
CONTENT-NUMBER OF FEMALE CHILDREN	19.25	1.50
CONTENT-NUMBER OF MALE ANIMALS	0.00	0.00
CONTENT-NUMBER OF FEMALE ANIMALS	4.00	2.70
MALES IN STERO. NONOCC. ROLES	0.50	1.00
FEMALES IN STERO. NONOCC. ROLES	1.00	1.41
TOTAL MALES IN NONOCC. ROLES	1.25	1.50
TOTAL FEMALES IN NONOCC. ROLES	2.50	3.00
MALES IN STERO. OCCUPATIONAL ROLES	1.25	0.95
FEMALES IN STERO. OCCUPATIONAL ROLES	0.50	1.00
TOTAL MALES IN OCCUPATIONAL ROLES	1.25	0.95
TOTAL FEMALES IN OCCUPATIONAL ROLES	0.50	1.00
TOTAL OCCUPATIONS DEPICTED FOR MALES	1.25	1.25
TOTAL OCCUPATIONS DEPICTED FOR FEMALES	0.75	0.95
NUMBER OF FAMOUS MEN	0.00	0.00
NUMBER OF FAMOUS WOMEN	0.00	0.00

FEMALES DRESSED ONLY IN SKIRTS	NO
DEMEANING OR STERO. STATEMENTS	NO
STERO. EMOTIONAL RESPONSES	NO
LANGUAGE EXCLUDING WOMEN	NO
SEPARATE FORMS	NO
SEPARATE NORMS	NO

PRIMARY SURVEY TEST BATTERY - LATE PRIMARY SURVEY TEST

	MEAN	STANDARD DEVIATION
ILLUSTRATIONS-NUMBER OF MALE ADULTS	6.00	8.04
ILLUSTRATIONS-NUMBER OF FEMALE ADULTS	0.25	0.50
ILLUSTRATIONS-NUMBER OF MALE CHILDREN	0.75	0.50
ILLUSTRATIONS-NUMBER OF FEMALE CHILDREN	0.25	0.50
ILLUSTRATIONS-NUMBER OF MALE ANIMALS	0.00	0.00
ILLUSTRATIONS-NUMBER OF FEMALE ANIMALS	0.00	0.00
CONTENT-NUMBER OF MALE ADULTS	14.00	1.63
CONTENT-NUMBER OF FEMALE ADULTS	8.25	1.50
CONTENT-NUMBER OF MALE CHILDREN	25.75	4.03
CONTENT-NUMBER OF FEMALE CHILDREN	18.00	3.55
CONTENT-NUMBER OF MALE ANIMALS	1.00	0.00
CONTENT-NUMBER OF FEMALE ANIMALS	0.25	0.50
MALES IN STERO. NONOCC. ROLES	0.50	0.57
FEMALES IN STERO. NONOCC. ROLES	0.00	0.00
TOTAL MALES IN NONOCC. ROLES	0.50	0.57
TOTAL FEMALES IN NONOCC. ROLES	0.00	0.00
MALES IN STERO. OCCUPATIONAL ROLES	1.25	0.50
FEMALES IN STERO. OCCUPATIONAL ROLES	0.75	1.50
TOTAL MALES IN OCCUPATIONAL ROLES	1.25	0.50
TOTAL FEMALES IN OCCUPATIONAL ROLES	0.75	1.50
TOTAL OCCUPATIONS DEPICTED FOR MALES	1.00	0.00
TOTAL OCCUPATIONS DEPICTED FOR FEMALES	0.66	1.15
NUMBER OF FAMOUS MEN	0.00	0.00
NUMBER OF FAMOUS WOMEN	0.00	0.00

FEMALES DRESSED ONLY IN SKIRTS	NO
DEMEANING OR STERO. STATEMENTS	NO
STERO. EMOTIONAL RESPONSES	NO
LANGUAGE EXCLUDING WOMEN	NO
SEPARATE FORMS	NO
SEPARATE NORMS	NO

PRIMARY SURVEY TEST BATTERY - VOCABULARY SURVEY TEST

	MEAN	STANDARD DEVIATION
ILLUSTRATIONS-NUMBER OF MALE ADULTS	17.00	6.08
ILLUSTRATIONS-NUMBER OF FEMALE ADULTS	9.66	2.30
ILLUSTRATIONS-NUMBER OF MALE CHILDREN	41.66	21.50
ILLUSTRATIONS-NUMBER OF FEMALE CHILDREN	33.00	16.37
ILLUSTRATIONS-NUMBER OF MALE ANIMALS	0.00	0.00
ILLUSTRATIONS-NUMBER OF FEMALE ANIMALS	0.00	0.00
CONTENT-NUMBER OF MALE ADULTS	0.00	0.00
CONTENT-NUMBER CF FEMALE ADULTS	0.00	0.00
CONTENT-NUMBER CF MALE CHILDREN	0.33	0.57
CONTENT-NUMBER OF FEMALE CHILDREN	0.33	0.57
CONTENT-NUMBER OF MALE ANIMALS	0.00	0.00
CONTENT-NUMBER CF FEMALE ANIMALS	0.00	0.00
MALES IN STERO. NONOCC. ROLES	4.00	1.00
FEMALES IN STERO. NONOCC. ROLES	2.33	1.52
TOTAL MALES IN NONOCC. ROLES	5.00	1.00
TOTAL FEMALES IN NONOCC. ROLES	2.66	2.08
MALES IN STERO. OCCUPATIONAL ROLES	4.33	1.15
FEMALES IN STERO. OCCUPATIONAL ROLES	1.00	0.00
TOTAL MALES IN OCCUPATIONAL ROLES	5.00	1.73
TOTAL FEMALES IN OCCUPATIONAL ROLES	1.66	0.57
TOTAL OCCUPATIONS DEPICTED FOR MALES	2.66	2.51
TOTAL OCCUPATIONS DEPICTED FOR FEMALES	0.66	0.57
NUMBER OF FAMOUS MEN	0.00	0.00
NUMBER OF FAMOUS WOMEN	0.00	0.00

FEMALES DRESSED ONLY IN SKIRTS	YES
DEMEANING OR STERO. STATEMENTS	NA
STERO. EMOTIONAL RESPONSES	NO
LANGUAGE EXCLUDING WOMEN	NO
SEPARATE FORMS	NO
SEPARATE NORMS	NO

STANFORD DIAGNOSTIC READING TEST - FORM A, GREEN LEVEL

	MEAN	STANDARD DEVIATION
ILLUSTRATIONS-NUMBER OF MALE ADULTS	•	•
ILLUSTRATIONS-NUMBER OF FEMALE ADULTS	•	•
ILLUSTRATIONS-NUMBER OF MALE CHILDREN	•	•
ILLUSTRATIONS-NUMBER OF FEMALE CHILDREN	•	•
ILLUSTRATIONS-NUMBER OF MALE ANIMALS	•	•
ILLUSTRATIONS-NUMBER OF FEMALE ANIMALS	•	•
CONTENT-NUMBER OF MALE ADULTS	0.66	0.57
CONTENT-NUMBER OF FEMALE ADULTS	2.33	0.57
CONTENT-NUMBER OF MALE CHILDREN	6.33	0.57
CONTENT-NUMBER OF FEMALE CHILDREN	7.00	1.00
CONTENT-NUMBER OF MALE ANIMALS	0.66	0.57
CONTENT-NUMBER OF FEMALE ANIMALS	0.00	0.00
MALES IN STERO. NONOCC. ROLES	0.33	0.57
FEMALES IN STERO. NONOCC. ROLES	0.33	0.57
TOTAL MALES IN NONOCC. ROLES	1.66	1.15
TOTAL FEMALES IN NONOCC. ROLES	2.66	0.57
MALES IN STERO. OCCUPATIONAL ROLES	0.00	0.00
FEMALES IN STERO. OCCUPATIONAL ROLES	0.00	0.00
TOTAL MALES IN OCCUPATIONAL ROLES	0.33	0.57
TOTAL FEMALES IN OCCUPATIONAL ROLES	1.50	0.70
TOTAL OCCUPATIONS DEPICTED FOR MALES	0.00	0.00
TOTAL OCCUPATIONS DEPICTED FOR FEMALES	1.33	0.57
NUMBER OF FAMOUS MEN	0.00	0.00
NUMBER OF FAMOUS WOMEN	0.00	0.00

FEMALES DRESSED ONLY IN SKIRTS	NA
DEMEANING OR STERO. STATEMENTS	NA
STERO. EMOTIONAL RESPONSES	NO
LANGUAGE EXCLUDING WOMEN	NO
SEPARATE FORMS	NO
SEPARATE NORMS	NO

STANFORD DIAGNOSTIC READING TEST - FORM A, RED LEVEL

	MEAN	STANDARD DEVIATION
ILLUSTRATIONS-NUMBER OF MALE ADULTS	9.66	2.08
ILLUSTRATIONS-NUMBER OF FEMALE ADULTS	2.66	1.15
ILLUSTRATIONS-NUMBER OF MALE CHILDREN	32.00	17.52
ILLUSTRATIONS-NUMBER OF FEMALE CHILDREN	24.66	11.37
ILLUSTRATIONS-NUMBER OF MALE ANIMALS	0.00	0.00
ILLUSTRATIONS-NUMBER OF FEMALE ANIMALS	0.00	0.00
CONTENT-NUMBER OF MALE ADULTS	2.00	1.00
CONTENT-NUMBER OF FEMALE ADULTS	1.33	0.57
CONTENT-NUMBER OF MALE CHILDREN	14.00	1.73
CONTENT-NUMBER OF FEMALE CHILDREN	10.33	0.57
CONTENT-NUMBER OF MALE ANIMALS	0.00	0.00
CONTENT-NUMBER OF FEMALE ANIMALS	0.00	0.00
MALES IN STERO. NONOCC. ROLES	0.33	0.57
FEMALES IN STERO. NONOCC. ROLES	0.00	0.00
TOTAL MALES IN NONOCC. ROLES	2.66	1.52
TOTAL FEMALES IN NONOCC. ROLES	3.00	0.00
MALES IN STERO. OCCUPATIONAL ROLES	2.00	1.00
FEMALES IN STERO. OCCUPATIONAL ROLES	0.66	0.57
TOTAL MALES IN OCCUPATIONAL ROLES	2.33	0.57
TOTAL FEMALES IN OCCUPATIONAL ROLES	1.00	0.00
TOTAL OCCUPATIONS DEPICTED FOR MALES	2.00	0.00
TOTAL OCCUPATIONS DEPICTED FOR FEMALES	1.00	0.00
NUMBER OF FAMOUS MEN	0.00	0.00
NUMBER OF FAMOUS WOMEN	0.00	0.00

FEMALES DRESSED ONLY IN SKIRTS	YES
DEMEANING OR STERO. STATEMENTS	NO
STERO. EMOTIONAL RESPONSES	NO
LANGUAGE EXCLUDING WOMEN	YES
SEPARATE FORMS	NO
SEPARATE NORMS	NO

TEST FOR AUDITORY COMPREHENSION OF LANGUAGE

	MEAN	STANDARD DEVIATION
ILLUSTRATIONS-NUMBER OF MALE ADULTS	22.25	3.94
ILLUSTRATIONS-NUMBER OF FEMALE ADULTS	15.25	3.77
ILLUSTRATIONS-NUMBER OF MALE CHILDREN	64.75	13.59
ILLUSTRATIONS-NUMBER OF FEMALE CHILDREN	46.25	8.01
ILLUSTRATIONS-NUMBER OF MALE ANIMALS	0.25	0.50
ILLUSTRATIONS-NUMBER OF FEMALE ANIMALS	0.25	0.50
CONTENT-NUMBER OF MALE ADULTS	5.00	2.82
CONTENT-NUMBER OF FEMALE ADULTS	1.00	0.00
CONTENT-NUMBER OF MALE CHILDREN	6.00	0.00
CONTENT-NUMBER OF FEMALE CHILDREN	9.00	1.41
CONTENT-NUMBER OF MALE ANIMALS	0.00	0.00
CONTENT-NUMBER OF FEMALE ANIMALS	0.00	0.00
MALES IN STERO. NONOCC. ROLES	9.25	3.30
FEMALES IN STERO. NONOCC. ROLES	2.25	0.95
TOTAL MALES IN NONOCC. ROLES	11.00	2.44
TOTAL FEMALES IN NONOCC. ROLES	3.00	1.41
MALES IN STERO. OCCUPATIONAL ROLES	3.25	1.25
FEMALES IN STERO. OCCUPATIONAL ROLES	2.00	2.70
TOTAL MALES IN OCCUPATIONAL ROLES	3.50	1.29
TOTAL FEMALES IN OCCUPATIONAL ROLES	2.75	3.50
TOTAL OCCUPATIONS DEPICTED FOR MALES	4.25	1.89
TOTAL OCCUPATIONS DEPICTED FOR FEMALES	1.00	0.00
NUMBER OF FAMOUS MEN	0.00	0.00
NUMBER OF FAMOUS WOMEN	0.00	0.00

FEMALES DRESSED ONLY IN SKIRTS	YES
DEMEANING OR STERO. STATEMENTS	NO
STERO. EMOTIONAL RESPONSES	NO
LANGUAGE EXCLUDING WOMEN	NO
SEPARATE FORMS	NO
SEPARATE NORMS	NO

THEMATIC APPERCEPTION TEST

	MEAN	STANDARD DEVIATION
ILLUSTRATIONS-NUMBER OF MALE ADULTS	14.66	3.05
ILLUSTRATIONS-NUMBER OF FEMALE ADULTS	16.66	3.21
ILLUSTRATIONS-NUMBER OF MALE CHILDREN	3.66	0.57
ILLUSTRATIONS-NUMBER OF FEMALE CHILDREN	1.66	0.57
ILLUSTRATIONS-NUMBER OF MALE ANIMALS	0.00	0.00
ILLUSTRATIONS-NUMBER OF FEMALE ANIMALS	0.00	0.00
CONTENT-NUMBER OF MALE ADULTS	.	.
CONTENT-NUMBER OF FEMALE ADULTS	.	.
CONTENT-NUMBER OF MALE CHILDREN	.	.
CONTENT-NUMBER OF FEMALE CHILDREN	.	.
CONTENT-NUMBER OF MALE ANIMALS	.	.
CONTENT-NUMBER OF FEMALE ANIMALS	.	.
MALES IN STERO. NONOCC. ROLES	1.50	0.70
FEMALES IN STERO. NONOCC. ROLES	1.00	0.00
TOTAL MALES IN NONOCC. ROLES	1.50	0.70
TOTAL FEMALES IN NONOCC. ROLES	1.50	0.70
MALES IN STERO. OCCUPATIONAL ROLES	0.66	1.15
FEMALES IN STERO. OCCUPATIONAL ROLES	0.00	0.00
TOTAL MALES IN OCCUPATIONAL ROLES	0.66	1.15
TOTAL FEMALES IN OCCUPATIONAL ROLES	0.00	0.00
TOTAL OCCUPATIONS DEPICTED FOR MALES	0.66	1.15
TOTAL OCCUPATIONS DEPICTED FOR FEMALES	0.00	0.00
NUMBER OF FAMOUS MEN	0.00	0.00
NUMBER OF FAMOUS WOMEN	0.00	0.00

FEMALES DRESSED ONLY IN SKIRTS	YES
DEMEANING OR STERO. STATEMENTS	NA
STERO. EMOTIONAL RESPONSES	YES
LANGUAGE EXCLUDING WOMEN	NA
SEPARATE FORMS	NO
SEPARATE NORMS	NO

WESCHLER ADULT INTELLIGENCE SCALE

	MEAN	STANDARD DEVIATION
ILLUSTRATIONS-NUMBER OF MALE ADULTS	19.25	3.77
ILLUSTRATIONS-NUMBER OF FEMALE ADULTS	5.00	1.15
ILLUSTRATIONS-NUMBER OF MALE CHILDREN	2.25	0.50
ILLUSTRATIONS-NUMBER OF FEMALE CHILDREN	0.00	0.00
ILLUSTRATIONS-NUMBER OF MALE ANIMALS	0.00	0.00
ILLUSTRATIONS-NUMBER OF FEMALE ANIMALS	0.00	0.00
CONTENT-NUMBER OF MALE ADULTS	9.33	3.51
CONTENT-NUMBER OF FEMALE ADULTS	0.66	0.57
CONTENT-NUMBER OF MALE CHILDREN	0.00	0.00
CONTENT-NUMBER OF FEMALE CHILDREN	0.66	1.15
CONTENT-NUMBER OF MALE ANIMALS	.	.
CONTENT-NUMBER OF FEMALE ANIMALS	0.00	0.00
MALES IN STERO. NONOCC. ROLES	1.33	0.57
FEMALES IN STERO. NONOCC. ROLES	1.00	0.00
TOTAL MALES IN NONOCC. ROLES	2.00	1.73
TOTAL FEMALES IN NONOCC. ROLES	1.00	0.00
MALES IN STERO. OCCUPATIONAL ROLES	5.50	0.57
FEMALES IN STERO. OCCUPATIONAL ROLES	.	.
TOTAL MALES IN OCCUPATIONAL ROLES	5.75	0.50
TOTAL FEMALES IN OCCUPATIONAL ROLES	.	.
TOTAL OCCUPATIONS DEPICTED FOR MALES	5.75	0.50
TOTAL OCCUPATIONS DEPICTED FOR FEMALES	0.00	0.00
NUMBER OF FAMOUS MEN	2.33	0.57
NUMBER OF FAMOUS WOMEN	0.00	0.00

FEMALES DRESSED ONLY IN SKIRTS	YES
DEMEANING OR STERO. STATEMENTS	YES
STERO. EMOTIONAL RESPONSES	YES
LANGUAGE EXCLUDING WOMEN	NA
SEPARATE FORMS	NO
SEPARATE NORMS	NO

WECHSLER INTELLIGENCE SCALE FOR CHILDREN - REVISED

	MEAN	STANDARD DEVIATION
ILLUSTRATIONS-NUMBER OF MALE ADULTS	16.50	2.38
ILLUSTRATIONS-NUMBER OF FEMALE ADULTS	7.50	1.73
ILLUSTRATIONS-NUMBER OF MALE CHILDREN	5.00	2.00
ILLUSTRATIONS-NUMBER OF FEMALE CHILDREN	5.00	3.46
ILLUSTRATIONS-NUMBER OF MALE ANIMALS	0.00	0.00
ILLUSTRATIONS-NUMBER OF FEMALE ANIMALS	0.00	0.00
CONTENT-NUMBER OF MALE ADULTS	6.50	6.13
CONTENT-NUMBER OF FEMALE ADULTS	1.66	1.15
CONTENT-NUMBER OF MALE CHILDREN	10.66	3.21
CONTENT-NUMBER OF FEMALE CHILDREN	2.66	0.57
CONTENT-NUMBER OF MALE ANIMALS	0.00	0.00
CONTENT-NUMBER OF FEMALE ANIMALS	0.00	0.00
MALES IN STERO. NONOCC. ROLES	1.75	2.87
FEMALES IN STERO. NONOCC. ROLES	0.50	0.57
TOTAL MALES IN NONOCC. ROLES	1.75	2.87
TOTAL FEMALES IN NONOCC. ROLES	0.50	0.57
MALES IN STERO. OCCUPATIONAL ROLES	3.50	1.00
FEMALES IN STERO. OCCUPATIONAL ROLES	1.00	0.81
TOTAL MALES IN OCCUPATIONAL ROLES	3.50	1.00
TOTAL FEMALES IN OCCUPATIONAL ROLES	1.50	1.00
TOTAL OCCUPATIONS DEPICTED FOR MALES	3.25	0.50
TOTAL OCCUPATIONS DEPICTED FOR FEMALES	1.50	1.00
NUMBER OF FAMOUS MEN	3.75	1.50
NUMBER OF FAMOUS WOMEN	0.00	0.00

FEMALES DRESSED ONLY IN SKIRTS	YES
DEMEANING OR STERO. STATEMENTS	YES
STERO. EMOTIONAL RESPONSES	YES
LANGUAGE EXCLUDING WOMEN	YES
SEPARATE FORMS	NO
SEPARATE NORMS	NO

WECHSLER PRESCHOOL AND PRIMARY SCALE OF INTELLIGENCE

	MEAN	STANDARD DEVIATION
ILLUSTRATIONS-NUMBER OF MALE ADULTS	0.00	0.00
ILLUSTRATIONS-NUMBER OF FEMALE ADULTS	2.00	0.81
ILLUSTRATIONS-NUMBER OF MALE CHILDREN	1.75	0.50
ILLUSTRATIONS-NUMBER OF FEMALE CHILDREN	1.25	0.50
ILLUSTRATIONS-NUMBER OF MALE ANIMALS	0.00	0.00
ILLUSTRATIONS-NUMBER OF FEMALE ANIMALS	0.00	0.00
CONTENT-NUMBER OF MALE ADULTS	2.00	0.00
CONTENT-NUMBER OF FEMALE ADULTS	2.33	3.21
CONTENT-NUMBER OF MALE CHILDREN	7.00	4.00
CONTENT-NUMBER OF FEMALE CHILDREN	5.66	2.30
CONTENT-NUMBER OF MALE ANIMALS	0.50	0.70
CONTENT-NUMBER OF FEMALE ANIMALS	.	.
MALES IN STERO. NONOCC. ROLES	0.25	0.50
FEMALES IN STERO. NONOCC. ROLES	0.25	0.50
TOTAL MALES IN NONOCC. ROLES	0.25	0.50
TOTAL FEMALES IN NONOCC. ROLES	0.25	0.50
MALES IN STERO. OCCUPATIONAL ROLES	0.50	0.57
FEMALES IN STERO. OCCUPATIONAL ROLES	0.00	0.00
TOTAL MALES IN OCCUPATIONAL ROLES	0.75	0.95
TOTAL FEMALES IN OCCUPATIONAL ROLES	0.00	0.00
TOTAL OCCUPATIONS DEPICTED FOR MALES	0.50	0.57
TOTAL OCCUPATIONS DEPICTED FOR FEMALES	0.00	0.00
NUMBER OF FAMOUS MEN	0.00	0.00
NUMBER OF FAMOUS WOMEN	1.25	1.89

FEMALES DRESSED ONLY IN SKIRTS	YES
DEMEANING OR STERO. STATEMENTS	NA
STERO. EMOTIONAL RESPONSES	NO
LANGUAGE EXCLUDING WOMEN	NA
SEPARATE FORMS	NO
SEPARATE NORMS	NO

WIDE RANGE INTELLIGENCE PERSONALITY TEST

	MEAN	STANDARD DEVIATION
ILLUSTRATIONS-NUMBER OF MALE ADULTS	33.75	5.79
ILLUSTRATIONS-NUMBER OF FEMALE ADULTS	27.75	5.25
ILLUSTRATIONS-NUMBER OF MALE CHILDREN	10.00	3.26
ILLUSTRATIONS-NUMBER OF FEMALE CHILDREN	12.75	5.56
ILLUSTRATIONS-NUMBER OF MALE ANIMALS	0.00	0.00
ILLUSTRATIONS-NUMBER OF FEMALE ANIMALS	0.00	0.00
CONTENT-NUMBER OF MALE ADULTS	0.00	0.00
CONTENT-NUMBER OF FEMALE ADULTS	0.00	0.00
CONTENT-NUMBER OF MALE CHILDREN	0.00	0.00
CONTENT-NUMBER OF FEMALE CHILDREN	0.00	0.00
CONTENT-NUMBER OF MALE ANIMALS	0.00	0.00
CONTENT-NUMBER OF FEMALE ANIMALS	0.00	0.00
MALES IN STERO. NONOCC. ROLES	1.66	1.52
FEMALES IN STERO. NONOCC. ROLES	4.00	1.00
TOTAL MALES IN NONOCC. ROLES	2.00	1.73
TOTAL FEMALES IN NONOCC. ROLES	4.00	1.00
MALES IN STERO. OCCUPATIONAL ROLES	9.66	5.50
FEMALES IN STERO. OCCUPATIONAL ROLES	6.33	6.65
TOTAL MALES IN OCCUPATIONAL ROLES	10.33	6.50
TOTAL FEMALES IN OCCUPATIONAL ROLES	6.33	6.65
TOTAL OCCUPATIONS DEPICTED FOR MALES	9.50	4.50
TOTAL OCCUPATIONS DEPICTED FOR FEMALES	3.25	1.89
NUMBER OF FAMOUS MEN	0.00	0.00
NUMBER OF FAMOUS WOMEN	0.00	0.00

FEMALES DRESSED ONLY IN SKIRTS	YES
DEMEANING OR STERO. STATEMENTS	NA
STERO. EMOTIONAL RESPONSES	YES
LANGUAGE EXCLUDING WOMEN	NO
SEPARATE FORMS	NO
SEPARATE NORMS	NO

```
WOODCOCK READING MASTERY TEST - FORM A
```

	MEAN	STANDARD DEVIATION
ILLUSTRATIONS-NUMBER OF MALE ADULTS	5.00	0.00
ILLUSTRATIONS-NUMBER OF FEMALE ADULTS	3.33	0.57
ILLUSTRATIONS-NUMBER OF MALE CHILDREN	0.00	0.00
ILLUSTRATIONS-NUMBER OF FEMALE CHILDREN	0.00	0.00
ILLUSTRATIONS-NUMBER OF MALE ANIMALS	0.00	0.00
ILLUSTRATIONS-NUMBER OF FEMALE ANIMALS	0.00	0.00
CONTENT-NUMBER OF MALE ADULTS	15.00	6.24
CONTENT-NUMBER OF FEMALE ADULTS	5.00	4.00
CONTENT-NUMBER OF MALE CHILDREN	8.66	4.04
CONTENT-NUMBER OF FEMALE CHILDREN	4.33	3.05
CONTENT-NUMBER OF MALE ANIMALS	0.66	1.15
CONTENT-NUMBER OF FEMALE ANIMALS	0.00	0.00
MALES IN STERO. NONOCC. ROLES	0.33	0.57
FEMALES IN STERO. NONOCC. ROLES	1.00	0.00
TOTAL MALES IN NONOCC. ROLES	0.33	0.57
TOTAL FEMALES IN NONOCC. ROLES	1.00	0.00
MALES IN STERO. OCCUPATIONAL ROLES	2.66	2.08
FEMALES IN STERO. OCCUPATIONAL ROLES	1.33	0.57
TOTAL MALES IN OCCUPATIONAL ROLES	3.00	1.73
TOTAL FEMALES IN OCCUPATIONAL ROLES	1.33	0.57
TOTAL OCCUPATIONS DEPICTED FOR MALES	4.50	0.70
TOTAL OCCUPATIONS DEPICTED FOR FEMALES	1.50	0.70
NUMBER OF FAMOUS MEN	4.33	0.57
NUMBER OF FAMOUS WOMEN	1.00	0.00

FEMALES DRESSED ONLY IN SKIRTS	YES
DEMEANING OR STERO. STATEMENTS	NO
STERO. EMOTIONAL RESPONSES	NO
LANGUAGE EXCLUDING WOMEN	YES
SEPARATE FORMS	NO
SEPARATE NORMS	NO

References

American Psychological Association. 1974. *Standards for educational and psychological tests* (Rev. ed.). Washington, DC: Author.

Anastasi, A. 1976. *Psychological testing* (4th ed.). New York: Macmillan.

Association for Measurement and Evaluation in Guidance. 1973. AMEG Commission report on sex bias in interest measurement. *Measurement and Evaluation in Guidance, 6*, 171-177.

Association for Measurement and Evaluation in Guidance. 1977. A case history of change: A review of responses to the challenge of sex bias in career interest inventories. *Measurement and Evaluation in Guidance, 10*, 148-152.

Birk, J. M. 1974. *Reducing sex bias: Factors affecting the client's view of the use of career interest inventories*. Washington, DC: National Institute of Education (ERIC Document Reproduction Service No. ED 095 367).

Boehm, A. 1980. The follow-up of research: A request. *American Psychologist, 35*, 473-474.

Boyd, V. S. 1978. Neutralizing sexist titles in Holland's Self Directed Search: What difference does it make? In C. K. Tittle and D. G. Zytowski (Eds.), *Sex-fair interest measurement: Research and implications* (pp. 21-26). Washington, D.C.: National Institute of Education (ERIC Document Reproduction Service No. ED 166 416).

Breland, H. M. 1974. *An investigation of cross-cultural stability in mental test items*. Princeton, NJ: Educational Testing Service. (ERIC Document Reproduction Service No. ED 093 916).

Brown, F. G., and Moss, J. 1979, April. Empirical methods for studying sex bias in achievement test items. Paper presented at the annual meeting of the National Council on Measurement in Education, San Francisco.

Buros, O. K. (Ed.). 1972. *Seventh mental measurements yearbook*. Lincoln: University of Nebraska Press.

Buros, O. K. 1974. *Tests in print.* Lincoln: University of Nebraska Press.

Buros, O. K. (Ed.). *Eighth mental measurements yearbook.* Lincoln: University of Nebraska Press.

Burrill, L. E. 1975, December. Statistical evidence of potential bias in items and tests assessing current educational status. Paper presented at the Fourteenth Annual Southeastern Conference on Measurement in Education, Atlanta.

California State Department of Education. 1978. *Guidelines for evaluation of instructional materials with respect to social content.* Sacramento, CA: Author.

Campbell, D. P. Crichton, L., Hansen, J. I., and Webber, P. 1974. A new edition of the SVIB: The Strong-Campbell Interest Inventory. *Measurement and Evaluation in Guidance, 7,* 92-95.

Campbell, J. 1976. Differential response for female and male law students on the Strong-Campbell Interest Inventory: The question of separate sex norms. *Journal of Counseling Psychology, 23,* 130-135.

Cleary, T. A. 1968. Test bias: Prediction of grades of Negro and white students in integrated colleges. *Journal of Educational Measurement, 5,* 114-124.

Coffman, W. E. 1961. Sex differences in responses to items in an aptitude test. *Eighteenth Yearbook, National Council on Measurement in Guidance, 11,* 117-124.

Cole, N. S. 1972. *Bias in selection* (ACT R51). Iowa City, IA: The American College Testing Program.

Cole, N. S., and Hanson, G. R. 1975. Impact of interest inventories on career choice. In E. E. Diamond (Ed.), *Issues of sex bias and sex fairness in career interest measurement* (pp. 1-17). Washington, DC: U.S. Government Printing Office.

Cook, J. 1978. Counseling and guidance programs. In C. K. Tittle and D. G. Zytowski (Eds.), *Sex-fair interest measurement: Research and implications* (pp. 145-146). Washington, DC: National Institute of Education. (ERIC Document Reproduction Service No. 166 416).

Cormany, R. B. Undated. *Standardized testing: Sexist or neutral?* Harrisburg: Pennsylvania Department of Education.

Darlington, R. B. 1971. Another look at "culture fairness." *Journal of Educational Measurement, 8, 71-82.*

Darlington, R. B. 1976. A defense of "rational" personnel selection, and two new methods. *Journal of Educational Measurement, 13,* 43-52.

Datta, L. E. 1977, June. He and she: Sex fairness in selection and guidance based on educational testing. Paper presented at the International Symposium on Educational Testing, University of Leyden, The Netherlands.

Dewey, C. R. 1974. Exploring interests: A non-sexist method. *Personnel and Guidance Journal, 52,* 311-315.

Diamond, E. E. 1972, September. The masculinity-femininity scale in interest measurement: An idea whose time has passed. Paper presented at the annual meeting of the American Psychological Association, Honolulu.

Diamond, E. E. (Ed.). 1975. *Issues of sex bias and sex fairness in career interest measurement.* Washington, DC: U.S. Government Printing Office.

Diamond, E. E. 1976. Minimizing sex bias in testing. *Measurement and Evaluation in Guidance, 9,* 28-34.

Diamond, E. E. 1978. Dealing with male-female differences on separately normed scales in the career development inventory. In C. K. Tittle and D. G. Zytowski (Eds.), *Sex-fair interest measurement: Research and implications* (pp. 89-93). Washington, DC: National Institute of Education. (ERIC Document Reproduction Service No. ED 166 416).

Diamond, E. E. 1980, March. The AMEG Commission report on sex-bias in achievement testing. Paper presented at the annual meeting of the American Personnel and Guidance Association, Atlanta.

Donlon, T. F. 1973. *Content factors in sex differences on test questions.* (ETS RM 73-28). Princeton, NJ: Educational Testing Service.

Donlon, T. F., Ekstrom, R., Lockheed, M., and Harris, A. 1977. *Performance consequences of sex bias in the content of major achievement batteries.* Princeton, NJ: Educational Testing Service. (ERIC Document Reproduction Service No. ED 151 415).

Dwyer, C. A. 1976, April. Test content in mathematics and science: The consideration of sex. Paper presented at the annual meeting of the American Educational Research Association, San Francisco.

Einhorn, H. J., and Bass, A. R. 1971. Methodological considerations relevant to discrimination in employment testing. *Psychological Bulletin, 75,* 261-269.

Equal Employment Opportunity Commission. 1970. Guidelines on employee selection procedures. *Federal Register, 35,* 12333-12336.

Fishbein, R. L. 1975, April. An investigation of the fairness of the items of a test battery. Paper presented at the annual meeting of the National Council on Measurement in Education, Washington, DC.

Fiske, E. B. 1980, July 8. Colleges place greater weight on test scores. *New York Times,* pp. C1, C4.

Fitzgerald, L. E., and Fisher, B. J. 1975. The legal implications of sex bias in interest inventories. In E. E. Diamond (Ed.), *Issues of sex bias and sex fairness in career interest measurement* (pp. 201-211). Washington, DC: U.S. Government Printing Office.

Frazer, W. G., Miller, T. L., and Epstein, L. 1975. Bias in prediction: A test of three models with elementary school children. *Journal of Educational Psychology, 67,* 490-494.

Gottfredson, G. D. 1976. A note on sexist wording in interest measurement. *Measurement and Evaluation in Guidance, 8,* 221-223.

Gottfredson, G. D., and Holland, J. L. 1978. Toward beneficial resolution of the interest inventory controversy. In C. K. Tittle and D. G. Zytowski (Eds.), *Sex-fair interest measurement: Research and implications* (pp. 43-51).

Washington, DC: National Institute of Education. (ERIC Document Reproduction No. ED 166 416).

Graf, R. G., and Riddell, J. C. 1972. Sex differences in problem-solving as a function of problem context. *Journal of Educational Research*, *65*, 451-452.

Hanson, G. R., Prediger, D. J., and Schussel, R. H. 1977, March. *Development and validation of sex-balanced interest inventory scales* (ACT RR 78). Iowa City, IA: American College Testing Program.

Harmon, L. 1973. Sexual bias in interest measurement. *Measurement and Evaluation in Guidance*, *5*, 496-501.

Harway, M., Austin, H. S., Suhr, J. M., and Whiteley, J. M. 1976. *Sex discrimination in guidance and counseling*. Washington, DC: National Center for Education Statistics. (ERIC Document Reproduction Service No. ED 132 499).

Herman, D. O. 1975, March. Aptitude tests: Sexy, sexless, or sexist? Paper presented at the annual convention of the American Personnel and Guidance Association, New York.

Holland, J. L. 1975. The use and evaluation of interest inventories and simulations. In E. E. Diamond (Ed.), *Issues of sex bias and sex fairness in career interest measurement* (pp. 19-44). Washington, DC: U.S. Government Printing Office.

Holland, J. L., and Gottfredson, G. D. 1976. Sex differences, item revisions, validity, and the Self-Directed Search. *Measurement and Evaluation in Guidance, 8,* 224-228.

Holman, M. G., and Docter, R. F. 1972. *Educational and psychological testing: Study of the industry and its practices*. New York: Russell Sage Foundation.

Jensen, A. R. 1980. *Bias in mental testing*. New York: Free Press.

Johnson, R. W. 1978. Relationships between female and male interest scales for the same occupations. In C. K. Tittle and D. G. Zytowski (Eds.), *Sex-fair interest measurement: Research and implications* (pp. 95-101). Washington, DC: National Institute of Education. (ERIC Document Reproduction Service No. 166 416).

Kerlinger, F. N. 1964. *Foundations of behavioral research*. New York: Holt, Rinehart and Winston.

Linn, R. L. 1973. Fair test use in selection. *Review of Educational Research*, *43*, 139-161.

Lockheed-Katz, M. 1974. *Sex bias in educational testing: A sociologist's perspective*. (ETS RM 74-13). Princeton, NJ: Educational Testing Service.

Lunneborg, C. E., and Lunneborg, P. W. 1978. *Sex composition of criterion groups in the discrimination of college graduating major groups*. Seattle: University of Washington. (ERIC Document Reproduction Service No. ED 169 108).

Maccoby, E. E., and Jacklin, C. N. 1978. *The psychology of sex differences* (Vol. 1). Stanford, CA: Stanford University Press.

Milton, G. A. 1959. Sex differences in problem solving as a function of role appropriateness of the problem content. *Psychological Reports*, *5*, 705-708.

Nondiscrimination on basis of sex. (Rules and regulations: Education programs and activities receiving or benefiting from federal financial assistance). 1975, June 4. *Federal Register*, *40*, 24128-24145.

Peterson, N. S., and Novick, M. R. 1976. An evaluation of some models for culture-fair selection. *Journal of Educational Measurement*, *13*, 3-28.

Plake, B. S., Hoover, H. D., and Loyd, B. A. 1978, March. An investigation of differential item performance by sex on the Iowa Tests of Basic Skills. Paper presented at the annual meeting of the National Council on Measurement in Education, Toronto.

Prediger, D. J. 1978, August-September. Basic vocational interest scales: The problem of sex restrictiveness and alternatives. Paper presented at the annual meeting of the American Psychological Association, Toronto.

Prediger, D. J., and Cole, N. S. 1975. Sex-role socialization and employment realities: Implications for vocational interest measures. *Journal of Vocational Behavior*, *7*, 239-251.

Prediger, D. J., and Hanson, G. R. 1976, September. Evidence related to issues of sex bias in interest inventories. Paper presented at the annual meeting of the American Psychological Association, Washington, DC.

Project on Equal Education Rights. 1975. *Summary of the regulation for Title IX Education Amendments of 1972.* Washington, DC: Association of American Colleges. (ERIC Document Reproduction Service No. ED 119 585).

Rayman, J. R. 1978. Sex and the single interest inventory: The empirical validation of sex-balanced interest inventory items. In C. K. Tittle and D. G. Zytowski (Eds.), *Sex-fair interest measurement: Research and implications* (pp. 27-34). Washington, DC: National Institute of Education. (ERIC Document Reproduction Service No. ED 166 416).

Rowell, E. H. 1977. *Are reading tests sexist? An investigation into sex bias in three frequently used individualized reading tests.* Providence: Rhode Island College. (ERIC Document Reproduction Service No. ED 145 362).

Scheuneman, J. Undated. *A new method of assessing bias in test items.* New York: Harcourt, Brace, Jovanovich.

Schiffer, L. J. 1978. Legal issues regarding sex bias in the selection and use of career interest inventories. In C. K. Tittle and D. G. Zytowski (Eds.), *Sex-fair interest measurement: Research and implications* (pp. 135-144). Washington, DC: National Institute of Education (ERIC Document Reproduction Service No. ED 166 416).

Schneider, J. W., and Hacker, S. L. 1973. Sex role imagery and use of the generic "man" in introductory texts: A case in the sociology of sociology. *American Sociologist*, *8,* 12-18.

Shaffer, W. M. 1976, April. The use of item-favorability data as evidence of sex bias in interest inventories. Paper presented at the annual meeting of the National

Council on Measurement in Education, San Francisco.

Shaffer, W. M. 1977. March. Separate-sex norms for tests: Status under Title IX. Paper presented at the annual meeting of the American Personnel and Guidance Association, Dallas.

Strassberg-Rosenberg, B., and Donlon, T. F. 1975. *Content influences on sex differences in performance on aptitude tests.* Buffalo: State University of New York at Buffalo. (ERIC Document Reproduction Service No. ED 110 493).

Tanney, M. F. 1974. *Face validity of interest measures: Sex role stereotyping.* Washington, DC: National Institute of Education. (ERIC Document Reproduction Service No. ED 095 368).

Thorndike, R. L. 1971. Concepts of culture-fairness. *Journal of Educational Measurement, 8,* 63-70.

Title IX—Prohibition of Sex Discrimination. Education Amendments Act of 1972. Public Law 92-318. 1972, June 23. *Federal Register, 37,* 444-447.

Tittle, C. K. 1973. Women and educational testing. *Phi Delta Kappan, 55,* 118-119.

Tittle, C. K. 1974. Sex bias in educational measurement: Fact or fiction? *Measurement and Evaluation in Guidance, 6,* 219-225.

Tittle, C. K. 1978a. Implications of recent developments for research in career interest measurement. In C. K. Tittle and D. G. Zytowski (Eds.), *Sex-fair interest measurement: Research and implications* (pp. 123-128). Washington, DC: National Institute of Education. (ERIC Document Reproduction Service No. ED 166 416).

Tittle, C. K. 1978b. *Sex bias in testing: A review with policy recommendations.* San Francisco: Women's Educational Equity Communications Network.

Tittle, C. K. 1979. *What to do about sex bias in testing.* San Francisco: Far West Laboratory for Educational Research and Development.

Tittle, C. K., McCarthy, K., and Steckler, J. F. 1974. *Women and educational testing: A selective review of the research literature and testing practices.* Princeton, NJ: Educational Testing Service.

Tittle, C. K., and Zytowski, D. G. 1978. *Sex-fair interest measurement: Research and implications.* Washington, DC: National Institute of Education. (ERIC Document Reproduction Service No. ED 166 416).

Troll, E. W. 1976, September. The Barbee Doll mentality and the Goodenough-Harris Drawing Test. Paper presented at the annual meeting of the American Psychological Association, Washington, DC.

Van der Flier, H., and Drenth, P. J. D. 1977. Fair selection and comparability of test scores. Paper presented at the International Symposium on Educational Testing, Leyden, The Netherlands.

Wade, T., and Baker, T. 1977. Opinions and use of psychological tests: A survey of clinical psychologists. *American Psychologist, 32,* 874-882.

Wesman, A. G. 1949. Separation of sex groups in test reporting. *Journal of Educational Psychology, 40,* 223-229.

Wild, C. L., and Dwyer, C. A. 1977, June. *Sex bias in selection.* Paper presented at the Third International Symposium on Educational Testing, Leyden, The Netherlands.

Women on Words and Images. *1975. Dick and Jane as victims.* Princeton, NJ: Author.

Index

About the Author

Paula Selkow is a licensed psychologist in private practice in Somerset, New Jersey. She has contributed to *Sex Roles*: *A Journal of Research*.